# Lebanon: Dynamics of Conflict

B.J. Odeh

For beautiful Liana
Daughter of the land
Child of the poor

# Lebanon: Dynamics of Conflict

## A Modern Political History

B.J. Odeh

Zed Books Ltd.

*Lebanon: Dynamics of Conflict* was first published by
Zed Books Ltd., 57 Caledonian Road, London N1 9BU, in
1985.

Cover design by Andrew Corbett
Printed by The Pitman Press, Bath

**British Library Cataloguing in Publication Data**
Odeh, B.J.
Lebanon: dynamics of conflict
  1. Lebanon — History — 1946-
  I. Title
  956.92'043          DS87
  ISBN 0-86232-212-X
  ISBN 0-86232-213-8 Pbk

**US Distributor**
Biblio Distribution Center, 81 Adams Drive,
Totowa, New Jersey 07512

# Contents

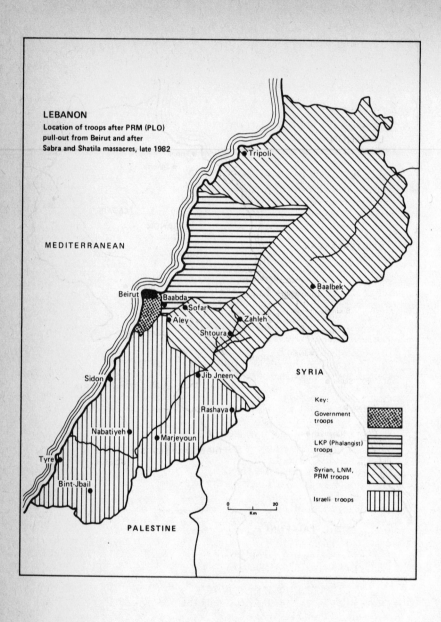

LEBANON
Location of troops after PRM (PLO)
pull-out from Beirut and after
Sabra and Shatila massacres, late 1982

MEDITERRANEAN

Tripoli

Baalbek

Beirut
Baabda
Sofar
Aley
Zahleh
Shtoura

Sidon
Jib Jneen

SYRIA

Rashaya

Nabatiyeh
Marjeyoun

Tyre

Bint-Jbail

Key:

Government
troops

LKP (Phalangist)
troops

Syrian, LNM,
PRM troops

Israeli troops

0          20
      Km

PALESTINE

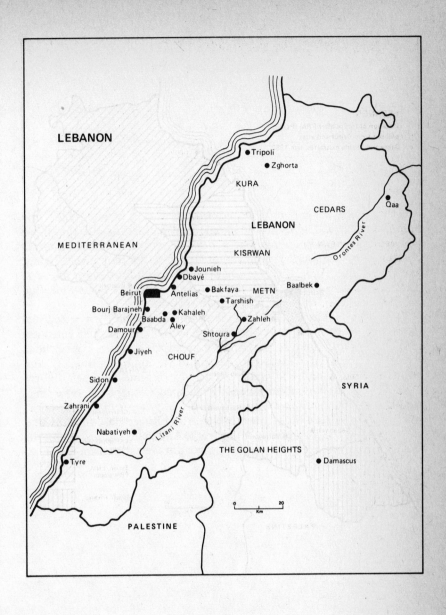

LEBANON

MEDITERRANEAN

Tripoli
Zghorta

KURA

CEDARS

Qaa

LEBANON

KISRWAN

Orontes River

Jounieh
Dbayé
Beirut
Antelias
Bakfaya
Baalbek
METN
Tarshish
Bourj Barajneh
Kahaleh
Baabda
Aley
Zahleh
Damour
Shtoura
Jiyeh
CHOUF
SYRIA
Sidon
Zahrani
Litani River
Nabatiyeh
THE GOLAN HEIGHTS
Tyre
Damascus

0        20
Km

PALESTINE

# Acknowledgements

It is impossible for me to mention all those who have made this work become a reality. The reality of Middle East politics dictates that most will have to remain anonymous. They are workers, revolutionaries, businesspeople, students, professors, researchers and housewives. They are people I have talked with at length or lived with for days or months. They are people I have political agreements and disagreements with. But they all wanted to help me in writing this work.

I am deeply indebted to Nabil, Ahmad and Ibrahim for setting up important interviews and to Muhammad and Dunia for their extended hospitality. To Ibrahim I. and Sami for giving me access to confidential research material. To Sayyed for taking me around. To Nabil Q. for photocopying volumes of material. To my parents for their understanding and support. I am especially indebted to Liana for reviewing, editing and contributing extensively to the improvement of the work. Many thanks to my editor Robert Molteno and Roger Hardy for the fine job they did in the final editing of the work. And thanks to Zed Books for bringing the work out. All errors in the work are my responsibility alone.

**B.J. Odeh**

# A Chronology

**1920-57**

1 September 1920: France creates Greater Lebanon

21 September 1943: Greater Lebanon achieves independence from France
Khoury is elected President of the Republic

15 May 1948: The Zionist entity — Israel — is created

19 September 1952: President Khoury is forced to resign through mass action

23 July 1952: The Egyptian Free Officers led by Nagib and Nasser depose King Farouk

5 January 1957: The US Congress approves the Eisenhower Doctrine

16 March 1957: President Chamoun of Lebanon accepts the Eisenhower Doctrine

**1958**

1 February: Egypt and Syria form the United Arab Republic (UAR)

8 May: The first Lebanese civil war begins

14 July: The Iraqi monarchy is deposed in a violent coup

15 July: US marines land in Lebanon

14 October: The first Lebanese civil war ends. US marines leave during the same month

**1964/67/68**

October 1964: The first Arab summit meeting establishes the Palestine Liberation Organization (PLO)

31 December: Al-Fateh begins military operations inside occupied Palestine

5 June 1967: The Six-Day Arab-Israeli war begins

21 March 1968: Palestinian guerrillas defeat superior Israeli forces at Karameh

28 December 1968: Israeli commandos raid Beirut International Airport

**1970**

25-29 March: The LKP (Phalangists) clashes with the Palestinian Resistance

17 August: Franjieh is elected President of Lebanon

September: Black September

**1973**

10 April: Israeli commandos assassinate three top Fateh officials in Beirut

May: The Palestinian Resistance (PLO) clashes with the Lebanese army

November: In an Arab summit meeting the PLO is recognized as the sole legitimate representative of the Palestinian people

**1974**

29–30 July: The PLO fights the LKP

21 August: A Lebanese policemen kills a Palestinian guerrilla in Sidon

22 September: The LKP clashes with the SPP in Tarshish

**1975**

28 February: Sidon fishermen demonstrate against the licensing of the Protein company. The Lebanese army clashes with the demonstrators and critically wounds Marouf Sa'd, the city's deputy

6 March: Marouf Sa'd dies

13 April: The second Lebanese civil war begins with the massacre of Ayn al-Rummaneh committed by the LKP

23 May: A military cabinet is formed

26 May: The military cabinet resigns under LNM mass action

24 June: The LKP and the Lebanese army attack the LNM in Chiyyah — a Beirut suburb

30 June: Kamal Jumblatt leaves for Egypt to consult with President Sadat on the Lebanese situation

1 July: Karami forms his cabinet

July: The Palestinian Resistance is occupied defending the Palestinian refugee camps against Israeli air raids

July–August: Israel attacks towns and villages in the south of Lebanon

24 September: The National Dialogue Committee (NDC) is formed

25 October: The Lebanese Islamic summit meeting convenes in Aramoun
              The 'battle of the hotels' begins

24 November: The NDC period ends

6 December: Black Saturday — the LKP massacres 70 innocent civilians and kidnaps 300 others

**1976**

4 January: LKP and PFN troops attack the Palestinian refugee camp of Tal al-Zatar

9 January: Interior Minister Chamoun orders the Lebanese army to fight the LNM

14 January: The Dubayye Palestinian refugee camp falls to LKP and PFN troops

15 January: The LKP and PFN troops attack the LNM area of Karantina
Lebanese army units begin to withdraw from the army to form
the Lebanese Arab Army (LAA) under the command of Lieutenant Ahmad Khatib

18 January: Karantina falls. LKP and PFN troops butcher residents

19 January: The Palestinian Resistance orders the Combined Forces to overrun all right-wing areas south of Beirut

20 January: All right-wing positions south of Beirut fall; including Damour

22 January: The Maronite right-wing agrees to the Syrian solution to the Lebanese problem

24 January: Jumblatt announces that the war is over

31 January: Pro-Syrian forces attack *Al-Muharrer* newspaper in Beirut as part of a campaign of terror against those who oppose the Syrian solution
    The Maronite right-wing forms the Front of Freedom and Man

2 February: Israel attacks the south

7 February: President Franjieh visits Damascus, Syria

14 February: The Constitutional Document is declared. The CD consecrates confessionalism

11 March: Brigadier Ahdab stages the 'Television Coup'.

14 March: 66 members of Parliament sign a petition asking President Franjieh to resign

23 March: The LNM establishes full control over the hotel area and Starco in Beirut

25 March: Franjieh is forced to flee the Presidential Palace due to LNM and LAA shelling

26–27 March: The LNM liberates several areas in the Mountain

31 March: Dean Brown, the US envoy, arrives in Beirut

15 April: Couve de Murville, the French envoy, announces his approval of Syria's role in Lebanon

16 April: The Palestinian Resistance reaches agreement with Syria on Lebanon

19 April: The Maronite right-wing attacks the Syrian–Palestinian agreement on Lebanon

9 May: Elias Sarkis is elected President of Lebanon through Syrian intimidation and threats

11 May: Dean Brown holds a press conference to urge reconciliation among the warring parties

14 May: Jumblatt, Ahmad Khatib and George Habash denounce Syria's military role in Lebanon on the side of the LKP

24 May: The LKP occupies Jubail and kills 30 Maronite supporters of the National Bloc leader Eddé

25 May: The LKP–PFN plot to assassinate Eddé fails

1 June: Syria invades Lebanon

2 June: Jumblatt meets with President-elect Sarkis and agrees to end the fighting and enter negotiations with the right-wing

6 June: The Combined Forces occupy the pro-Syrian Lebanese and Palestinian parties' offices and arrest many of their leaders

9 June: The Arab Foreign Ministers meet and agree to send a symbolic Arab force to replace the Syrians in Lebanon

17 June: President Asad of Syria visits France

19 June: France and Syria issue a joint communiqué to show their agreement

on Lebanon and the Middle East

1 July: Saudi and Sudanese army units arrive in Lebanon and take positions in Beirut and Sidon

13 July: The Arab Foreign Ministers call for a ceasefire and dialogue between the Palestinian Resistance and Syria

26 July: The Damascus agreement between Syria and the Resistance is signed

12 August: Tal al-Zatar falls after 52 days of daily right-wing attacks

28 September: Syria launches a four-day offensive on LNM mountain positions
The LKP and the Lebanese army also fight the LNM

17 October: The Riyadh mini summit meeting is held

25 October: The Cairo Arab summit meeting rubber stamps the Riyadh mini summit agreement

8 December: President Sarkis asks Dr Hoss to form a Lebanese cabinet

## 1977/1978/1979

18–19 January: The Egyptian working class moves against the Sadat regime

March: Israel invades Lebanon and establishes a six-mile buffer zone on Lebanese territory

16 March: Kamal Jumblatt is assassinated

19 November: Sadat visits Jerusalem

2 November 1978: The Baghdad ninth Arab summit meeting is held

26 March 1979: The Israeli–Egyptian 'peace' treaty is signed

## 1982

6 June: Israel invades Lebanon

June: The Lebanese Resistance Front (LRF) is formed

August: Bashir Gemayel is elected President of Lebanon
The Palestinian Resistance (PLO) leaves Lebanon

1 September: President Reagan announces his initiative for 'peace' in the Middle East

14 September: President-elect Bashir Gemayel is assassinated

17 September: Massacres at Sabra and Chatila perpetrated by Israel and the LKP

## 1983

15 May: Rebellion within Al-Fateh

17 May: The Israeli–Lebanese agreement

24 June: Arafat is ousted from Syria

4 September: Israel withdraws from the central mountains to the south of Lebanon

23 October: The US marines and French compounds in Beirut are destroyed

November: Arafat withdraws from Tripoli in the north of Lebanon
A conference of Lebanese warlords is held in Geneva, Switzerland

**1984**

4 February: Lebanon's Prime Minister Chefic Wazzan resigns

7 February: The US announces its decision to withdraw from Lebanon

29 February: President Amin Gemayel visits Syria in an attempt to save his presidency

21 March: A conference of Lebanese warlords is held at Lausanne, Switzerland
US forces are officially pulled out of Lebanon

25 April: President Amin Gemayel asks Rashid Karami to form a cabinet

# List of Abbreviations

## The Fascist Right Wing

**LKP**      Lebanese Kataeb Party (Phalange)
**PFN**      Party of Free Nationalists

## Other Right-Wing Parties

**CB**      Constitutional Bloc
**NB**      National Bloc

## Lebanese National Movement Organizations

**ABSP**      Arab Ba'ath Socialist Party (pro-Iraq)
**ASAP**      Arab Socialist Action Party
**LCP**      Lebanese Communist Party
**OCA**      Organization of Communist Action
**SPP**      Socialist Progressive Party (also referred to as PSP)

## Pro-Syrian Lebanese Organizations during the 1975–76 War

**AMAL**      Lebanese Resistance Battalions
**BPO**      Ba'ath Party Organization
**SNP**      Syrian Nationalist Party (also referred to as PPS)

## Palestine Liberation Organization Groups*

**ALF**      Arab Liberation Front
**Al-fateh**      Palestine National Liberation Movement
**PDFLP**      Popular Democratic Front for the Liberation of Palestine (also referred to as DFLP)

| | |
|---|---|
| **PFLP** | Popular Front for the Liberation of Palestine |
| **PFLP-GC** | Popular Front for the Liberation of Palestine — General Command |
| **PLF** | Palestine Liberation Front |
| **NSF** | National Struggle Front |

\* The PLO also includes the pro-Syrian Saiqa forces.

## Main Lebanese Fronts Created after the Israeli 1982 Invasion of Lebanon

| | |
|---|---|
| **LRF** | Lebanese Resistance Front (mainly includes OCA, LCP, ASAP and the Palestinian PFLP) |
| **NSF** | National Salvation Front (defunct since April 1984) |

# Preface

This book is primarily about Lebanon and how internal contradictions developed and interacted with regional politics, through the Palestinian link, to bring about the Lebanese Civil War of 1975-76; it provides an essential background analysis for an understanding of Lebanese and regional politics since 1976. The Israeli invasion of Lebanon on 6 June 1982, and the events that follow cannot be fully understood without addressing historical contradictions that arose in the area, not only through the impingement of a Zionist, exclusivist entity upon the region but also the economic and political contradictions concomitant with development and underdevelopment and imperialist interests in the area.

Class formations and transformations, the material basis of confessionalism, the impact of colonialism, as well as dependency relationships between Lebanon and the dominant capitalist countries, are central to the analysis. Ethnicity and religion are also placed in a materialist context to better understand old loyalties, class formations and the various alliances between different sectors of Lebanese society.

The Lebanese Civil War of 1975-76 provides us with an opportunity to study revolutionary development. To this end I have examined the contending forces and their economic and political underpinnings. The continuity of revolutionary development of the LNM prior to and during the 1975-76 battle is also demonstrated, as well as positions the LNM assumed in combating status quo (pro-system) forces and effecting reforms and the effect of the Syrian invasion on revolutionary development. The lack of revolutionary ideology to guide the LNM, the loose coalition that characterized it, and errors in strategic political and military analysis and tactics are brought into focus.

In the chapter dealing with the 6 June 1982 Israeli invasion of Lebanon, the political developments in the region since the Riyadh mini-summit and the Cairo summit in 1976 which wrapped up the 1975-76 Lebanese Civil War are highlighted. The various imperialist and Arab reactionary plans (Camp David, Fahd Plan, Fez II) to bring about stability for capitalism in the area, the Reagan Initiative, the Arafat-Hussein negotiations, the Israeli-Lebanese 17 May 1983 agreement and the development of the revolutionary movement, including the 15 May 1983 rebellion within Al-Fateh and Arafat's ouster from Tripoli are discussed.

Primary sources on Lebanon's political economy were obtained from studies available in the Arab world, where also, in 1977 and 1978, many meetings and interviews were conducted with people directly or indirectly involved with the Lebanese Civil War of 1975-76. I was able to secure an extended interview with a top official in the Central Political Council of the LNM, and also an interview with a leader of the Arab Baath Socialist Party in Lebanon. Another extended interview was conducted with a top PLO official who also is a member of Al-Fateh, and, too, with two top officials of Fateh — the Revolutionary Council, an off-shoot of Al-Fateh; an intermediate level PFLP leader was also interviewed. Many other interviews or meetings were conducted with people who witnessed major events in the battle of Lebanon during 1975-76, and with party members and sympathizers of the Socialist Progressive Party (SPP), Baath, PFLP, Al-Fateh, the Lebanese Kataeb Party (LKP), and others. I was also able to study the documents, speeches, party organs, and statements and so on of these various groups, and during my visits to the Arab world in 1980, 1982, 1983 and 1984, I was able to secure other information pertinent to the analysis presented in this book.

**B.J. Odeh**
New York 1984

# 1. Lebanon and its Arab Setting

The Republic of Lebanon, an area of 10,040 square kilometres with a population of just under three million people, lies on the eastern shores of the Mediterranean. The country has a moderate Mediterranean climate which makes its coastal plains ideal for citrus fruit growing. In between two mountain chains, Mount Lebanon, which is adjacent to the coastal plains, and Anti-Lebanon, lies the Bekaa Valley, which is noted for its grain. Lebanon is also rich in water resources, which include two major rivers, the Litani in the south and the Orantes in the north.

Historically, culturally and economically, Lebanon has been an integral part of the Arab world. The population is predominantly Arab Muslim and Christian. The Sunnis, Shiites and Druze comprise the Muslim sects, while the Maronites, Catholics and Eastern Orthodox comprise the major Christian sects, with the Maronites being in the majority among them.

On 13 April 1975 a civil war erupted in Lebanon that destroyed its economy, fragmented its population and disintegrated its political institutions. To many, the war came as a surprise. To others, it was part of a plan. A look at the historic and political process of nation-building, and at the social forces that brought about Lebanese independence from France in 1943, will give us insight into the political and economic causes of this conflagration. For our purposes, it is necessary to deal with the Arab East, since geographically, culturally and politically Lebanon is linked to this part of the world. It is important, therefore, to talk, by way of introduction, about Arab politics, especially since the late 1940s, to appreciate the way in which Lebanese politics has been integrally connected.

The Second World War had severely weakened the traditional European colonial powers and made it very difficult for them to control the revolutions for national independence that were accelerating throughout their colonies. Ultimately many of these colonies achieved independence in the late 1940s. Lebanon's and Syria's independence was part of this process that continued through the 1950s and 60s in Asia and Africa.

## The Creation of a Zionist Entity in Palestine

A counterweight to this anti-colonial process was represented by the creation in Palestine of the colonial-settler state of Israel, which came into being with the aid of the United States and Great Britain (the colonial power in Palestine since the First World War). The creation of the Zionist entity showed the doggedness with which colonialism sought to maintain its power in the area, and the way in which neo-colonialism tried to broaden its options in subjugating the Arab world.

The task of guaranteeing Western European and US interests in the Arab East was given to the newly formed United Nations. In November 1947, against the will of the majority of Palestine's inhabitants, the United Nations voted to partition it into Jewish and Arab states. At the time of the UN resolution, there were 600,000 Jews and 1,300,000 Arabs living in Palestine. Zionist landholdings at that time consisted of less than 8% of Palestine's territory, yet the UN resolution allocated 55% of Palestine to the Zionist state. In May 1948 Israel had become a state, and by that time she had destroyed 400 Arab villages. These villages were completely destroyed, 'their houses, garden walls, and even cemeteries and tombstones, so literally a stone does not remain standing and visitors passing are being told, "It was all desert" ' (Professor Israel Shahak). Eighty per cent of what now makes up the state of Israel is on territory that once belonged to 700,000 Arab Palestinians. These Palestinians were terrorized into fleeing the land that their ancestors had lived on for thousands of years.[1]

As a consequence of the creation of the Zionist entity, a new political element came into being in the Arab world — the Palestinian refugee. To date the Palestinian refugee remains the central element in the politics of the area. Initially under one million in 1948, the refugees spread to Lebanon, Syria, Jordan, Iraq and Egypt, and ultimately to every Arab country and other parts of the world. Those who did not leave Palestine either stayed within the confines of the Zionist entity or in the West Bank and Gaza, two Palestinian areas that were taken over by Jordan and Egypt respectively.

'An-Nakbah' (the catastrophe), the Arab debacle in Palestine, galvanized the masses in the Arab world. In a major way, this incident hastened the process of anti-colonialism and structural change within the Arab world. On 23 July 1952, Egypt deposed the monarchy and, under Gamal Abdel Nasser, she led the anti-colonial struggle in the Arab world and beyond. As things stood, the test for anti-colonialism in the area was the posture of each Arab state or political organization regarding the Palestinian question and Arab unity. On this score, Egypt had a near perfect record sheet. The nationalization of the Suez Canal in 1956, and the Suez war which followed, had, overnight, as it were, catapulted the Egyptian revolution into a position of leadership in the area.

The defeat of Britain, France and Israel in the Suez war marked the end of an era and the beginning of a new one — imperialism had entered a new phase. Britain and France were no longer able to embark on such an undertaking as the Suez war if this was in conflict with US interests. The United States had consolidated its hegemony in the area to the point where it became meaningful to talk about United States-led imperialism. The United States opposed the invasion of Egypt, since that would have made a colony out of Egypt. The United States had a vested interest in clearing the world of colonies that belonged to her rivals. In this way US capital could compete with European powers in the neo-colonies.[2] In only a few cases had the United States been unable to invest heavily in the newly independent countries that achieved a semi-colonial status rather than a colonial one. Egypt was a case in point. It had opted for state-capitalist development led by a petty-bourgeois nationalist class.

What ensued was no less momentous. The Arab masses found themselves fighting military pacts and other arrangements that attempted to strengthen imperialism. The major battles that took place during the 1950s centred around the Baghdad Pact, the Eisenhower Doctrine and the Point Four Program.[3]

## The Formation of the United Arab Republic

Arrayed against Nasser and the Arab masses were the Saudi Arabian, Iraqi, Jordanian and Lebanese regimes. To counter this array, Egypt allied herself with the nationalist Syrian regime. The alliance culminated in the union of the two countries in February 1958 with the formation of the United Arab Republic (UAR). Now Egypt was in a better position to deal with her enemies. It is important to note that, while the overwhelming majority of the people were pro-Nasser, union with Syria would not have been possible without the support and activity of the Baath Party in Syria and the Syrian national bourgeoisie. These petty-bourgeois nationalist and national-bourgeois interests were in conflict with those Arab states that sought alliances with imperialism, since these alliances blocked their own development as a national bourgeoisie.

The union of Syria and Egypt in the form of the UAR quickly came under attack. A union between the two Hashemite monarchies in Jordan and Iraq was hastily constructed. Lebanon began to move to a position of open animosity towards the UAR and identified herself with the UAR's sworn enemies (Saudi Arabia, Iraq and Jordan).

The attempted encirclement of the UAR through these moves backfired on its perpetrators. The internal dynamic of Lebanese society quickly brought Lebanon to civil war in May 1958. The majority of the Lebanese did not regard these imperialist developments in the area, as the Lebanese regime did, to be in their favour. Furthermore, a major sector of the traditional establishment opted to ride the wave of this mass discontent in an attempt to tilt the balance of power within the Lebanese political system in its favour. This move was especially inviting to this sector of the establishment when it was common knowledge that the UAR, which the Lebanese masses looked up

5

to, was also in support of the mass movement in Lebanon.

Another development, the Iraqi coup of 14 July 1958, had completely shattered the Baghdad Pact and the encirclement of the UAR. It also tilted the balance of power in Lebanon, and in the entire area, in favour of the radical nationalists. The Iraqi coup did away with the monarchy and declared itself in favour of Arab unity. It also declared itself to be opposed to all imperialist pacts.

Along with the 1958 Lebanese civil war, the Iraqi coup destabilized the region for US imperialism and posed a threat to other imperialist powers in the Arab East. Although a coup failed to materialize in Jordan, the situation in the area was so grave for imperialism that Britain and the United States were compelled to intervene. Relying on the Eisenhower Doctrine of 1957 (which gave the US the 'right' to intervene militarily in Lebanon upon request of that country's president), US marines landed in Lebanon on 15 July 1958. British troops also landed in Jordan as a response to the Iraqi coup.

The US intervention showed that imperialism fully understood the new situation that existed in the region. The Baghdad Pact was dead. Arab nationalism was carrying the day. Rather than fight with Arab nationalism, the US agreed with Nasser to resolve the Lebanese civil war by supporting General Fuad Chehab to succeed the pro-US Camille Chamoun to the Lebanese presidency. To the US, Chamoun was dispensable. The key to imperialist interest in Lebanon was the salvaging of Lebanon's archaic political system (confessionalism). On the other hand, in supporting Chehab, Nasser ensured that a friendly regime existed on his borders.

In general, this agreement symbolized the politics of the area from the late 1950s until the mid-1970s. The region's politics reflected the commonality of interests between the United States and the Arab national bourgeoisie. To varying extents, both wanted to get rid of colonialism and both were anti-communist. In doing what it did, US imperialism recognized the primacy of the Arab national bourgeoisie and its influence on the mass movement in at least a part of the Arab East. In protecting and enhancing its interests, the United States could no longer depend solely upon such reactionaries as the Saudi and Jordanian regimes. The US realized that the Arab national bourgeoisie's fight against feudalism could be conducive to capitalist development. The UAR was not socialist; in time, given the development of the international capitalist system, the UAR and other Arab countries would become fully integrated into this United States-dominated capitalist system.

## Arabism and Some of its Internal Problems

In Lebanon, the Chehab regime was both pro-United States and friendly towards the UAR in foreign policy. To achieve stability, the regime's domestic policy attempted to effect certain political and economic reforms. Lebanon remained friendly towards the UAR even after Syria separated from the union with Egypt in 1961. The Syrian coup of 1961 was the first setback to Arabism in the area since the creation of Israel in 1948. By February 1963, however, Arabism recovered, albeit temporarily, from its setbacks when the Iraqi Baath Party seized power after toppling the dictator Abdel-Karim Qassem. Also, in March 1963, the Syrian Baathists were able to seize power in a coup that toppled the 'separatists'. All seemed to be going well for Arab unity at that point. Both Baathist regimes were intending to unite Egypt, Syria and Iraq as a first step towards full Arab unity. Such a first step would have been of tremendous importance to the Arab masses in their fight against Israel and Arab reaction. Such hopes were soon dashed, however, after the Baathists began to have major differences with Nasser about the nature of the proposed union. Basically, Baathist differences with Nasser had to do with his perception of political parties. Nasser simply did not believe that political parties should play any role in the union. In effect, he wanted the Baathists in both countries to dissolve themselves, as they had done in 1958 when Syria joined the union with Egypt (UAR). This was something that the Baathists were unwilling to do.

Another problem that exacerbated this unification attempt was the inability of the two Baathist regimes to stabilize and consolidate their power in Syria and Iraq. This problem was especially glaring in Iraq. There the Baathists went on a rampage, killing thousands of communists in a bid to settle accounts. In 1958 the communists had tried to enhance their position under the Qassem regime at the expense of the Baathists. After weakening the Baathists, Qassem then turned around and dealt a heavy blow to the communists, killing and imprisoning thousands. At any rate, the infamous Baathist regime in Iraq came tumbling down after a reign of terror that lasted for nine months. The Baathists were replaced by the Aref regime. Abdel-Salam Aref was an officer in the Iraqi army who had participated with Qassem in 1958 in toppling the Iraqi monarchy. Both had shared power after the coup, until Qassem was able to oust Aref. In 1963 Aref participated with the Baathists in the coup against Qassem, but remained aloof. After the Baathists discredited themselves, he was in a position to assume power.

In Syria, the Baathist regime had purged all the non-Baathist officers from the state in an attempt to consolidate power. The result, however, was continued instability in the form of attempted coups, and purges among the Baathists themselves.

## 'Chehabism' — 1958–70

In the midst of all this turmoil, Lebanon was able to remain on friendly terms with both Syria and Egypt. Internally, much of what had occurred under Chehab amounted to an attempt at modernization. But modernization was antithetical to the existence of the Lebanese state. The National Pact (1943), which regulated the relationships within the exploiting class, was the political basis on which the Lebanese state rested. This pact affirmed the sectarian (confessional) basis of Lebanese politics. Any modernizer had to confront confessionalism (a system of government whereby the various religious sects of a polity are proportionally represented according to the population of each sect), and its corollary, the politics of the *zuama* (political bosses). Of necessity, a consistent modernizer came into conflict with confessionalism. Chehab, though a modernizer, was neither willing nor able to do so. His dilemma was that he did not think it feasible to restructure the state on a non-confessional basis. Consequently, his attempts at modernization were inconsistent, haphazard and, by and large, ineffective. From the outset, the majority of the zuama checked his efforts. Also, Chehab was unable to develop a non-confessional mass base to support modernization. Such a step on his part would have meant forsaking capitalist development and opting for socialism, something he was not prepared to do.

Chehabism (that modernizing trend and its corollaries in Lebanese politics) remained the dominant trend under Charles Helou, who succeeded Chehab to the presidency in 1964 for a six-year term. Although Chehabism was weaker without Chehab, its policies towards the Arabs remained firmly entrenched. These policies were a requirement of the Lebanese domestic situation. To maintain stability, the regime was forced to appease pan-Arabism in Lebanon and the region.

In this second period of Chehabism, a number of events converged upon Lebanon. To begin with, the recession of 1965 brought about a host of economic problems. This disturbance provided the basis for political moves by the labour movement and the left-wing political parties in an effort to pressure Helou into social and political reforms.[4]

## The Rise of the Palestinian Movement

Coupled with these events was the rise of the Palestinian revolutionary movement. In 1964 an Arab summit meeting created the Palestine Liberation Organization (PLO). The PLO was conceived by the Arab regimes to appease the Palestinian and Arab masses and keep them under their control. The PLO was allowed to open offices in all the Arab capitals, and immediately began to contact and organize the Palestinians in the Arab world, ostensibly for the liberation of Palestine. The Palestinian who was appointed to head the PLO, Ahmad Shuqairy, was a pro-Saudi reactionary. However, despite the fact that the PLO was compromised and under the control of the Arab reactionaries, progressive Palestinians were able to work within its institutions to reach Palestinians in the refugee camps. The main thrust of Palestinian revolutionary work was represented by the creation of the Assifa paramilitary units which belonged to Fateh (the Arab acronym for Palestine National Liberation Movement, read in reverse to mean 'conquest'). On 1 January 1965, the Fateh organization conducted its first military operations in occupied Palestine against the Zionist entity. These events signalled the beginning of a new era in the Arab world among the Palestinian and Arab masses.

Since its inception, Fateh galvanized the Arab masses. But it also had the ruling classes in the Arab world worried. In Lebanon, Fateh had a few units that were intermittently conducting strikes against Israel. The guerrilla organization also had Palestinian youth recruited for military training. Fateh had given the Palestinians hope. Palestinians had begun to operate in their own name, independently, or so it seemed, of any Arab state.

Fateh's headquarters were in Syria, where Yasser Arafat and others were directing Palestinian units striking Israel from Jordan, Lebanon and Gaza. Jordan and Lebanon immediately tightened their already tight grip on the Palestinians. And in Lebanon, in an attempt to silence the Assifa, the Chehabist Deuxième Bureau (military intelligence) assassinated Jalal Kawash, an Assifa guerrilla, in captivity. The assassination backfired on the Lebanese government. The Arab masses were outraged and almost up in arms against the Lebanese state. Contrary to what was intended, Fateh emerged stronger than before, due to the popular support it enjoyed after Kawash's murder. The Lebanese state responded with more repression against the Palestinians in Lebanon, in an attempt to rout the secret Assifa forces.

For Lebanon, however, this was only the tip of the iceberg. The humiliating defeat of the Arab nationalist regimes in the 1967 Six-Day War confirmed to the Arab masses and especially the Palestinians that: (1) all Arab regimes in the area (including Nasser's) were incapable of liberating Palestine or solving their own problems, and (2) the only force capable of carrying out the revolution was the PLO. Consequently, the Palestinian movement was catapulted to prominence. The PLO came under the hegemony of the guerrilla movement and Arafat replaced Shuqairy as chairman. Fateh and the Popular Front for the Liberation of Palestine (PFLP) increasingly came out in the open in Jordan and Lebanon. This open armed presence of the PLO prompted the formation of more guerrilla organizations. Currently there are eight guerrilla organizations in the PLO (Fateh, the PFLP, the Democratic Front for the Liberation of Palestine, the PFLP-General Command, Saiqa, the Popular Struggle Front, the Arab Liberation Front and the Palestine Liberation Front), in addition to the Palestine Liberation Army (PLA), the original military arm of the PLO.

On 21 March 1968 another dramatic change occurred in the status of the Palestinian movement that made it the leading force in the fight of the Arab masses against Zionism and imperialism. In Karameh, a village on the east bank of the Jordan river, a few hundred Palestinian fighters were capable of inflicting heavy damage upon thousands of Israeli troops who crossed over from the other side in an attempt to wipe out the guerrilla forces.[5] This new status of the Palestinian fighters allowed them to take over the PLO in the same year of the Karameh triumph.

For Lebanon, the Palestinian issue was an important component of Lebanese domestic politics. This became more pronounced when Israel invaded Beirut's international airport and damaged 13 civilian planes in December 1968. The progressive forces within Lebanon that later comprised the Lebanese National Movement (LNM) which led the fight in the civil war against the right wing, demanded that the Lebanese state assume a confrontational position vis-à-vis Israel. The right-wing forces, on the other hand, primarily the Phalangists (the Lebanese Kataeb Party-LKP), the Party of Free Nationals (PFN) and the National Bloc (NB), came out against the Palestinian presence in Lebanon. It soon became clear that, under the pressures of regional and national politics, Lebanon's internal stability was precarious.

## 'Black September' 1970

Meanwhile, the PLO was dealt a heavy blow in Jordan. The Palestinians comprise the majority of the population in Jordan, and the PLO was openly operating in the streets with their jeeps and artillery. Ostensibly, this meant that King Hussein of Jordan was unable to exercise power within his own kingdom. Hussein conspired with the Arab regimes to conduct an assault upon the revolutionary Palestinian influence, which was then militarily at its peak. Hussein also saw a certain role for himself in Arab politics that required the complicity of Israel. He wanted to negotiate with Israel to take the West Bank to create a certain entity (a greater Jordan or whatever). In this way he could rid himself of the PLO and at the same time do Israel a favour — provided he could persuade Israel to negotiate with him rather than someone else. Hussein began politicking with the other Arab states and forced the PLO to withdraw from the towns and camps, corralling them in the woods of Jarash and Ajloun, close to the Syrian border. Once the Palestinian fighters were isolated from their mass base in the towns and camps around Amman, the Jordanian army began pounding them. During 'Black September' of 1970, over 20,000 Palestinians, mostly non-combatants, died. Many of the remaining PLO forces went to Syria and Lebanon.

This defeat was due to a host of reasons. For our purposes, however, suffice it to say that the defeat was the result of erroneous strategic and tactical planning by the PLO leadership. Essentially, that leadership compromised on its presence in Jordan and accepted Arab intercessions that ultimately worked against it.

Black September and Nasser's death in 1970 signalled the end of an era in Arab politics. In the same year, a coup occurred in Syria in which Hafez al-Assad assumed power. The previous Baathist regime of Salah Jedid and Nouredin al-Ataasi was viewed as responsible for Syria's defeat in the 1967 Six-Day War. Assad installed his own Baathist regime to rule Syria.

## The Election of Franjieh

Nineteen-seventy was also a year of presidential elections in Lebanon, where the parliament elects a president for a six-year term. The right wing was able to make the Palestinian presence in Lebanon a major issue in the elections.

However, the issue that dominated the elections was 'Chehabism'. The main traditional leaders were divided on the wisdom of continuing Chehabism for a third term. Ultimately, Suleiman Franjieh was elected instead of Elias Sarkis, the Chehabist candidate of the Deuxième Bureau (military intelligence).

The progressive forces within Lebanon played a pivotal role in this election. It was Kamal Jumblatt, the leader of the Socialist Progressive Party (SPP) and of the progressive movement, that tipped the balance in parliament in Franjieh's favour. The progressive forces sought to weaken the Deuxième Bureau and the Phalangist influence in domestic politics. The army and its intelligence service, who were encouraged by the right wing, had increasingly come up against the labour movement and the Palestinians. The progressive forces hoped that Franjieh (who was viewed as more sympathetic to them than Sarkis) would not allow the army to break strikes or interfere with or suppress their political activity.

Since 1968, it had been clear to the Lebanese right wing (the Phalangists, NB and PFU) the US, Israel and the Arab reactionaries that the Palestinian movement had become a force to contend with. These powers were soon conspiring to rid Lebanon of the PLO as they had done in Jordan during Black September. With the PLO out of the picture, imperialism could eliminate the last vestiges of effective resistance to its hegemony in the area. It was important to hit the PLO before it could entrench itself by establishing stronger ties with the Lebanese population and the Lebanese National Movement (LNM), which represented the majority of the Lebanese. Furthermore, an LNM alliance with the Palestinians would certainly threaten the pro-US regime in Lebanon.

## Egypt's 'No War – No Peace' Situation

For Egypt, meanwhile, Nasser's death and the succession of Anwar Sadat to the presidency symbolized the end of national capitalist development and the triumph of the comprador bourgeoisie. The Egyptian comprador class was interested and anxious to assume its 'rightful' place in the international capitalist market. This comprador class, therefore, had to open up its economy to the United States. At the same time it had to bring an end to the 'no war-no peace' situation that had existed with Israel since the 1967 Six-Day War. This situation did not allow the comprador to attain stability as long as a large part of Egypt's resources were diverted to the military. Equally important was the fact that overtures to the capitalist West could not have been justified to the Egyptian people while Israel, the US's imperialist ally, remained holding Egyptian territory.

The 1973 October War solved the problem for the comprador class. Egyptian forces crossed the Suez Canal and initially defeated Israeli forces. The war itself was a political decision intended to force Israel to the negotiating table. Sadat could have gone all the way but only ventured six miles into Israeli-occupied Sinai. The hand-shaking that occurred between Egypt and

Israel on Kilometre 101 symbolized a new reality in politics — Egypt and Israel were on the way to signing a treaty. Syria, Egypt's ally in the October War, felt betrayed by Egypt's decision to go it alone in negotiations with Israel. This Egyptian move derailed the Geneva Conference initiative, which was on the cards prior to October 1973 and was favoured by Syria as a way to resolve the Arab-Israeli conflict and its core, the Palestinian problem. Kissinger's shuttle diplomacy, however, made it plain that the United States, Egypt and Israel were not interested in bringing the Russians into the negotiations. Nor were they interested in a comprehensive settlement of the conflict.

The Arab masses were arrayed against this Egyptian–Israeli rapprochement. Furthermore, some conservative Arab states, including Saudi Arabia, did not support the Egyptian position and remained publicly aloof from the entire process. Other Arab states (Syria, Libya, Algeria, South Yemen and Iraq) were openly opposed to the negotiations. Iraq was still playing a progressive role in Arab politics at this time. Under Baathist rule since the coup of 1968, it was pursuing a policy of extreme animosity towards both Israel and the United States. Despite its antagonism to Baathist Syria, Iraq had played a major role in the October War in Syria's defence.

The US wanted a settlement in the area that would guarantee its interests. All the obstacles mentioned above, however, prevented US imperialism from bringing about an agreement to its liking between Egypt and Israel. Another major impediment was the PLO. For US imperialism to stabilize the region and protect its hegemony in the area, the PLO had to be rendered ineffective and Palestinians had to be found who were willing to sign an accord in the name of the Palestinian people, thus 'solving' the Palestinian–Israeli problem. Imperialist logic went as follows: if the Palestinians were to sign an accord with Israel, then no one would be able to fault Egypt for signing a 'peace' treaty with Israel. This would then lead other Arab states to do likewise and a new capitalist era would be established in the region.

The logical place to strike at the PLO was in Lebanon, where the Palestinians were the strongest and where they enjoyed an open armed presence. Other areas such as the West Bank and Gaza were already under Israeli occupation and repression, and in Jordan King Hussein had effectively suppressed the PLO during the massacres of Black September.

There were other favourable conditions for imperialism that existed in Lebanon which would facilitate a strike against the PLO and weaken the revolutionary movement in the Arab world. These were: (1) The Lebanese right wing would be utilized as the main tool for effecting the strike. (2) Israel could help by intensifying her attacks against the Palestinian forces, especially in the south of Lebanon. (3) Israel could also help in training, advising and arming these right-wing forces. (4) The LNM could also be hit along with the Palestinians.

The LNM factor was important, since the LNM was gaining in strength and popularity as a challenger to the Lebanese system. It was a classic case of hitting two birds with one stone.

Basically, due to its internal contradictions, Lebanon was ripe for conflict. The LNM was a threat to capitalist interests in Lebanon. The Palestinian movement was a threat to imperialism's regional interests. The United States, Israel and Arab reactionaries converged to bring about the Lebanon conflagration of 1975-76.

It is against this background and in this context that the 1975-76 Lebanese Civil War can be more fully understood.

# Notes

1. *People's Tribune*, Chicago, 20 June 1983.
2. *Rally, Comrades!*, Voice of the Central Committee of the Communist Labor Party of the United States of North America, Vol. 3, No. 3, April 1983.
3. The Baghdad Pact of 1955 included Iraq, Turkey, Iran, Britain and the United States. The Eisenhower Doctrine of 1957 provided the US with the 'right' to intervene militarily in Lebanon in July 1958. The Point Four Program was originally the fourth point of President Truman's inaugural address of 1949. The Program was a US technical assistance programme to 'undeveloped' countries.
4. Elias El-Bwary, *History of the Labor and Trade Union Movement in Lebanon: 1947-1970*, Vol. 2 (Beirut, Dar-El-Farabi, 1980).
5. *Arab Palestinian Resistance* (Voice of the Palestine Liberation Army), March 1981, 12-14.

# 2. The Muslim-versus-Christian Myth

The Lebanese right-wing parties and the imperialist media have promoted the notion that the Lebanese Civil War of 1975–76 and all conflicts within Lebanon are conflicts between Muslims and Christians. Respectability was conferred on this misconception by academic literature on political development that asserted Lebanese politics was a matter of competition and/or conflict between Muslims and Christians.

This chapter takes issue with this false notion of Lebanese politics and deals with the literature that directly utilizes the Muslim-versus-Christian model. A refutation of this model is extremely important, since the model transcends the walls and ivory towers of academia to reinforce and support imperialist mass propaganda.

## Lebanese Conventional Literature

The Lebanese civil war of 1958 spurred a number of writers to focus upon the 'causes' of this war and/or to suggest ways to modernize Lebanon as a preventive measure against future crises. The more basic questions dealing with the political and economic arrangement behind the creation of the confessional polity or the 1958 crisis were circumvented or dismissed.[1]

Writers such as Kamal Salibi and S. Khalaf emphasize the religious cleavages in Lebanon, assuming they constitute the main contradiction in Lebanese society. Most of these writers consider the class nature of the polity to be at best superficial. They assess the political system as 'basically sound'; but for a few adjustments its rationality could be maintained.[2]

The second major war, in 1975, brought into question not only the literature of the inter-war years (1958–75), but also the inadequacy of the thesis that Lebanon's politics represent a contention between Christians and Muslims.[3] The several political and economic crises of these inter-war years prompted a number of studies that delved into the reasons behind Lebanon's instability and suggested ways of restabilizing the system.[4] However, none of the studies of which I am aware addressed the basic tenets of the system or the development model upon which it is based.

To most writers in the conventional literature, primordial ties are not conducive to modernization. Writers contend, however, that despite primordial ties, Lebanon is capable of developing, because it possesses other factors that favour modernization (education, democracy, etc.).[5] Writing within this tradition and noting 'the forces making for dissolution',[6] Hourani describes Lebanon's political development in a hopeful tone. He characterizes Lebanon as having 'a frail sense of common citizenship' and other permanent institutions, some of which are liberal, but all being important in nation-building, especially the presidency, which stands 'above communities, clans and families' and is 'the final guarantee both of the unity and of the Christian character of Lebanon' (sic).[7]

With the exception of Chehab's presidency (1958–64), all presidents had relied upon families, clans and so on. Even Chehab had to rely on some equivalent as a power base — military intelligence and other political bosses with primordial ties. However, because Chehab tried to bypass most of the traditional *zuama* (bosses), a formidable anti-Chehab alliance arose which later was successful in stripping the president of his influence.[8]

On a more basic level, Chehab's term of office and his 'modernization' attempts, as witnessed by institutional development, were an aberration. Even if one stays within the confines of the conventional paradigm, it is not difficult to see that the 'Christian character of Lebanon' is hardly a secular modernizing achievement, given the literature on modernization.[9]

The National Pact (1943), which legitimizes the confessional nature of the Lebanese state, despite claims of its rationality,[10] cannot be seen as a modernizing formula. It is a formula that consecrated primordial ties and more basically preyed upon and encouraged the development of primordial religious feelings.[11] This is hardly a development that corroborates the conventional paradigm. Hourani, writing at the end of Chehab's term, should have been aware of these developments.

In a vein that at face value appears to be in opposition to Hourani's characterization of nation-building, Khalaf concedes that Lebanon hardly possesses any of the instruments of a civil polity. He is of the opinion that political modernization does not necessarily mean secular and ideological commitments as opposed to primordial alliance. He informs us that the break need not be final, 'the viability of the political system will not appear so curious if one understands the nature of social and political change in Lebanon.' Further, the central theme that he wishes to discuss is that 'primordial ties and loyalties are not, as often assumed, impediments to national solidarity and political unity.' At once we see that Khalaf's concern is with nation-building and with the need 'to account for persistence of primordial ties in the political life of Lebanon.'[12] The approach he takes is cultural: 'How to assimilate traditional culture into the culture of a rational and secular society without destroying both?'[13] He repeats, after Halpern, that 'modernization involves the ability to absorb and generate change, not the repudiation of traditional values.'[14]

His theme leads to a discussion of the *zuama* and their role in articulating their constituent demands, a point which, he maintains, corroborates the rationality of the National Pact and of religion in Lebanese politics.[15] He advocates the view, shared by Salibi, Entelis and others, that the pact and religion gave stability and democracy to the polity and that the zuama were instrumental in maintaining its political continuity.

Khalaf also contends that the benefits enjoyed and generated by the system are due to confessionalism. 'The consecration of confessional loyalties through the National Pact is a realistic and effective formula.'[16] However, unable to set Lebanon's crisis aside, he claims that the ills the system experiences are caused by bureaucracy and not by confessionalism. Essentially, he has no problem with confessionalism or primordial ties; maintaining that one can still build and modernize further with them.[17]

It seems that, in Khalaf's analysis, the polity can be modern without being civil. Since modernity is rational, the National Pact is rational and carries the polity into a realm of modernity. This rationality of the pact appears to be the box within which all elements of primordialism reside. However, it is a Pandora's box: once uncovered, the polity cannot be contained within the path of nation-building designed by such mainstream literature.

To blame the problem on one element of modernity, namely bureaucracy, is inconsistent with any variation of the paradigm with which one may choose to work. If one maintains that the bureaucracy is to blame because it still has influence of a primordial nature, and because of friction originating from the zuama system (in the case of Lebanon both exist),[18] then it follows that these primordial ties and influences are at the least hurdles to bureaucracy and, by implication, to modernity. It then follows that either the modern or the zuama system is not rational.

On another level, to separate the influences of the pact from those of bureaucracy is irrational, since the pact is extended, in practice, within the bureaucracy.[19] Whatever administrative arrangement a polity has, there is by necessity the function of management and administration. However, to solve the problems that arise within the structures of the polity, one would have to understand its political, economic and social nuances, as well as the bureaucratic implementation one resolves to utilize. Khalaf chooses to ignore these more basic questions.

Another mainstream writer of significance is J.P. Entelis. His problematic is the survival of the state through the Lebanese Kataeb Party (LKP) or the Phalangists. He, like the other mainstream writers assumes that 'Lebanism' (Lebanonism), a pluralistic society and elite politics are essential for conflict resolution.[20] Entelis contends that a rational confessional arrangement has no place for dogmatic politics which try to assimilate Lebanon through Arab nationalist ideology, or politics that seek an alternative system. He informs us that:

> [Lebanon's] experience has demonstrated that an accommodative attitude toward parochial interests can actually accelerate national integration, enhance the legitimacy of the political system, and maximize the possibility of peaceful adjustment of social conflicts. Moreover, the

adaptive elements of Lebanon's modernization process have helped to cope with internal tensions and discontinuities resulting from rapid social change.[21]

Here Entelis relies on the work of Khalaf and E. Harik, among others.[22] As is obvious from this analysis, 'rapid social change', and not the model of development utilized (laissez-faire grafted on to a confessional polity), is responsible for 'tensions and discontinuities'. Furthermore, Entelis contends that the confessional system is positive in this regard because it helps Lebanon to 'cope' with development.

As the history of Lebanon has shown, the long-awaited society Entelis speaks of has failed to materialize. Instead of helping Lebanon to 'cope', the country's 'modernizing' structures have legitimized unequal relationships in politics and economics among the population and regions.

Entelis defines his problematic as 'modernization', etc., and dismisses challenges to the system from anti-system parties and groups as ideology or demagogy. He then proceeds 'objectively' to examine system maintenance and system development ('challenge'). The LKP, we are told, is the 'genuinely democratically-inspired and modern political [organization which seeks] an evolutionary form of social integration based upon the legitimate recognition of confessional interests.'[23]

Entelis, like the other writers reviewed thus far, chooses well-defined categories (Christian, Muslim) that have the force of tradition. In choosing other categories, one would first have to challenge the previous ones. Furthermore, questioning the traditional language of the 'modern' system maintenance, nation-building, etc. leads to an examination of reasons behind the creation of such categories, and to an analysis of the material conditions that were responsible for the prevalence of such categories in the literature.

If, as is shown in chapters 3 and 4, development means more than just modernization and involves the universe of political economy of the polity, then it is obvious that political development involves more than system maintenance. It certainly involves more than stability, pro-system parties (like the LKP) and zuama or other traditional 'relevant' institutions ('relevant' to what, and to whom?).

Entelis finds many flaws in the Lebanese modernization effort. However, his flaws are not the fault of the system; on the contrary, he proclaims that 'confessionalism is the Lebanese response to this democratic problem in a plural society.'[24]

Michael Hudson, who is one of the most important students of Arab politics, contends that in Lebanon

Democratic institutions have brought about and maintained stability in an unfavourable political environment. The Lebanese case suggests that formal institutions, although neglected in behavioural political science, deserve new attention as causal agents in the process of political modernization. At the same time, it raises the question of whether such institutions can supply enough systematic flexibility to meet the social mobilization demands of a rapidly changing society.[25]

As a pluralist body politic, Hudson says Lebanon needs

> . . . a political system based upon the balance of power . . . In turn, the balance of power has required institutions that promote democratic values . . . Lebanon's representative institutions are an essential condition of its stability, not a lucky by-product.[26]

Although Hudson shares with Entelis, Salem and others the problematic of stability and modernization of new states (Lebanon in this instance), his keen insight into the problem allows him to reach conclusions which are at variance with Salibi's visualization of 'traditional Muslims versus modernizing Christians'. Hudson recognizes that the 'system is democratic only in a limited sense'.[27] And modernization presents a problem of adding new social demands to a weak government apparatus. Meeting these demands and becoming responsive to the people 'will threaten the existing democratic values that are a product of the balance of power among autonomous traditional groups'.[28] One can already infer that modernization and development will not be conducive to that political system. The system is based on a static balance of power which is irrational since it cannot cope with political and economic development.

Hudson assumes that the basic question to investigate is the effect of social mobilization on the Lebanese body politic. He does not analyze the underlying reasons for instability. Instead, he sets out to study 'the environment of the Lebanese political system'.[29]

This formulation of the problem confines Hudson, as it does other writers, to the study of élite politics. This also allows most writers to relegate to the realm of 'ideology' and demagogy pan-Arab feelings and political practice among the Lebanese. It further allows these writers to dismiss such practices as unworthy of serious consideration by social scientists investigating political-science questions such as modernization and nation-building. Hudson studies 'the connection between traditional pluralism, the balance of power, democratic values and stability'.[30] While relegating the weakness of the system to 'elements beyond its control',[31] he poses

> . . . the most interesting and perplexing question about Lebanese politics: considering all the factors weighing against it — a divided citizenry, low national feeling, the pressure of Arab politics, the strains of modernization — how can it perform so successfully?[32]

Instead of being seen as 'interesting and perplexing', this state of affairs should have been seen as an indicator of rapidly developing and deepening problems of the confessional polity. Despite 'the regularity of institutionalized instability', the problems created by social mobilization such as the regional and 'structural unevenness' and 'the growing politicization' of the Lebanese, Hudson isolates what he calls 'two important characteristics that mitigate to some extent [the system's] weaknesses' and which give it 'a certain capacity for muddling through'. They are: (1) increasing institutional strength; and (2) a degree of democratic procedure.[33]

He sets out to discuss the modernization that occurred in the office of the presidency and the Chamber of Deputies. He points out some of the reforms that took place under Chehab (a social-security programme, administrative reform and the creation of the social development office) and the changes in Lebanon's foreign policy (closer Arab solidarity). These discussions allow him to conclude:

> The events of the last decade suggest that while sectarians at the popular level show no signs of disappearing, the political system can to some extent transcend the confessional, corporate society.[34]

And, in opposition to Entelis's later thesis about the LKP:

> For Lebanon more than most states, survival today requires political responsiveness to broadly populist demands, and this fact is recognized by Lebanese politicians. Lebanon does not need a party system to make these realities apparent and a determinant in policy-making. Indeed, the vulnerability of the system increases its responsiveness.
>
> This is not to say, however, that Lebanon will overcome the persistent challenges of modernization in the long run. Institution growth and democratic procedures are palliatives, not cures . . . [but Lebanon's dilemma remains]: too little democracy may lead to social disorder and revolution; too much may bring down upon the state the wrath of the traditional leaders.[35]

Unlike Entelis, Hudson does not see confessionalism as Lebanon's answer to the democratic problem. And, unlike Salem, he does not believe evolutionary modernization has good prospects.

Although Hudson is at variance with important conclusions of mainstream writers on Lebanon, his commitment to 'their' model prevents his from considering revolutionary change as a solution to Lebanon's development. Given his problematic, Hudson tends to think of such change, though indirectly, as a danger to democracy and institution-building.[36] Although he puts his finger on Lebanon's perennial dilemma, his model does not allow him to cross the threshold.

It took a civil war to bring an analyst of Hudson's calibre to criticize the major treatments of the Lebanese polity. It is, I believe, an indictment of the conventional literature from one working within it. In what I feel is to some extent an honest self-criticism, Hudson contends:

The civil war in Lebanon makes it imperative to reassess the conventional pluralist interpretations of Lebanese politics, in particular those of the 'optimistic' school of Lebanese specialists and those of the consociational theorists.[37]

He further states, 'It needs no further demonstration that the optimistic pluralist analyses of Lebanese politics, including the consociational model, were inadequate.'[38]

Despite Hudson's criticism of the 'conventional pluralist interpretations', this type of literature on Lebanon, and especially its cruder form using the Muslim-versus-Christian model, is still dominant. Consequently, legitimacy and credence are being conferred by academia upon the false notion that the 1958 and 1975 civil wars in Lebanon were in fact conflicts between Christians and Muslims. In this type of literature, these wars are treated as being the continuation of sectarian (confessional) politics by other means.

Writers such as Kamal Salibi and Frank Stoakes, writing on these wars, continue to use the Muslim/Christian categories. Salibi, for instance, asserts:

> In 1958, the confrontation between the Muslims and Christians of the country had resulted in a general political collapse, which shook Lebanon to its foundations, opening the way for social changes on a more rapid and radical scale.[39]

In fact, Salibi's entire book *Crossroads to Civil War: Lebanon 1958–1976* is full of assertions that the wars of 1958 and 1975 were the result and continuation of sectarian politics, or more specifically, Muslim-versus-Christian politics. Salibi's usage of Muslim/Christian categories, to the exclusion of virtually all others, robs the Lebanese of his humanity. The Lebanese is suddenly abstracted and simplified. He becomes one-dimensional: either Muslim or Christian.

As a leading representative of this brand of writers, Salibi tries to induce the reader to believe that the Lebanese is classless and has no position in the production process or in the economy as a whole. The Lebanese neither belongs to, nor has allegiance to, a political party unless it is religious. Salibi's book conjures up in the reader's mind images of the Muslims competing with or fighting the Christians of Lebanon in an effort by each of these religious groups to protect its existence and interests. According to Salibi, the interests of Muslims (all Muslims) lie in pan-Arabism. The interests of Christians (all Christians) lie in Lebanonism. Salibi does not analyse the reasons for 'Muslims' being pan-Arab or for 'Christians' being Lebanonists. Further, he does not analyse the relationship between the Muslim bourgeoisie and the Muslim masses, the Christian bourgeoisie and the Christian masses, or the bourgeoisie that is in fact multi-confessional, and the confessional and other cleavages in the mass of the population that may have much to do with the Lebanese conflict.

What is also so unsatisfactory about the Muslim/Christian categorization is the sense of the absolute that is embedded in it. Things are clear-cut. But even Salibi finds problems in using this categorization. When it becomes outrageous to force events to fit the absolute categories that dominate his book, Salibi suddenly allows us to meet the 'communists' and the 'radicals' who descend upon us out of thin air. Discussing 1968 events, Salibi informs us:

> Popular demonstrations upholding the Palestinian right to unrestricted commando action from Lebanon against Israel condemned the attempts on the part of the Lebanese authorities to keep commando movement under control, and the Communists and Ba'th Socialists, working in close association with Kamal Janbalat [Jumblatt] and his Progressive Socialist Party, invariably appeared at the head of these demonstrations.[40]

Further, in discussing 1974 events:

> Meanwhile, the Kata'ib Party had also reactivated its old political front against the radical National Movement in Lebanon. Ever since its formation in 1969, this National Movement, under the leadership of Kamal Janbalat, had pressed and agitated in favour of a radical reform of the Lebanese political system.[41]

In dealing with 1975 events:

> The fishermen of Lebanon, prompted by the Communists and other radical parties, saw the establishment of the Protein Company as an attempt to monopolize the Lebanese fishing industry, and a threat to their livelihood.[42]

Once particular events are smoothly discussed by using the 'radical' and other categories, Salibi jettisons them to rescue the Muslim/Christian dichotomy. This recurring practice in Salibi's book demonstrates the inconsistency in any discussion of Lebanese politics that utilizes the Muslim/Christian categorization.

It is well known that the 'radical' parties have members of all religious sects and many of them operate in all the Lebanese regions. If so, why does Salibi insist on a 'Christian position' versus a 'Muslim position'? Possibly by the 'Christian position' Salibi means that of the 'militantly conservative Christians'? But who are these? And the 'Muslim position' might, for Salibi, mean that of the 'Muslim bourgeoisie'. Again, he does not tell us. One suspects that the usage of these seemingly innocuous terms conceals an entire history of political and economic development in Lebanon. And that the consequences of such development are explained away through the Muslim/Christian dichotomy.

Salibi also identifies two cultures and societies in Lebanon: one Christian and modern, the other Muslim and traditional. According to Salibi, the

Christian society is 'socially and culturally homogenous' and not prone to conflict, as is the lot of the Muslim society. Further, because the Christian intellectuals do not form a distinct class, they are links at every level between the different parts of their society and so 'they promote a unity of purpose among all classes'.[43]

Salibi characterizes 'westernization' in Asia and Africa and the Muslim Arab states in the Arab East as:

> ... an urban phenomenon, setting towns apart from rural areas and emphasizing within each town the distinction between the rich upper class and the working folk. Hence in Westernizing societies, cultural incongruity is naturally coupled with increased social tension. The traditional culture, when it is relegated to slums and depressed villages, rapidly loses its original vitality and becomes a leading cause of national sensitivity.[44]

However, Salibi makes an exception for what he describes as 'westernization' in Lebanon:

> Lebanon presents a striking contrast to the general pattern of Westernization in the Arab Middle East. Because of the influence of its Christian population, this country stands apart from its surroundings, displaying those marked Western tendencies by which it is chiefly distinguished.[45]

Those negative aspects of 'westernization' of which Salibi speaks are explained in terms of 'false pride' and 'devious reasoning'.

> The West, which they generally admire, in challenging them to meet its standards, often appears to them as a threat. Paradoxically, these Westernizing people while seeking to understand the causes of their own cultural inertia, are usually obsessed by a false pride which inhibits them from accepting unfaltering realities and compels them to resort to devious reasoning. They are hence prone to lay the blame for their most serious problems on outside forces ... They are also inclined to stress, as a reason for their social and cultural failings, their comparative lack of national power, a condition which is actually the outcome rather than the cause of their backwardness. It is probably because of their insistent association of progress with power that newly independent Asian and African nations have tended to hold their armies in high esteem ... military dictatorships have easily superseded constitutional governments in most Afro-Asian countries.[46]

The tensions created along class lines in Afro-Asian countries Salibi speaks of, are part and parcel of the capitalist model and hardly due to cultural inertia or backwardness. Tensions between town and country, the association of progress with power, and modernization using the military are more than merely the 'outcome' of the 'western' model of modernization (South Korea, Taiwan, the Philippines).

Lebanon's case, which Salibi opposes to the general development that occurred in Africa and Asia, is also questionable. By Salibi's admission, Lebanon experienced primordial and sectarian conflict on a similar scale to other Afro-Asian countries. Many of these countries were able to find working formulas to resolve conflicts until such times as conflagrations occurred, as for example in Cyprus (1974) and Nigeria (1960s). Before Salibi's writing, Lebanon experienced a coup in 1961, a civil war in 1958, a serious crisis in 1952 and a coup in 1949. According to Salibi, however, Lebanon is stable and unique because of its 'Christian' character. But there are Christians in other Afro-Asian countries. Ethiopia is a strategically located country, with a rich history, predominantly Christian, but extremely under-developed.

In Salibi's analysis, development and underdevelopment are not connected with the effects of colonialism — expropriation and exploitation of human and natural resources, dependency, underdevelopment, and so on, and the creation of a privileged sector of the population that, in various ways, per-petuates the link to the colonial power after independence. Many colonial countries failed to develop evenly precisely because they adopted the Western (i.e. capitalist) model of development.

Lebanon's political and economic development will be dealt with in detail in chapters 3 and 4, but some comments are, however, in order here. If the level of observable phenomena alone was considered, it would become clear that this Muslim/Christian categorization has no merit. The history of growth and development of the Lebanese National Movement (LNM) groups such as the Communist Party, the Organization of Communist Action, etc., is integral to the development of the Lebanese social formation. In giving them such cursory mention, however, Salibi would have us believe that these are fringe groups marginal to Lebanese politics. Further, he would have us believe that, in fact, major LNM components — such as Jumblatt's Socialist Progressive Party (SPP) — espouse sectarian politics.

While it is true that the base of the SPP is primarily Druze, the party was throughout the 1960s and 1970s against confessionalism. Salibi himself reports Jumblatt's opposition to sectarian politics:

> Even since its formation in 1969, this National Movement, under the leadership of Kamal Janbalat, had pressed and agitated in favour of a radical reform of the Lebanese political system. It had called for amendments to the Lebanese Constitution and changes in the Electoral Law, which would secure the abolition of the principle of sectarian representation in public office, and in parliament, in favour of what it called 'social' or 'popular' representation.[47]

Salibi contradicts himself, too, when he opposes the LNM stance to the 'Muslim' one:

On the issue of the amendment of the Constitution and the 'National Covenant', the National Movement found itself fighting side by side with the Sunnite Muslim front, demanding full Muslim participation in the functions of government. While the National Movement, however, was ideologically opposed to the sectarian principle on which the 'National Covenant' was based, the Sunnite front represented by Saib Salam, Rashid Karami, and Mufti Hasan Khalid, and the 'National Front' (al-Hay'a al-Wataniyya) headed by Amin al-'Uraysi, merely insisted that the terms of the 'National Covenant' should be more fairly applied to give the Muslim Lebanese their rightful political share in the state.[48]

These contradictions do not corroborate Salibi's Muslim/Christian categorization. Neither does the history of any 'radical' party in Lebanon. The Lebanese Communist Party's history, for instance, and its struggles in the labour movement since the 1920s are well documented. In considering momentous political development, the Communist Party cannot be dismissed. Further, it is well represented in the south, the north, the Bekaa and in Beirut, and its members come from all religious groups.

What is so disquieting about this Muslim/Christian categorization is that it goes beyond academic circles, of which Salibi is the foremost representative. Israel and the Western media have always categorized the 1975 war as a Muslim/Christian affair. This has served Israel well. It has concealed the true nature of the conflict. However, those Muslims and Christians who fought side by side against the so-called 'Christian' forces can attest to the fact that, at root, the conflict was not sectarian, despite the assertions of Israel, Salibi and others.

The presence of Christians in the top leadership of the LNM, and the role that the traditional (confessional) Muslim leaders played in maintaining the system, underscore the fallacy behind the sectarian argument. Furthermore, the Christians are divided into sects. The LKP (the Phalangists), the PFN and other groups do not represent 'the Christians'. To begin with, about 95% of the LKP members come from the Maronite Christian sect. The LKP's strength is in Kisrwan (in the Mountain) and in parts of Beirut. Most members of other Christian sects are either neutral or actively support the LNM.

In addition, the LKP does not even represent the Maronites. Franjieh, Chamoun and Eddé have their own organizations. While at times these Maronite leaders have entered into coalitions with each other, they have often been at odds. Eddé, for instance, was against the LKP throughout the 1975 war and until now (1984). There is bad blood between Franjieh and the LKP, who brutally murdered his son Tony and his family, after raping Tony's wife; LKP butchers mutilated all their bodies. On 23 July 1983 Walid Jumblatt (Kamal's son) announced the formation of a National Salvation Front that included Franjieh, Karami and Jumblatt; working against the LKP regime in Beirut and against Israel. Under such circumstances, it is rather difficult to imagine the existence of a 'Maronite position', much less a

'Christian position'.

As a representative of a clearly ideological trend in academia, Salibi tries to bestow academic respectability upon fallacious arguments. It is regrettable to note, moreover, that the sorry state of the mainstream literature on political development has simplified Salibi's task.

To simply relegate all 'backward' elements in Lebanon to the 'traditional Muslims' is no substitute for hard analysis of politics and economics. There is a need to trace the origins and development of the conflict from its beginning in order to discover why and how confessionalism became a form of 'the political', a form of the capitalist state. Class formation and the impact of the colonial power upon the development of new classes and the economy are subjects worthy of attention. Lebanon and its society has one economy. The political system reinforces the economy, which in turn creates uneven development among the country's regions and population. This in turn reinforces the political set-up and its attendant zuama system. Explaining 'backwardness' by concocting an inherent evil in the aboriginal culture is superficial, subjective, and skirts the underlying reasons that prevented Lebanon from even development. It is obvious in Lebanon's case that the ruling élite — of all sects, but predominantly Maronite — perpetuates the status quo and controls the state.

On another level, as E. Shils and others have noted, classes do cut across religious lines.[49] Besides, Christians in Lebanon are not a monolithic community, as Salibi leads us to believe. Maronites, Catholics, Greek Orthodox and Protestants comprise some of the country's Christian sects. In many Christian villages one sees various political affiliations: Arab nationalists, Syrian nationalists, Communists and Kataeb (Phalangists). These affiliations are reflections of various ideological and class positions. This observation does not support Salibi's characterization of the Christian intellectuals.

The confessional nature of the state does not allow an honest analyst to categorize the Christians as liberals and the Muslims as traditionalists. Confessionalism, though it may possess certain liberal symbols, is not really liberal, because it is replete with primordial ties that infiltrate liberal symbols. It behoves Salibi to remember that the 1949 coup was attemped by the Syrian nationalists, whose leader was a Christian; that the 1952 crisis was instigated by the Christian president, which later prompted Christians and Muslims to force the president to resign; and that the 1958 civil was was also initiated to uphold the National Pact, which was being violated by a Christian president.[50] After that war Chehab, the new president, instituted social, economic and political reforms, keeping the confessional system intact and mitigating the radicalization of the masses. As Salibi very well knows, those parts of the country which are predominantly Christian could not have won the social benefits they enjoy without the ruling Christian élite dominating the political process, and using it to support the economic sectors that favoured their areas at the expense of the rest of Lebanon.[51] Salibi's analysis extols the inequities of uneven development and legitimizes the confessional political process. The history of Lebanon, before and after Salibi's analysis, belies his observations on the nature of the confessional polity.

# Notes

1. Qubain, Issawi, Salibi, Meo and Harik are examples of these writers.
2. See L. Binder, 'Political Change in Lebanon', in L. Binder, ed., *Politics in Lebanon* (New York, John Wiley and Sons, 1966). E. Salem, *Modernization Without Revolution: Lebanon's Experience* (Bloomington, Indiana University Press, 1973).
3. See Hudson's critique referred to in pp. 17–20 of this chapter.
4. Hudson, who comes the closest to such a critique, elects to remain within the mainstream paradigm à la Deutsch; see pp.17–20 of this chapter.
5. E. Shils, 'The Prospect for Lebanese Civility', in L. Binder, op. cit.
6. A. Hourani, 'Lebanon: The Development of a Political Society', p. 29, in L. Binder, op. cit.
7. Ibid.
8. A. Hottinger, 'Zu'ama in Historical Perspective', p. 100, op. cit. P. Rondot writes, 'Shivabism therefore risks being no more than an exceptional episode, at the end of which the problems of the Lebanese Executive will reappear in their previous and, so to speak, classic form'; in L. Binder, op. cit. Rondot was right.
9. One has only to recall Parsons pattern variables and the Liberal theory that gave rise to structural functionalism. Talcott Parsons, *The Social System* (Glenco, Free Press, 1951).
10. See H. Saab, 'The Rationalist School in Lebanese Politics', in L. Binder, op. cit.
11. See, for instance, C. Maksoud and G. Shukri in L. Binder, op cit., and *Urs Ed-Dam Fi Lubnan* (Beirut, Dar-et-Taliya, 1976) respectively.
12. S. Khalaf, 'Primordial Ties and Politics in Lebanon', *Middle East Studies*, IV, 244–5.
13. Ibid.
14. M. Halpern, 'Toward Further Modernization of the Study of the New Nations', *World Politics*, XVII, 158–81.
15. S. Khalaf, op. cit., p. 260.
16. Ibid., p. 262.
17. Ibid., p. 265.
18. E. Shils, op. cit., p. 4, in L. Binder, op. cit.
19. Ibid.
20. J.P. Entelis, *Pluralism and Party Transformation in Lebanon: Al-Kata'ib, 1936-1970* (Leiden, Netherlands, E.J. Brill, 1974).
21. Ibid., p. 8.
22. Ibid., pp. 5–8.
23. Ibid., p. 7. Frank Stoakes agrees with Entelis on the LKP; see 'Lebanese Kata'eb Party as a Builder, Surrogate and Defender of the State', *Middle East Studies*, XII (October, 1975), 215–16.
24. Ibid., p. 6.
25. M. Hudson, 'Democracy and Social Mobilization in Lebanese Politics',

*Comparative Politics*, (January, 1969), 245.

26.   Ibid.
27.   Ibid.
28.   Ibid., pp. 245–6.
29.   Ibid.
30.   Ibid.
31.   Ibid., p. 248.
32.   Ibid., pp. 248–9.
33.   Ibid., pp. 252–9.
34.   Ibid., p. 261.
35.   Ibid., p. 262.
36.   Ibid., p. 263.
37.   M. Hudson, 'The Precarious Republic Revisited: Reflections on the Collapse of Pluralist Politics in Lebanon'. Presented at the Annual Meeting of the Association of Arab-American University Graduates (AAUG), New York, 2 October 1976, p. 5.
38.   Ibid., p. 11.
39.   Kamal S. Salibi, *Crossroads To Civil War: Lebanon 1958–1976* (Delmar, NY, Caravan Books, 1976), p. 7.
40.   Ibid., p. 38.
41.   Ibid., p. 82.
42.   Ibid., p. 92.
43.   K. Salibi, 'The Personality of Lebanon in Relation to the Modern World', p. 266, in L. Binder, op. cit.
44.   M. Hudson, op. cit., p. 262.
45.   Ibid., p. 265.
46.   Ibid., p. 264.
47.   K. Salibi, *Crossroads* . . . op cit., p. 82.
48.   Ibid., p. 83.
49.   See F. Khuri, 'The Changing Class Structure in Lebanon', *Middle East Journal*, XXIII, pp. 29–43.
50.   P. Rondot, op. cit., p. 138 in L. Binder, op. cit.
51.   Tourism, fruit, banking and transit trade all favour Mount Lebanon and Beirut.

# 3. Political History: From the Ottoman Period to Independence

In the fourth decade of the 7th Century AD, Muslim Arabs conquered Syria (then comprising Lebanon, Palestine and modern Syria). In order to repel Byzantine attacks, Muslim tribes settled in the conquered areas. The displaced Christians, who were mostly Maronite, took refuge in the northern part of Mount Lebanon (the Mountain).[1]

During the Crusades, Mardites were brought from the Amanus and Taurus mountains (in southern Turkey) to protect coastal towns from Muslim Arab attack. At the end of the Crusade period, Muslim Arabs forced these Mardites to resettle in the Mountain, where they intermingled with the Maronites.

Under the influence of the Crusaders, Maronite relations with Rome began to take form in the 12th Century. Rome's influence also touched upon Maronite religious doctrines. It was not until 1439, however, that partial union with Rome was achieved at the Council of Florence. Full union was effected only in 1736 at the Synod of Al-Luwzayah.[2]

Catholic missionaries in the Mountain and trade with Italian city-states further reinforced relations between the Maronite Mountain and the West. During the 17th Century, the Maronites referred to the area around the Cedars as Mount Lebanon. Not until the 18th Century did the name also refer to areas further south which bordered Jabal ash-Shuf (the Chouf mountains), where Arabs of the Druze religion had lived since the Crusade period.[3]

The Druze religion is an offshoot of Islam. It originated in Egypt during the reign of the Fatimid Caliph Hakim, who ruled from 996 to 1021. Not meeting with much success in Egypt, Muhammad al-Darazi, founder of the Druze religion, took refuge in the Chouf after Hakim's assassination. There, the Druze began to convert other Muslim tribes to their belief. Families who played important roles in Lebanon's history, such as the Tannukhs, the Arslans, the Maans and the Jumblatts, were among the converts.[4]

In this setting a feudal system began to emerge in the Maronite and Druze areas. When Ottoman Selim I defeated the Mamluks (rulers of Syria and Egypt) in Syria in 1516, feudalism was already firmly established in the Mountain. Selim I named Fakhr-ed-Din from the Maan family 'Sultan of the Mountain'. His grandson Fakhr-ed-Din II (ruled 1586–1635) is regarded as the father of modern Lebanon. Fakhr-ed-Din II was able to unite the Mountain with the Chouf into the 'Emirate of Mount Lebanon'. During his reign the Ottomans did not interfere much in the internal affairs of the emirate, since they regarded it as a 'tax farm'.[5]

Bashir Chehab I was elected governor in 1697 by the council of emirs (landlords) after the last of the Maans died childless.[6] During the 1700s the Chehabis (converts to Christianity from Islam) were ruling the emirate. However, the decline of the Maans prompted the Hamadeh family (Shiites) to annex the northern areas of the emirate to its Hirmil region (northern Bekaa area).[7] In 1759, however, the Maronite peasants rebelled against the Hamadehs and asked the Chehabis to reestablish them in their domain. In keeping with their predecessors' policies, the Chehabis encouraged Maronite peasants to migrate south to Kisrwan and the Chouf where they were needed for agricultural production. This migration, however, resulted in the permanent push of the Shiites out of the emirate. Furthermore, exclusive Druze areas were also witnessing a sustained and steady Maronite peasant migration since these peasants were also needed to till the land of landlords who were seeking to increase their revenues.[8]

In the emirate, social stratification consisted of two main socio-economic groups, lord and peasant. Peasants were also subdivided into landowners and tenants. In this feudal system, social relations were somewhat secular. However, in the Iqta (feudal) system, party groupings cut across religious lines.[9] Although the Druze landlords were more influential than their Maronite counterparts, 'nevertheless, it is clear that religious affiliation was not a factor in shaping the politics of the Imarah (emirate) before the end of the eighteenth century.'[10]

Druze landlords were more powerful than their Maronite counterparts, since they had a strong social organization and since the Druze were historically the pillars of the emirate while the Maronites had been integrated relatively recently. While northern Maronite lords were not much better off than their peasants, influential Druze lords exercised political and economic power in areas outside their villages.[11]

In vying for power over the emirate, Bashir Chehab II (a Maronite) depended upon Druze lords to fight other Chehabi contenders. Bashir II, who ruled the emirate from 1788 to 1840, also encouraged the complete integration of the Maronites into the emirate, as they were needed as labourers and scribes. For these reasons, Maronites were treated on an equal basis with Druze and Muslims. They were also allowed to own land and to participate in the politics of the emirate.

The political office of *mudabbir* (manager and adviser to the emir) was an extremely sensitive position. Earlier Chehabi rulers had Maronite mudabbirs to counter the power of Druze lords.[12] When Bashir II became ruler, he rewarded his Druze supporters by appointing one of them as mudabbir. This was an opportune moment for the Druze lords to check the power of the Maronite lords and regain the power which they had lost earlier. Although the office of mudabbir '... made political conflict inevitable between the Maronite and Druze Manasib (lords), who were the main custodians of power in the system',[13] the feudal system still remained secular, and political conflict among lords also cut across religious lines.

Up until the middle of the 18th Century, landlords and peasants were the main social forces in the feudal system. However, the development of the emirate brought about another highly organized social force whose role was to become decisive in 18th- and 19th-Century Lebanon.

## The Rise of the Maronite Church as a Socio-Economic Institution

The Maronite church's traditional organization and its poverty were not conducive to making it an independent and powerful social force on the political scene. However, reform in the church and the integration of the Maronite areas into the emirate were favourable conditions for the growth of its prestige and power. Church reorganization brought about formal hierarchy and limited bribery in seeking religious positions. It also regulated and made church functions more efficient. These steps were aided by the education of the clergy at the Maronite college which Pope Gregory XIII opened in Rome in 1584. Integration of Maronite areas into the emirate had put the Maronites on an equal footing with the rest of the population in the secular system.

At first, the reorganized church remained poor and completely dependent upon the upper class 'for general support, for seats where they could carry on their religious work, and for the establishment and maintenance of new monasteries. In return for these benefits, the notable clans exercised influence over the church and secured most of the top offices for members of their families.'[14] Thus we see a symbiotic relationship between church and nobility and, in many cases, the church was an institution through which the nobility could exercise influence over the peasants.

When the Khazins (Maronite lords of Kisrwan) wished to encourage Maronite peasants to migrate to their fiefdom, they accomplished this through the church. They also supplied the church with protection and influenced its policies by transferring much of their lands into mortmain (non-transferable ecclesiastical possession). Non-Christian lords did not interfere with the church, but on various occasions donated land in the south of the emirate for the building of monasteries. This was one means of attracting the much-needed peasants to the south of the Mountain. Return for their 'altruism' came in the form of revenues from taxes that the church had to pay. Furthermore, Christian donor families regarded mortmains as investments and exercised property rights over them by having bishops elected from their families. A member of these clans once wrote to the Pope: 'The monasteries are ours founded by our fathers and grandfathers, and we will admit to them whomever we want to admit . . . We remain obedient to the Holy See in all matters religious.'[15]

A significant development gave much political and economic power to the clergy in the 18th and 19th Centuries. Around 1700 the Maronite Order of Monks was founded as an autonomous organization within the church. The order was formally under the bishop, but each monastery was in fact run by its abbot. Monks were recruited from among the peasants and they lived a communal and ascetic life. Since they did not need much to live on, they were capable of working the land and saving money to acquire more land. Seeing how efficient these monks were, the lords began donating more non-productive land to them. With so much land to cultivate, the monks encouraged Maronite peasants to congregate around and work for them. 'For these reasons many of the *muqati'jis* (feudal lords) preferred to see monks serving their subjects rather than the village secular priest, for the secular priest, as an individual working by himself, was not the productive force the organization of the monks was.'[16] In this way, the Maronite Order of Monks became 'one of the largest propertied sectors of Lebanese society'.[17] These corporate bodies became wholly integrated into the system, which they served well.

Towards the end of the 18th Century, as the Maronite Order of Monks became wealthier, a power struggle developed between it and the Maronite and Druze lords. Earlier, the monks had paid taxes to the lords, who took their share and passed the rest on to the ruler of the emirate. By the 19th Century they had begun to pay their taxes directly to the ruler, who was also interested in curtailing the lords' power.[18]

The church also began to encourage the oppressed peasants to revolt against the feudal privileges of their lords. Because of the social and economic functions that the church exercised in society through its daily contacts with the people, it was capable of wielding more influence among the people than the lords did. Interests of both clergy and peasants converged against the feudal system. The clergy were capable of leading the opposition due to their organization, education and the communal alternative to the feudal system which they could offer.

## The Ammiyah Revolt

During the rule of Bashir Chehab II, his commitment to Westernization and his war efforts demanded an ever increasing budget which he sought to bolster by levying more taxes on the peasantry. The peasantry came out openly against Bashir in the *ammiyah* (commoners') revolt of 1820.[19] Bishop Istfan, who had earlier had disagreements with Bashir concerning the latter's religious practices, participated with other clergy in the revolt. Class alliances shifted during the revolt. Bashir had to rely upon the Jumblatt family to fight the ammiyah, while other Druze and some Shiite lords sided with the ammiyah. The revolt also attracted two Chehabi emirs who wanted Bashir deposed. Maronite lords either fought the revolt or stayed neutral, as did some of the Druze lords.

The ammiyah revolt and the alliances concocted around it were powerful enough to depose Bashir II, who fled the emirate to Huran in Syria. The revolt was significant in various ways. (1) It was organized into village communes, with each village electing a representative to a general council. This was something unheard of in the feudal system. (2) Commoners and clergy exercised leadership roles. (3) Church ideology overlapped with peasant communal ideas and was effective in challenging the feudal system.

The new relationship the peasants were championing sought to transcend the patron/client one. To this effort Maronite districts of Al-Matn, Batrun, Jibbat Bsharri, Kisrwan and Jubail all took part in the revolt. Harik contends: 'The class consciousness [of the peasants] is also evident from the fact that peasants participated in the uprising against the wishes of their *muqati'jis* (landlords), particularly the Khazins and the Abillamas who stood with the Druze *manasib* and signed their compact.'[20]

The two Chehabi emirs who participated in the revolt against Bashir II lost the ammiyah's support when they tried to levy taxes upon the peasantry to meet their financial obligations to the Ottomans. Meanwhile, Bashir II had arranged with the Ottoman ruler to return to the Mountain, where he immediately began to reconcile the Druze lords. Once this was done, he sent his son to collect taxes. Peasants protested and gathered in a place called Lihfid. Bashir II negotiated with the ammiyah and agreed to their demands of equal treatment with the Druze lords in tax matters. Certain political demands, however, were not acceptable to Bashir II, who still had most of his support base among Druze lords loyal to the Ottomans. The demand that the emir ruling over them should not be appointed by the Ottoman ruler but should be one of them (a reference to Bashir's wavering religious affiliation, 'Christian by baptism, Moslem by matrimony, Druze through convenience rather than conviction ...')[21] precipitated fighting in Lihfid, Kisrwan, Jibbat Bsharri and other places. The outcome of the fighting was disastrous for the ammiyah and the nobility that supported it.

Most of the Druze lords became supporters of the Jumblatt family, who aided Bashir II in the battles against the ammiyah in 1821. When Bashir fled to Egypt due to a quarrel with the Ottoman ruler, the Jumblatts became extremely powerful. On his return from exile, Bashir II felt very uncomfortable about this rising new power in the emirate.

From 1822 until 1825 Bashir worked to consolidate his position. To this end he searched for new allies. He found the church and the masses most useful in suppressing Druze competition. The most powerful Druze and Maronite families were completely subdued in the battle of Mukhtarah. The effects of this battle were far-reaching. Although the feudal system remained a viable institution, it nevertheless underwent fundamental structural changes. The church entered the political scene as a challenger to the lords, thus curtailing much of·their previous power. A symbiotic relationship between the emir of the emirate and the Maronite patriarch emerged, and the latter was encouraged to settle differences among the Maronite lords. At times the patriarch was even capable of intervening with the emir on behalf of Druze lords. That was an activity that Emir Bashir discouraged. 'Thus the patriarch became a man of much political influence, but not a holder of political office.'[22]

What the church could not achieve through the ammiyah, it came closer to achieving through its alliance with Bashir. As a powerful institution, the church aspired for dominant, if not exclusive, power in the polity of Mount Lebanon. To this end, the church encouraged in various ways (through writing, its influence in the ammiyah, its daily contact with the peasantry, etc.), the breakdown of social relations between the Druze and the Maronites and gave this a sectarian flavour. The goal of a Christian emirate, dominated by a church which enjoyed mass support, brought together the weak Maronite lords in an alliance with the church against the Druze lords.[23]

## Egypt's Invasion of Syria, 1831

Meanwhile, Egypt was preparing to conquer Syria. The church allied itself with the Egyptian conqueror, Ibrahim Pasha, and his ally Bashir II. Bashir was interested in getting rid of Ottoman influence over the emirate, which he thought Ibrahim Pasha would aid him in doing. The church also found it propitious to ally with Egypt to get rid of the Ottomans and their allies, the Druze lords. In this way, the church thought that it could get closer to its goal of a Maronite emirate. When Egypt invaded Syria in 1831, the church was extremely effective in mobilizing Maronite peasants to fight in Bashir II's army. Bashir and his son also utilized sectarian sentiments to incite the Maronite peasants to fight the Druze lords.[24]

Despite the fact that Egyptian tax policies were unpopular among the peasantry, and despite the problems that the clergy had in explaining to the peasants the reasons behind the Maronite alliance with Egypt, the clergy was unwilling to relinquish the alliance. The clergy did not want the tax issue to become a hurdle in the way of an exclusive, church-dominated Maronite Mount Lebanon, which they thought the Egyptian connection would help secure. This, however, remained an unrealized dream. After Egypt's rule became firmly established in Syria, Ibrahim Pasha became lukewarm towards Bashir and the church, and began contemplating radical changes for the Mountain. The clergy did not appreciate what they regarded as an encroachment on their privileges, and immediately asked the French Consul in Beirut to intervene and prevent such an occurrence.[25]

In essence, the clergy sought to keep all forces balanced in their bid for a Christian emirate. The people, however, were unable to carry the tax burden and contend with corvée (forced labour) and the fear of the conscription in the Egyptian army. Although the clergy and the Maronite lords were not really pleased with the situation either, they were unable to take action in favour of the people against Bashir II and Ibrahim Pasha. Druze peasants were also unable to act single-handedly against Ibrahim Pasha in Lebanon since they were leaderless. Their lords were still outside the emirate after they had been crushed resisting Egypt's conquest of Syria.

## The May 1840 Revolt Against the Egyptians

Divergence between clergy and peasants prompted the alliance of Druze and Maronite peasants who led the revolt of May 1840 against the Egyptians. The revolt was similar to the ammiyah revolt of 1820 in its organization and goals. It called for government reorganization, less taxation, an end to corvée in the iron mines of Al-Matn and to the privileges of Druze lords, since 'Lebanon is not the property of the Druze, it is ours . . .'[26] The leadership was made up of the commoners, while the lords who joined with the revolt were among the followers.[27]

Needless to say, the revolt upset the plans of the clergy, who tried in vain to pacify it. The peasants petitioned the Maronite patriarch with their grievances, but to no avail. In July, however, the church reversed its position and supported the revolt. This move coincided with the mid-July Treaty of London, which committed the European powers to oust Ibrahim Pasha from Syria.[28]

The first stage of the revolt failed when, in July 1840, Bashir II and Ibrahim Pasha defeated the commoners. In September of that year, however, British, Ottoman and Austrian troops landed at Junieh and encouraged the Maronites to revolt against the Egyptians. With this foreign support, the peasants succeeded in overthrowing the Egyptian yoke. The Ottomans appeased the Maronite peasants by exempting them from taxes for a period of three years. They also agreed to reorganize the emirate since, like the peasants, they were interested in curtailing the influence of the emir. The Ottomans wanted to centralize the political machine in the emirate so that they could control it. To this end, they agreed with the European powers to oust Bashir II and appoint Bashir Qasim Shihab (Bashir III) as ruler of the emirate. To further their interests in the emirate, the Europeans recognized the Maronite patriarch as the representative of his people and began to deal with him accordingly.

The Maronite church was still pursuing its goal of a Maronite emirate. This led the church to solidify its alliance with Bashir III, who was looking for a support base among the population. The returning Druze lords, however, saw such an alliance as an encroachment on their rights to fiefdom. What also worried the Druze lords was the Ottoman intention of reorganizing the emirate.[29] Such a reorganization necessitated limiting the power of the Druze and Maronite lords.

To avoid any premature eruption of hostilities, the church found it propitious, at times, to mediate between the Druze lords and Bashir III. Bashir's lack of tact in dealing with these lords had completely alienated them and eventually led to the October 1841 hostilities.[30] The result was frustrating to the clergy. While they wholeheartedly sided with Bashir III and sent him troops made up of Maronite commoners and lords, this army could not act due to internal bickering and the lack of a unified leadership. While the clergy and the commoners were out to destroy the feudal system, the Maronite lords were opposed to this position. On the one hand, they could not break away from the commoners, who were fighting their common enemy (the Druze lords). On the other, the demise of the feudal system was definitely not to their advantage. Ultimately, they sided with their Druze counterparts against the Maronite peasants. The attempt of the church to unite Maronite lords and peasants failed the test of class interests and class struggle.

In 1842 the Ottomans replaced Bashir III with an Ottoman ruler. Displeased with this alternative, the European powers intervened and called for a new arrangement within which they could exert more influence in Lebanon. In 1843 they initiated the two-governorate system. This comprised a northern governorate which was predominantly Maronite and a southern governorate with Druze lords but mostly Christian peasantry.

In 1845 clashes between Druze and Maronites brought about a situation in the southern governorate that stripped the Druze lords of most of their power over their Maronite subjects. The inclusion of intermediaries between Maronite subjects and their Druze lords further eroded the feudal system in the Mountain and contributed to the rise of sectarian sensitivities. The church at this time claimed that 'it was easier for Christians to die than consent to live under Druze rule.'[31] Such sectarianism encouraged by the church and by the European powers was absent during the revolts of 1820 and 1840. Hitti contends that the ammiyah 'starting from a wide base, with the thesis that all sons of the Arabic tongue constituted one nation toward the realization of which they all should strive, the nascent pan-Arab movement was soon confronted with specific local problems resulting in its fragmentation.'[32]

The ammiyah spirit was sacrificed to the sectarian conflict which the church utilized to reach the goal of a Maronite emirate. However, this goal was not attained and in the course of a few years led to another round of open class warfare that assumed (thanks to the Europeans and the church) the semblance of religious warfare. But before dealing with these events, it may be useful to look briefly at Lebanese society in the early 19th Century.

## Socio-Economic Development under Egyptian Rule

Great economic and social change occurred in the decade of Egyptian rule (1831-40). This new opening to the West had a far-reaching impact upon the social formation of 19th-Century Lebanon. Earlier, Lebanon had undergone change primarily because of the needs of the feudal system to become more productive. With this new Egyptian influence, tension propelling change was exacerbated further.

During the 17th and 18th Centuries Beirut had no more than 5,000 residents, and was fairly important for the purpose of trade on the eastern coast of the Mediterranean. Subsistence economy was prevalent in the Mountain, where the household loom complemented farming. Concerning social relations in that period, Hitti informs us that 'Christians, Druze and Shiites continued to live together in harmony and peace.'[33] Further, 'Neighbourliness, if not "familiness" characterized business transactions as they did social relations.'[34] Speaking of social relations and customs, Volney, a French traveller to Lebanon in the 1780s,

> ... was struck by the similarity between Druze and Maronites in the mode of life, system of government, language, customs and manners. Members of both communities live amicably side by side. Druze at times accompany Maronites to churches, make use of the holy water and, if pressed by missionaries, suffer themselves to be baptized.[35]

A few years earlier, in 1760, Abbot Mariti observed that the Druze 'behave with great friendship to Christians and respect their religion. They pray indifferently in the Greek churches and the Turkish mosques.'[36]

Improved means of transport and increased cultural contact with the West through missionaries had brought furniture from Paris and textiles from the mills of Manchester, along with other European commodities, to the local market. Local cottage industry and village handicraft could not compete with European goods. Consequently, dyeing, weaving and other manufacturing began to disappear. By 1841 European goods had almost completely replaced local goods. This dealt 'severe blows to the textile industry of Aleppo and Damascus'.[37]

The silk industry began to be dominated by outsiders who helped to incorporate the Lebanese mountain village into the world capitalist market economy. These outsiders began to invest in village lands and villagers were hired as part-time labourers to work the land, planting mulberry trees to grow the silk worm. 'These changes in the rural areas had adverse impact upon the number and proportion of agricultural workers.'[38] Unable to find jobs in the village, landless peasants migrated to urban centres in search of better work. Education and the expanding trade in Beirut and other cities also contributed to the rapid development and expansion of the urban population. Sericulture was among the few local economic activities that prospered due to European contact. Not until the First World War was it adversely affected.

The development of the division of labour and the impact of the West on Lebanon resulted in the emergence of new classes. Because the Druze lords fled the Mountain during the 1820s and 1830s, they were unable to participate in the new social and economic relations that were forming. Consequently, the Maronite peasants were able to increase their wealth partly at the expense of the Druze lords.

> Peasants of Druze lords in the 1820s were by the end of the 1830s their money lenders ... Druze middle and lower classes were almost entirely rural and were affected mainly by being drawn into a closer dependence on the foreign market while gaining rather less than their Christian and Muslim counterparts from the ferment of the economy in Beirut.[39]

In the 1840s control of the economy (at least those factors of production that are geared to modern industry, such as modern oil presses and steam reeling factories) was in the hands of foreign capitalist investors.[40] By the late 19th Century Beirut had a population of 120,000. The type of business-man who emerged was one who was geared to serving the international capitalist market by acting as a middleman. Gradually these men accumulated economic and social power and, along with lawyers, doctors and educators, formed a new class that began to share power with the upper class of land-owners and clergy. Another class in the Lebanese social formation was the producing class: tillers and manual workers.

## The Development of Sectarian Conflict

Having considered the main social and economic changes during the first half of the 19th Century, we can now take a look at the events that led to a change in the form of government in the Mountain.

When Bashir Ahmad Abillama became governor of the northern governor-ate in 1854, he posed as the champion of the Catholics. With the blessing of France and Austria, he began instigating sectarian conflict between Catholics and Orthodox Christians. Recognizing that Bashir Ahmad was supported by its rivals, England gave its support to his opponent, Bashir Assaf, who also enjoyed the support of the Maronite aristocracy. Three years later (1857) rebellion broke out in Kisrwan against the feudal lords. Clashes between rebels and lords prompted Bashir Ahmad to take action against both parties. This in turn spurred the two sides to organize separately against the governor. The lords wanted to replace him, while the peasants wanted to get rid of both lord and governor.[41]

In their attempt to win their demands, the peasants invited the lords to a meeting to present them with their grievances. The Khazins, Maronite lords of Kisrwan, refused to consider any of the grievances. Instead, they threatened the peasants, thus succeeding in antagonizing them even more. Seeing that the affair was leading to violence, the elected peasant chief Salih Sfayr resigned and the peasants elected Tanius Shahin. By January 1859, the revolt was in full flood and enjoyed the backing of the French, the Maronite church and the Ottomans.[42] Local revolts erupted against the Khazins, in which they were beaten up and evicted. The peasants then declared the formation of their own state in the north.

In organizing against the revolt, the Khazins had failed to get the support of the Druze lords in the southern governorate. Instead, these Druze lords tried to prevent anti-feudal action in their areas by relying on Druze *uqqal* (religious men), who resorted to sectarian propaganda. In this way, they tried to keep the Druze commoners under their wing and to effect an alliance between Druze lords and commoners against Maronite peasants in the south. The uqqal reminded the Druze peasants of earlier sectarian conflict and in general tried to conceal the class nature of the uprising. This, however, did not prevent many Druze communities from revolting against their lords. But the scattered and spontaneous revolts were doomed to failure and the Maronite peasants were left to fend for themselves in the south. From the summer of 1859 through April 1860, Maronite peasants tried to organize themselves in anticipation of hostilities.[43]

Massacres of Christian peasants in the south began in April 1860. This was the weapon that the Druze lords utilized to defend their feudal system in the south. These lords were also already in touch with Ottoman governors and garrison commanders, who aided in this conflagration. Scores of Maronite villages were burned to the ground in Al-Matn and the Chouf districts, and in a few days the whole of the southern governorate was a theatre of conflict.[44] What was significant in all this was that the peasant state in the north did not come to the aid of their fellow Maronite peasants in the south. There were several reasons for this. The northern state was in a precarious position, facing constant threat from the Maronite feudalists. Added to this were the threats and promises that peasant leaders in the north received from the Ottomans and the European powers.

The British, it seemed, had a hand in much of what took place in April. The attack on the town of Zahle, for instance, 'was planned by Colonel Churchill . . .'[45] The various foreign powers were stirring sectarian conflict through the support they gave the competing factions. The British supported the Druze, the French the Maronites and the Russians the Greek Orthodox. Although the conflict seemed to be motivated by sectarian allegiance, the underlying causes were competition over which powers (local and/or foreign) were to control the political and economic destiny of the Mountain and the area in general.[46]

Within a few days the conflict had cost over 11,000 lives. At this point, Britain, France and other powers agreed to send 12,000 troops to bring an end to the conflict, which had also spread to Damascus. When, however, 7,000 French troops landed in Lebanon, the Ottoman Fuad Pasha was already in full control of the situation. He had already clamped down on those directly responsible for the massacres.[47]

## The Mutassarrifiyya: Class Rule in Sectarian Guise

As a subsequent development, in the autumn of 1860, an international commission met to negotiate an agreement for the political reorganization of Lebanon. The commission represented Britain, France, Russia, Austria and Prussia, and was presided over by Fuad Pasha, who represented Ottoman interests. Eight months after its first meeting on 5 October 1860, on 9 June 1861, the commission reached an agreement, 'the Reglement Organique', comprising 17 articles. This accord established the Mutassarrifiyya (governorate) system that united Lebanon (the two governorates) under an Ottoman ruler and abolished feudalism in the Mountain.[48]

Under the new Ottoman administration, which lasted until 1915, Lebanon was divided into six (later seven) districts according to the distribution of religions in the population. The Mutassarrif (governor) was appointed by the Ottoman Sultan, subject to the approval of the European powers. The Ottoman ruler (the Mutassarrif) was always a non-Lebanese Christian and an Ottoman subject aided by a central administrative council of twelve. This council was to be made up of four Maronites, three Druze, two Greek Orthodox, one Shiite, one Sunni (both Muslim sects) and one Greek Catholic.[49]

Each district was run by a governor aide, picked from the local population, who was assisted by a council of three to six representatives of the various sects. Deir al-Kamar, a Christian town, was the seat of the government. To appease the weakened nobility, the governors appointed them to the central council. In this new arrangement, Druze and Maronite peasants agitated for ownership of agricultural land and equitable representation. Maronite peasants, however, left the Mountain, as land became too scarce and expensive for them to own.

Although a stable Mount Lebanon was conducive to French political and economic interests, this did not prevent the French from attempting to gain a better position in the Mountain vis-à-vis the other powers.[50] To this end, France encouraged the Maronite Yusuf Karam to rebel against Daoud Pasha, the first Ottoman governor, whose appointment was not popular with the Maronites. Before Fuad Pasha had gained control of the 1860 events, Karam was promised the governorship by the big powers. This was probably one reason why he and others in the north did not move to aid the southern peasants in 1860. France began promoting Karam as a national hero who was seeking more political independence for Lebanon. This French move failed, however, and Karam was subsequently banished from the Mutassarrifiyya.[51] For the next 53 years the region maintained stability. However, instead of political representation being based on class lines openly and directly, the Mutassarrifiyya system legitimized sectarian representation and foreign intervention in Lebanon and in the area generally.

Even after the Karam debacle, France did not stop trying to improve her position in Lebanon. Through other surrogates, such as Paul Nujaym and Jesuit father Henri Lammans, France tried to promote Lebanese nationalism. Writing from Paris, the Lebanese Nujaym agitated for Lebanese territorial expansion that was in congruence with French expansionism at that time. Nujaym wrote:

> The statutes of 1861 and 1864 have mutilated Lebanon and robbed it of some of its most fertile districts. Most of all, they have deprived it of its great port of Beirut ... Lebanese commerce, very active and flourishing, has no opening to the sea, as the Porte does not permit the creation of a port on the Lebanese coast ... It is necessary that the guaranteeing Powers should intervene to defend the autonomy and accomplish the necessary reforms. But the most serious and most urgent problem of all is the extension of the Lebanese frontiers

> . . . The live forces of the Lebanese nation must be made use of in Syria itself, rather than be dispersed in all parts of the world . . .[52]

## Colonialism versus Pan-Arabism

A Lebanese nation, however, dominated by Christians and in congruence with French interests was not particularly appealing to the Druze. A dominant trend at this time was the 'liberal' one which called for 'pan-Arabism' and Syrian unity. Its main proponents were Christians, mostly Maronite literary figures, and leaders of the 'Arab Renaissance' movement in politics and literature. Al-Bustani, Al-Yaziji, Sarruf and Faris Nimr were among these 'pan-Arab' literary pillars.[53]

The First World War had subjected Lebanon to various economic and social dislocations. The newly-formed commercial classes in the coastal area were waiting deliverance. The Maronite commercial class was hoping for French intervention, while the other sectors of society were hoping for Arab independence.

The Sykes-Picot agreement of 1916 between France and Britain divided the Arab East between them. Britain was to take over Iraq, Jordan and Palestine; and France, Syria and Lebanon.[54] The terms of the agreement, however, ran counter to the hopes of the Sharif Hussein of Mecca and were partly in conflict with what the British had promised him in return for his help against the Ottomans in the war.

To exercise more influence on the local political movements, France helped to create the Central Syrian Committee in Paris in 1917, which called for a Syrian state extending over much of 'Natural Syria under French Mandate'.[55] On 1 October 1918, the Ottoman Ismail Bey handed over power to Umar Bey Dauq in Beirut. Umar proclaimed the establishment of an Arab Government, which was supported by Faisal (Sharif Hussein's son) who had already declared himself king of Syria after the Ottoman's defeat in the war. Shukri Pasha al-Ayyubi, a representative of Faisal, arrived from Damascus at the head of a small force to legitimize the Arab Government in Beirut. Shukri reactivated the Central Mutassarrifiyya Council in Lebanon to act as a branch of the Arab government in Syria and raised the flag in Baabda (near Beirut), the seat of the council.[56]

## The Establishment of a 'Greater Lebanon'

To arrest such unfavourable developments, France was compelled to support the Maronite clergy, who were articulating separatist tendencies against the Arab nationalists' call for the unification of Syria and Lebanon. The Maronite clergy were demanding the creation of a 'Greater Lebanon' (the Mountain and other parts of Syria) which would be under French Mandate. Consequently, two Maronite delegations headed by the clergy went to Paris in 1919 and 1920, respectively, to present their proposal for a 'Greater Lebanon'. However, these new developments forced France to relinquish its dream of a Syrian state as espoused by the Central Syrian Committee.[57]

French designs for the area were in conflict with the principle of self-determination called for by the League of Nations, established after the First World War. The King-Crane fact-finding commission, appointed by the League of Nations, had recommended a united Palestine-Syria with autonomy for the Mountain. This Palestine-Syria was to be under the domain of King Faisal, with the mandate for this area going to either the United States or Britain. The commission believed that Arab-French hostilities would not be prevented unless the French were to restrict their mandate to the Mountain.[58]

After his trip to Europe in early 1919, Faisal, due to French diplomatic pressure, relinquished his claim to Lebanon. He then accepted a separate Mountain area under France.[59] Hearing of Faisal's new position, the Arab nationalists reacted by convening a National Congress that proclaimed the independence of all Syria (including the Mountain). The French reacted by arresting the Lebanese who took part in the congress. With French encouragement and approval, 'representatives' of the Christian sects met in Baabda and proclaimed Lebanon independent of Syria.

Disregarding the King-Crane findings, the Supreme Allied Council approved the French Mandate for Syria and Lebanon on 25 April 1920. On 10 July the Central Council (of the old Mutassarrifiyya) resolved by majority vote to proclaim Lebanon independent of France and called for cooperation with Syria. To put an end to nationalist tendencies, France decided to occupy Syria. The Arab defeat in the battle of Maisaloun (24 July 1920) sealed the fate of Syria.[60] On 1 September 1920, France proclaimed 'Greater Lebanon' (modern Lebanon) independent of Syria.[61] The majority of the population in the annexed territories to the Mountain were non-Maronites and mostly Muslim; Greater Lebanon was established against their will.[62] With this expansion the Maronites were reduced to 30 per cent of the population.

The only significant development after the establishment of Greater Lebanon was the Druze revolt in Syria, in the summer of 1925, which spread to the areas annexed to Lebanon.[63] Although the Druze opposed French attempts to weaken their power, their revolt had a national character: it called for the unity of all Syria, the establishment of home rule and the withdrawal of French troops. The revolt was defeated in 1927. During the revolt, in an attempt to counter these moves, the French had drafted a Lebanese constitution, and on 24 May 1926 the Lebanese Republic was proclaimed with Charles Dabbas as president.[64]

In July 1928, the Syrian Constituent Assembly met and drafted a constitution reaffirming the unity and independence of Syria. The French, however, dissolved the assembly in May 1930 and redrafted a new Syrian constitution.[65]

Having secured the fragmentation of Syria, the French changed their tactics towards the Arab nationalists in Lebanon. They amended the constitution in 1927 and 1929, to guarantee proportional representation for all the sects and regions of Lebanon. They further guaranteed equitable sectarian representation in public employment. These French tactics resulted in the acceptance of the Lebanese Republic by the élite of the various sects.

The Maronite élite, however, was split on the issue of independence from France. Emile Eddé, an isolationist and the leader of the National Bloc, called for French protection of a Christian Lebanon. Khoury, the leader of the Constitutional Bloc, on the other hand, realized that without appeasing the Muslims he could not become president of an independent Lebanon.[66] The Muslim élite, who by and large were for pan-Arabism, also realized that if the issue remained a separate Lebanon versus a unified one with Syria, the French would stay in both Syria and Lebanon. In addition, the élite in the big cities realized that they would reap benefits from a non-restricted trade if political power were in their own hands.

To thwart any anti-French sentiments that would arise with these new developments, France aided Eddé in becoming president in 1937. Once in power, Eddé tried to convince some of the Muslim notables to support his policies. The independence movement, however, was strong and could not be redirected. During the Second World War de Gaulle promised Lebanon and Syria their independence. However, when the Vichy forces were defeated in the Arab East, de Gaulle reneged on his promise. Instead he sought to revert to the 1936 Franco-Lebanese Treaty, under which France was given certain economic concessions.[67]

In the run-up to the presidential elections, Maronite and Muslim notables joined forces within the Chamber of Deputies to out-manoeuvre Eddé and the isolationists. Consequently, Khoury was elected President of the Republic on 21 September 1943. This new political unity was developed into an informal understanding between Muslim and Christian élites which came to be known as the 'National Pact'. The National Pact consecrated confessionalism and gave Lebanon its peculiar polity arrangement. It stated:

> First, the Christians gave up the idea of an isolated Lebanon and accepted an independent and sovereign Lebanon within the Arab world. The Muslims in return, gave up the idea of giving back to Syria the territories which had been annexed to Lebanon; and also the aim of uniting Lebanon with the Arab world . . .
>
> Secondly, the Christians gave up the idea of foreign protection, either by way of occupation, military outposts or the concluding of treaties with the Western powers . . . In return, the Muslims agreed to stop working to make Lebanon submit to Syrian or Arab influence.
>
> Thirdly, the number of seats in Parliament was to be distributed in such a way as to ensure a majority to the Christians. Also, the President of the Republic was always to be a Christian while the Premier in the Government was always to be a Muslim . . .[68]

It is important to note that, as an informal understanding among the élite, the National Pact was not adopted as a part of the Constitution. The unity of the élite against the French was possible because the National Pact guaranteed proportional representation (based on the 1932 census) of all the different religious sects within Lebanon. The 5:6 Muslim–Christian ratio of parliamentary seats was, however, suggested by the British.

What was happening in Lebanon at that time was a power struggle between the Muslim and Christian élite on the one hand, and the French on the other. The latter arrested Khoury and appointed Eddé head of state. This incident touched off mass demonstrations in many parts of Lebanon in support of Khoury, who was finally reinstated on 22 November 1943 due in large measure to the Anglo-American pressure on France. This was followed by the withdrawal of foreign troops from Syria in April 1946 and from Lebanon in December 1946.[69]

## The Emergence of Modern Classes

Between the two world wars, great economic and social changes occurred in Syria and Lebanon. These changes were a continuation, on a larger and more direct scale, of the opening to the West that took place in the second half of the 19th Century with the invasion of Syria by Ibrahim Pasha of Egypt.

At the beginning of the French occupation of Syria and Mount Lebanon, agriculture, with its dominant feudal relations, was the main economic sector. In the coastal areas, however, especially in Beirut, a merchant class had been developing since the early 1800s.

When France carved out modern Lebanon from Syria in September 1920, it intended to dominate the region's economy and tie it to its own. It also wanted to weaken the nascent Syrian bourgeoisie that had been developing since the early 1800s, primarily on the basis of the textile industry.

Both the Syrian bourgeoisie and the feudal lords banded together in an attempt to fight French designs in Syria and Lebanon. As was shown earlier, these attempts were unsuccessful in defeating the imposed partition of Syria. The division of Syria created obstacles to the free flow of goods and encouraged competition among her sea ports.[70] This move discouraged local industry from developing, which in turn severely limited exports. It was no coincidence, therefore, that the balance of trade was constantly in deficit or that the sources of wealth remained in agriculture, stock breeding, commercial services and small-scale industry.[71]

To alleviate the effects of political fragmentation and to keep them within manageable proportions, the French opted for the use of a single currency, a commercial code and a unified customs system. In the 1930s one-third of trade with Syria and Lebanon was transit trade. Silk, fruits, carpets and similar goods were shipped out, and machinery, vehicles and cotton goods were flowing in. At the same time, cottage industries were giving way to more modern production techniques. In fact, one can trace the foundations of Lebanon's industry after independence (1943) to the innovations that occurred between 1928 and 1940, often with foreign capital. In that period old workshops were modernized and other factories were built to produce commodities that were new to the area or to increase production of existing items on the market.[72]

During French rule, capitalism deeply penetrated the agricultural sectors of both Syria and Lebanon. Land became a commodity. Agricultural production for sale and not for use accelerated and the number of agricultural wage workers increased.

The French Mandate also encouraged and contributed to the development of financial institutions in the area. In 1936 there were three French banks, one Italian and one Egyptian-Syrian in addition to the Banque de Syrie. This encouragement of the services sector, including banking, helped develop an urban petty bourgeoisie based in the services. The commercial class also began to develop into a fully-fledged comprador. It was on the basis of these developments that the comprador eventually became the dominant capitalist class fraction in the early 1940s.

Increased differentiation of Syria and Lebanon, despite the customs union, allowed two separate sets of classes to exist in two distinct, though mutually dependent, economies. By the late 1930s, the Syrian and Lebanese class structures were primarily comprised of a landed aristocracy (whose sector had been deeply penetrated by capitalist relations of production), a peasantry, a nascent industrial capitalist and proletariat (more developed in Syria than in Lebanon, however, and working primarily in textiles), a commercial class and an urban petty bourgeoisie (in the services and government sectors).

The Second World War gave opportunities for the further development of local industry and agriculture. Agriculture was able to experiment with new methods of increasing production. The shortage of petroleum products spurred the authorities to construct a refinery in Tripoli (north of Lebanon). In addition, banks helped finance many projects for irrigation, power, roads, etc.[73] They also gave out loans to avert severe famines and unemployment, both of which still occurred locally and intermittently. Army expenditures also helped compensate for loss of exports. All these developments during the war contributed to local accumulation of capital, which toward the end of the war was looking for investment opportunities which war controls had prevented.[74]

By 1943 the Lebanese economy and its attendant class structure had developed tremendously. Furthermore, the local accumulation of capital which occurred during the war, and which was primarily based in Beirut, helped to increase the separation between the Syrian and Lebanese economies.

In the Lebanese class structure a sector of the peasantry was transformed into agricultural wage workers. Feudal landlords were transformed into agricultural capitalists. Feudal families, such as Asaad, Osseiran, Khalil, Hamadeh (all Shiites) and Skaf (Catholic), had to deal with a capitalist market.

Local capitalists that benefited from the development of trade, banking and industry increased in strength. Leading comprador families were Chiha,

Pharaon, Taqla (all Catholic), Abu Chahla (Orthodox), Khoury, Eddé (both Maronite), Oueini, Solh, Yafi, Salam, Karami (all Sunni).

It was these capitalists (the comprador, the industrialists and the landed aristocracy) who joined forces to oust the French and declare Lebanon independent. Although the rising comprador did not challenge the powerful landed aristocracy before securing independence, the comprador was aware that the structures that were supporting the aristocracy were weakening. Specifically, land no longer remained the only source of wealth and 'landowners lost their function of tax collection'.[75] Furthermore, the international situation favoured the commercial and financial bourgeoisie and not agricultural landowners.

Directly after the war, it was necessary to return to free enterprise so as to meet the demand for imported goods, whose supply had been limited during the war.[76] Accumulated capital, seeking a quick return on investment with low risk, saw that these goals could be realized through commercial activity. An opportunity for industrialization was not possible because of the tradition of commercial activity that the few intervening years of war were unable to change. Also, the objective of the new comprador class coincided on the international level with that of the US policy of freedom of trade and competition.[77]

To be sure of mass support in its bid to control the state, the competing élite posed as representatives of various religious sects rather than of the respective competing bourgeois class fractions. What helped them to do so was that class conflict had a tendency to take the form of religious strife. This was primarily due to foreign intervention and the role that the clergy played in the political development of the Mountain.

The hegemony of the comprador in the power bloc in the capitalist state was largely due to the role that the comprador was playing in the economy. The other class fractions were the extremely weak industrialists and the still powerful landed aristocracy.

Although capitalism was already established in agriculture, the old feudal families (turned capitalists) maintained their fiefdoms after independence. The Asaad family, for instance, owned many southern villages that gave them the basis for political power in their region. As agricultural production became increasingly for exchange, the family's commercial ties further developed with the towns of Tyre, Sidon and Beirut. These ties added to the family's political power in the Lebanese social formation.

The situation was similar with other landlord families. The Khalil family developed its political power on the basis of its agricultural landholdings in the south. The family also dealt in real estate and developed its trade in agricultural products.

In the Bekaa Valley, the feudal Hamadeh family was the dominant leader of the Shiites and the Catholic Skaf family enjoyed political power on the basis of its agricultural landholdings.

In the mountainous Chouf region the two dominant Druze families were the rival feudal Jumblatts and the less powerful Arslans.

These were major landlord families that developed into agricultural capitalists and became part of the ruling bourgeoisie. This capitalist class fraction included Christian, Muslim and Druze families. This newly developed class fraction consecrated the traditional *zaim* (patron) power in 'modern' Lebanon. Basically, this zaim institution was an adaptation of the zaim/client relationship to a capitalist mode of production.

The comprador class fraction of the bourgeoisie was multi-confessional as well. It included Druze, Muslim (Sunni and Shiite) and Christian (Maronite, Catholic, Orthodox and Protestant). It is significant to point out that most members of the comprador did not own large tracts of land in comparison to what the old feudal families owned. Members of the comprador were primarily in the coastal towns of Beirut, Tripoli and Sidon. Many of them, especially the Christians, had ties with the hinterland, primarily with the Mountain.

The core of this bourgeois fraction comprised certain families who developed their political and economic power primarily on the basis of merchant and/or financial capital. The most prominent was the Solh family (Sunni), whose power base was in the south among the Sunni bourgeoisie and petty bourgeoisie whose livelihood depended mainly upon trade and services.

In Beirut, the traditional Yafi, Oueini and Salam families (all Sunni) were prominent in trade and services. In the case of the Salams their influence was also due to their large landholdings in Palestine. This was also the case with other families, such as the commerce-based Sursuks.

(It is interesting to note that the Salams, Sursuks, Tueinis and others had sold their landholdings in Palestine to the Zionists for a good price. These land sales helped such families increase their wealth and political power in Lebanon.)

In the north of Lebanon merchant capital was concentrated among a few families. The rival Karami, Muqqaddam and Jisr families (all Sunni) were powerful leaders in Tripoli.

Initially local finance was concentrated mainly in the hands of families such as Pharaon, Abu Chahla, Chiha, Khoury, Taqla and Eddé. Michel Chiha was the thinker and writer that called for independence from France. This man, the 'father of independence', was in fact a representative of comprador interests: that class fraction that led the fight for independence for the common interest of the capitalist class. This does not mean, however, that all the members of the comprador were for independence. In fact, France was behind Emile Eddé, who was against Khoury and Chiha. Eddé's opposition to independence, however, only reflected his relative weakness in relation to the other pro-independence financial families. He saw in continued French colonialism a boost to his own position.

The growth that occurred in the banking and trading sectors of the Lebanese economy after independence provided the basis for other merchant capitalist and petty-bourgeois individuals to become part of this financial oligarchy. Solh, Salam, Yafi, Oueini and others joined it. Petty-bourgeois individuals such as Camille Chamoun (who succeeded Khoury to the presidency), Fawzi al-Hoss and Najeeb Salha became multi-millionaires.

Although some members of the landed aristocracy developed financial wealth, they remained basically within the agricultural capitalist fraction of the ruling bourgeoisie. In general, the overlap that existed among the bourgeois fractions was not sufficient to blur the differences in the economic bases of these fractions.

In the struggle to establish its own state, the bourgeoisie was supported by the peasantry, workers (including agricultural workers) and the petty bourgeoisie of the towns and villages. It was in the interests of the petty bourgeoisie to act as a supporting class in the struggle for independence. The development of the services and government sectors presented opportunities for the development and upward mobility of this class.

This explains why the Lebanese Kataeb Party (LKP) and the Najjadah supported independence. The LKP (founded by Pierre Gemayel in 1936) was based in the Maronite Mountain area around Bikfayya and in Beirut. The party's class base was petty-bourgeois and its ideology capitalist. The Najjadah organization was based in Beirut among some petty-bourgeois and semi-proletarian Muslim Sunnis.

The nascent working class also fought the French colonialists in the hope that independence would improve its economic and social position. The working class fought under the banner of various bourgeois political groupings. At that time the only party that espoused proletarian ideology was the Communist Party of Syria and Lebanon. This party was young and weak, reflecting the level of development of the working class.

Despite the participation of the LKP, the Najjadah and other parties in the fight for independence, political parties were still relatively young in Lebanon and were unable to organize and lead this struggle. Consequently, the hegemonic class mainly relied on traditional institutions to organize the support given to it by the other classes.

Traditional zaim/client relations in agriculture and family loyalty secured the peasantry as a supporting class. Asaad, for instance, was assured of peasant support regardless of his political position. In the case of the Solh family, its prestige (due to its economic power) guaranteed it the allegiance of city-dwellers in the south. As will be shown later, however, the allegiance of the city-dwellers to a particular family was not as rigid as it was in the case of the peasantry after independence. This was due, in part, to the different levels and kinds of development (and underdevelopment) in the cities and towns as opposed to those that were taking place in the countryside.

The financial bourgeoisie also had its own political grouping: Khoury's Constitutional Bloc (CB). Like Eddé's National Bloc (NB), it was not a party in the proper sense of the word. It neither had a mass base nor a programme to be implemented through daily activity among the masses. At that time (during the fight for independence), the CB (as well as the NB) did not have real membership. However, it was able to attract people who supported the Khoury family. This allegiance was based on traditional and family ties.

These developments and characteristics in Lebanon's history coloured its

class composition up to the late 1930s. The peasantry, the developing proletariat, the landed aristocracy which became a fraction within the controlling
bourgeoisie and the petty bourgeoisie comprised the class make-up of the
Lebanese social formation. These classes were unanimous in their struggle for
independence from France. Independence, however, was primarily in the
interest of the bourgeoisie. The state that this bourgeois class created was a
capitalist state in which the comprador class fraction was dominant through its
hegemonic position in the power bloc.

Bourgeois class interests of certain families that were tied to geographic
and economic sectors of the Lebanese state developed and expressed
themselves in political terms since Lebanon's independence, up to and includ-
int both civil wars (1958 and 1975) and up to the present day. Names such
as Eddé, Karami, Salam, Khoury, Asaad, etc. played a leading role in shaping
and directing political and economic eventualities. In succeeding chapters
one can also see how the competition among these bourgeois class fractions
and/or families within the capitalist class as a whole brought into being different regimes to run the capitalist state.

## Conclusion

The history of Mount Lebanon has been an integral part of the historical
development of Syria. From the 9th Century, when the Maronites were
established in the north of the Mountain, Mountain society evolved through
an intricate interaction between the Maronites and the Druze living in the
south. Through integration these exclusive communities were capable of
establishing a secular feudal order that matured and prospered within the
emirate of Mount Lebanon.

The feudal mode of production, with its attendant political and social
institutions, further encouraged the integration of the two communities.
The needs of the system for more agricultural land and production to increase
landlord revenues greatly encouraged this integration. It also helped create
new social forces that became competing and independent on the political
scene. This explains, in great part, the role given by the landlords to the
Maronite Order of Monks in production and, consequently, their important
influence among the peasantry compared with that of the individual village
priest. Furthermore, monk organizations were efficient production units with
little conspicuous consumption.

An organized social force such as the clergy, sharing with the peasants
animosity toward the feudal system, made a formidable force which the
ruling emir used to consolidate his position against feudal lords. In its effort
to become a dominant or an exclusive force in the emirate, the church had
to unite with the emir and rely upon religion to separate Druze and Maronite
peasants from each other. Druze landlords resorted to the same tactics to
counter church designs. To a large extent and despite its influence on the
peasants, the church was unsuccessful in turning the class conflict into a

religious one. As Hourani contends:

> It is true that for generations Lebanon was torn by internal strife, but it was the strife of factions and families. It was only for a short time during the nineteenth century that it took the form of a religious war, and even then the fundamental causes were social and political rather than religious.[78]

In the bid for its emirate, the church had to betray many of the peasants' interests, as was the case during the 1840 revolt.[79] What the church wanted to achieve ran counter to the historical development of the Mountain. Instead, it helped in achieving the massacres of 1860 which later led to the introduction of the Mutassarrifiyya system.

Beginning with the Egyptian conquest in 1831, Western impact upon society in Syria and Lebanon was formidable and far-reaching. This impact was decisive in creating or helping to create new class formations. Social, political and economic upheavals occurred that spelled the end of feudalism as a political institution. The new classes that were formed came increasingly to share power with the landlord class, which remained the most powerful until independence.

As the commercial class (comprador bourgeoisie) gained in economic power, the feudal mode of production increasingly became less dominant because land as a source of wealth had lost its exclusive position.

French colonialism hastened the integration of Lebanon into the world capitalist system. It strengthened and encouraged the development of the comprador through the division of Syria to render the area economically weak and dependent upon foreign trade and commercial services.

The conflict within the dominant class centred around the struggle for independence. Some fractions of this class sided with the French while others opted for independence. The victory of the independence forces was a result of specific class alignments which established the first regime, El-Khoury's in 1943.

The peasantry, workers and petty bourgeoisie functioned as supporting classes for the bourgeoisie in the fight for independence. This was because these classes were already divided along confessional lines with allegiance to their respective zuama. At the dawn of independence (1943) the landlord class and the comprador fraction of the bourgeoisie were dominant in the Lebanese social formation. Their state displayed a power bloc in which high finance was hegemonic. The landlord class was, however, extremely powerful, and without it the power bloc could not have been possible. The Lebanese state displayed another important feature characteristic of its historic development. This feature, confessionalism, was the form of state that was capable of resolving intra-power bloc conflict and conflict among the class fractions of the dominant classes in the social formation. Confessionalism, then, was that form of state that attended to the 'common interests' of the dominant classes and provided polity cohesion.

# Notes

1. Fahim I. Qubain, *Crisis in Lebanon* (Washington, DC, Middle East Institute, 1961), 9.
2. Ibid., p.10.
3. Iliya F. Harik, *Politics and Change in a Traditional Society: Lebanon 1711–1845* (New Jersey, Princeton University Press, 1968), 13.
4. Qubain, op. cit., pp. 10–11.
5. K.S. Salibi, *The Modern History of Lebanon* (New York, Praeger, 1965), XXI, 3, pp. 5–7.
6. Qubain, op. cit., p. 11.
7. Salibi, op. cit., p. 4.
8. Ibid., pp. 10–12.
9. Harik, op. cit., pp. 46–7.
10. Ibid.
11. Salibi, op. cit., p. 10.
12. Harik, op. cit., pp. 169–72.
13. Ibid., p. 173.
14. Ibid., p. 84.
15. Ibid., p. 85.
16. Ibid., p. 114.
17. Ibid., p. 112.
18. Salibi, op. cit., p. 27.
19. Philip K. Hitti, *Lebanon in History* (New York, St Martin's Press, 1962), 416.
20. Harik, op. cit., p. 221.
21. Hitti, op. cit., p. 417.
22. Harik, op. cit., p. 232.
23. Ibid., p. 241.
24. Ibid., pp. 235–8.
25. Ibid., pp. 242–4.
26. Ibid., p. 249.
27. Hitti, op. cit., p. 245.
28. Harik, op. cit., p. 246.
29. Ibid., p. 253.
30. Ibid., p. 261.
31. Ibid., p. 271.
32. Hitti, op. cit., p. 478.
33. Ibid., p. 407.
34. Ibid., p. 471.
35. Ibid., pp. 407–8.
36. Ibid., p. 408.
37. William R. Polk, *The Opening of South Lebanon, 1788–1840* (Mass., Harvard University Press, 1963), 215.
38. Hitti, op. cit., p. 471.
39. Polk, op. cit., p. 174.
40. Ibid., p. 216.
41. Salibi, op. cit., p. 82.
42. Ibid., p. 84.
43. Ibid., p. 87.

44. Hitti, op. cit., p. 437.
45. Ibid., p. 438.
46. Salibi, op. cit., p. 87: 'Though the whole conflict was strongly sectarian in 1860, it continued to have the dimensions of class division.' Harik, op. cit., p. 276.
47. Hitti, op. cit., p. 439.
48. Ibid., p. 441. See also Salibi, op. cit., p. 109.
49. Salibi, op. cit., p. 110.
50. M. Emerit, 'The Syrian Crisis and French Economic Expansion of 1860', *Arab Studies* (March 1972), 11–13, 19. (Arabic Source)
51. Salibi, op. cit., p. 112–13.
52. Ibid., pp. 118–19.
53. Ibid., p. 154.
54. Ibid., pp. 159–60.
55. Ibid.
56. Stephen H. Longrigg, *Syria and Lebanon Under French Mandate* (New York, Oxford University Press, 1958), 66.
57. Ibid., p. 88.
58. Ibid., pp. 89–92.
59. Ibid., p. 87.
60. Ibid., p. 103.
61. Ibid., p. 99.
62. Ibid., pp. 89–92.
63. Salibi, op. cit., p. 169.
64. Ibid., p. 170.
65. Longrigg, op. cit., pp. 182, 187.
66. Salibi, op. cit., pp. 172–3.
67. Ibid., pp. 184–8.
68. George Dib, from his introduction to his own translation of 'Selections from Riadh Solh's speech in the Lebanese Assembly, October 7, 1943', *Middle East Forum* (Beirut, January 1959), 6.
69. Longrigg, op. cit., pp. 353–5.
70. A.H. Hourani, *Syria and Lebanon: A Political Essay* (New York, Oxford University Press, 1954), 89.
71. Longrigg, op. cit., p. 271.
72. Ibid., pp. 271, 274.
73. Ibid., p. 271.
74. Ibid., p. 339.
75. Hourani, op . cit., p. 92.
76. Longrigg, loc. cit.
77. Ibid.
78. Hourani, op. cit., p. 92.
79. Peasant revolts sought to undermine feudalism. Since most peasants were Maronites, there was much overlap between class and sect affiliation. Identification of peasants as Maronites, however, played into the hands of the church, which sought to play up the religious factor to use the anti-feudal sentiment of the peasants for its own goals: to have hegemony over the Mountain. The initial progressive nature of religious affiliation soon dissipated and sectarianism became a reactionary phenomenon. This was especially true under colonialism, which

heavily influenced Lebanon's political development by leaving its imprint on Lebanon after independence. It is important to note that sectarianism had been conditioned by social forces that utilized and developed it for their own class interests.

In his discussion of ethnicity in Africa, Wallerstein argues similarly. He also seeks to understand ethnicity within the context of the international capitalist system. This leads him to argue that ethnic and national liberation struggles are forms of class struggle. See, for example, I. Wallerstein, 'Social Conflict in Post-Independent Black Africa: The Concept of Race and Status Group Reconsidered', in I. Wallerstein, ed., *The Capitalist World Economy* (New York, Cambridge University Press, 1979). See also I. Wallerstein, 'Class and Class Conflict in Contemporary Africa', and 'Class Formation in the Capitalist World Economy', ibid. Perhaps the most devastating critique of those who talk of ethnicity and not class struggle (in any of its forms) is that they dismiss the international capitalist market and simply remain in the confines of the state or region under consideration.

# 4. Lebanon's Political Economy: 1943-1974

The struggle for independence and the class make-up of the political alliances that carried it through were largely influenced by and the product of the historical development of Syria and Lebanon. Of significance was the creation and development of new economic sectors and class formations.

Khoury, the first president, was tied to powerful local banking interests. Chiha (considered one of the 'fathers' of Lebanese independence) was a powerful banker and the brother-in-law of Khoury. Pharaon, an important financier, had sided with the 'fathers' of independence.[1] The Kataeb (Phalangist) Party, representing Maronite interests opting for independence, joined forces with El-Khoury, El-Solh (Sunni Muslim) and other members of the élite to bring about the confessional Lebanese independent state.

Confessionalism — a system of government whereby various religious sects of a polity are proportionally represented according to the population of each sect — organized relationships among the ruling élite and the classes it represented by invoking sectarian representation in an effort to conceal class conflict. Through the new arrangement, the ruling élite was able to guarantee itself mass following based upon sect and/or zaim (patron/client) relationships.

The balance that confessionalism and the National Pact had represented was not expected to last long. Writing in the 1940s, Albert Hourani contended that 'a state so deeply divided both in structure and in ideas as the Lebanese republic and without any unifying national spirit could not continue to exist, at least in its present form, unless there were some external power controlling it closely and intervening continually in its affairs.'[2] Hourani was mainly referring to the national spirit and to political structures and ideas. On another level, however, one could legitimately talk about economic structures and activities that significantly contribute to class formations and greatly influence the political class struggle in its methods and ultimate goals.

The dynamic of the economic structure obtaining in Lebanon at independence was (as mentioned in the previous chapter) supportive of the relatively new classes formed in Lebanon, and not of the archaic landed aristocracy. With the dynamic of the economy favouring certain sectors over others, economic dislocations were to be expected to spill over to the political arena and threaten the once-intact static balance of forces. To be sure, political crises occurred in the first 15 years of independence, two of which severely upset the balance of forces.[3]

To gain a fuller understanding of these crises, a discussion of the development of the economy is warranted at this point. Although Lebanon gained independence in 1943, it was not until the end of 1946 that all the functions of state were gradually handed over to the national government by the departing French. For this reason, an attempt will be made here to discuss the economy as of 1945. First, however, let us recapitulate the development of the economy during the Second World War.

Agriculture was the main sector of the economy at independence. The war years brought to Lebanon a relative growth of industry and runaway inflation (the wholesale price index in Beirut rose to a peak of 1,203 in January of 1945, taking 1939 as the base year). Allied expenditures of 800 million Lebanese pounds brought an expansion of the volume of money from a low of 38.4 million LL in 1939 to a high of 410 million in September 1945.[4]

Economic structures set up by the French (customs union, single currency, banks, etc.) favoured the rising comprador bourgeoisie. As an example, although the customs union alleviated some of the economic disadvantages of the division of Syria, it was beneficial to colonial interests and the local agents of colonial capital. To protect the Syrian market (Lebanon's most important one), the Syrian bourgeoisie severed the union in 1950.[5]

Due to these colonial economic set-ups, international capital was capable of further penetrating, weakening and disintegrating the local economy. Transit trade was facilitated by the capacity of Beirut's port to handle the large-size ships and the development of refrigerated and non-refrigerated storage areas at the port. The improvement of land transport and the opening of Beirut International Airport in 1950 added to the importance of transit trade and tourism. The 1948 dumping of exchange controls, which facilitated the buying and selling of currencies for Lebanon and the area in general, contributed greatly to the development of Lebanon as an international financial and gold trade centre.[6]

Table 1 provides some understanding of the position of the various economic sectors and subsectors and their dynamic in the first few years after independence.

It is clear from the table that the shares of 'services', 'transport and communication' and 'real estate' in the national income increased. Also, if one bears in mind that much of the industry was geared to exports and much of the construction was for office space, hotels, clubs and so on, the disparity between 'services', 'transport and communication' and 'real estate' on the one hand, and agriculture on the other, becomes clearer, even at this early stage of Lebanon's independence.

About half the workforce in Lebanon was engaged in agriculture.[7] This figure would have been higher were it not for the large-scale migration from the village to the town and to other countries. Per capita income in agriculture, even at this early stage, was lower than in other sectors. Increasing

Table 1
Lebanon: Net National Income by Industry[a] 1948 to 1950
(Millions of Lebanese Pounds)

| Sector | 1948 | 1949 | 1950 |
|---|---|---|---|
| Agriculture | 168.5 | 158.8 | 176.0 |
| Construction | 34.8 | 31.9 | 41.7 |
| Industry[b] | 133.4 | 135.5 | 137.3 |
| Services[c] | 91.4 | 93.1 | 100.5 |
| Transport & Communications | 33.5 | 35.3 | 37.7 |
| Real Estate[d] | 90.0 | 93.4 | 96.0 |
| Government[e] | 63.1 | 64.6 | 71.8 |
| Other[f] | — | — | 339.0 |
| Total | — | — | 1,000.0[g] |

a  All estimates are at factor cost, except agricultural income, which is at
  market price.
b  Including price utilities, mining and quarrying.
c  Including certain services and professional workers and agencies. Excluding
  government and domestic services.
d  Net rent of residential buildings only.
e  Including municipalities.
f  Trade, finance and income received from foreign countries.
g  Provisional estimate.

Source: Albert Y. Badre, 'National Income of Lebanon', Monographs 1 to 7
(Beirut: 1951 to 1954, mimeographed).

agricultural acreage as a possible way of boosting income was not readily
feasible. This effort needed capital which was not available, and large-scale
irrigation projects which take years to finish.

In the early fifties, efforts were made to increase the production of fruit
and vegetables, the net value of which was 50 and 10 per cent in 1948 and
1949, respectively. These and a few other industrial crops (olives, tobacco,
silk, onions, potatoes) provided export surplus. Increased production of
fruit and vegetables required heavy capital outlay, which came mostly from
commercial profits and income gained in the services area. Necessary irrigation projects were publicly financed.[8]

Although in Lebanon soils, topography and rainfall distribution offer a
variety of climatic conditions to allow tropical, sub-tropical and temperate-
zone crops, we see that most of the country's agriculture is geared toward
those crops needed for export at the expense of the needs of the local market.
Because of this, Lebanon has been a net importer of livestock, cereals and
grains.[9] Other reasons advanced for this export phenomenon were that the
prevalence of small-scale ownership and the mountainous nature of the land
did not encourage large-scale mechanization (except in the plains) but

favoured crops requiring little land (which happened to be export crops!).[10]

In 1953 land distribution in Lebanon was estimated as follows: 10% of the land was in holdings of 100 hectares and over; 15-20% was in holdings of 10-100 hectares. The total number of large and medium holders was 6,000. The rest of the land was held by 133,000 owners, most of whom owned less than two hectares. There were a few landless labourers, most of whom rented land from large landowners.[11] Cultivated land per capita of agricultural population was 0.4 hectares, less than 20% of which was irrigated.[12] Because of this land-holding profile, much of the necessary agricultural products were not profitable to plant. For example, in 1948 and 1949 cereals accounted for 20 and 12% of the gross value of agricultural production. In 1953 Lebanon was a deficit country in agricultural products. The only items that were in surplus were fruit, vegetables and 'industrial crops'.[13]

Table 1 shows that industry did not fare much better than agriculture vis-à-vis the services, 'transportation and communication' and 'real estate' sectors. The ascendancy of Lebanese industry in the immediate post-war period was mainly due to the initial scarcity of imported goods. Accordingly, productive capacity doubled between 1946 and 1952. The end of the Korean war had brought more foreign competition to the local market. Furthermore, the severance of the customs union with Syria and the shortage of raw materials contributed to greatly offset the gains initially won by Lebanese industry. Two things remained favourable to industry: one was the protective tariffs, the other was the low level of industrial wages due to the high rate of unemployment in the country.

The following figures will give a better picture of the early pattern of development achieved by Lebanese industry. Oil refineries had increased their output from 100,000 tons in 1940 to 545,000 tons in 1953. Power output had increased from 57 million kilowatt-hours in 1945 to 164 million in 1953. Construction maintained a 7 to 10% level of GNP. Its share of gross investment was over 50%, and consumed a large proportion of small savings. Production of building materials also expanded in these years. Food processing had a higher value of output and more capital employed than the other industries. This industry operated well below capacity and, except for sugar, provided a small surplus for export. The textile industry provided one-sixth of domestic consumption, although woollen cloth production remained well below its consumption levels and productive capacity.[14] Table 2 shows the status of the various industries in 1950.

Table 2 clearly shows that the most important industries were food processing, textiles and non-metallic minerals. Despite the conditions favouring Lebanese industry then, much of it was operating below capacity and was not satisfying the wants and desires of the local market.* What aggravated the

---

* The textile industry, for example, during the late 1940s and early 1950s was operating below capacity. Output of woollen cloth had failed to exceed 150 tons. That was a figure well below both consumption and production capacity. See, for example, figures from Ministry of National Economy, 1954. See also *Le Commerce du Levant*, 3 July 1954: special issue on industry for figures on food, soft drinks and alcoholic beverages, which were operating well below capacity.

Table 2.
Lebanon: Industrial Establishments, Employees, Capital, Cost of Materials and Output, 1950[a]

| Product or Industry | Number of Establishments | Number of Employees | Capital[b] | Investment Per Employee[b] | Gross Output[b] | Net Output[b] |
|---|---|---|---|---|---|---|
| Food Processing | 455 | 5,404 | 24.9 | 4,607 | 61.7 | 30.1 |
| Beverages | 123 | 1,292 | 10.7 | 8,282 | 12.2 | 5.6 |
| Textiles | 60 | 5,040 | 32.6 | 6,468 | 39.5 | 17.7 |
| Wearing Apparel | 15 | 1,036 | 3.3 | 3,185 | 2.3 | 1.2 |
| Wood and Cork | 48 | 241 | 1.4 | 5,809 | 3.8 | 1.6 |
| Furniture | 95 | 1,211 | 4.6 | 3,799 | 10.3 | 6.2 |
| Paper | 9 | 91 | 0.5 | 5,495 | 0.9 | 0.5 |
| Printing | 100 | 855 | 8.6 | 10,058 | 5.8 | 2.7 |
| Leather | 64 | 737 | 4.6 | 6,242 | 14.2 | 6.2 |
| Rubber | 6 | 447 | 1.0 | 2,237 | 2.1 | 1.4 |
| Chemicals | 64 | 1,104 | 5.9 | 5,344 | 16.4 | 7.9 |
| Non-Metallic Minerals | 156 | 2,768 | 35.5 | 12,825 | 21.5 | 13.5 |
| Metal Products | 30 | 639 | 2.6 | 4,069 | 11.1 | 6.5 |
| Machinery | 27 | 590 | 3.2 | 5,424 | 3.6 | 1.9 |
| Electrical Appliances | 4 | 217 | 1.6 | 7,373 | 1.9 | 0.8 |
| Concessions & Public Utilities | – | – | – | – | 38.8 | 13.9 |
| Other | 29 | 367 | 6.5 | 17,711 | 2.7 | 1.8 |
| Total | 1,285[c] | 22,039[c] | 147.4[c] | 6,688 | 248.8 | 119.7 |

a  Excluding handicrafts; net output of handicrafts in 1950 was LL 17.6 million.  b  Millions of Lebanese pounds (LL).
c  Excluding concessions and public utilities .

Source: Albert Y. Badre and Asad Y. Nasr, 'National Income in Lebanon', Monograph No. 3, 'Income Arising in the
Industrial Sector' (Beirut, May 1953, mimeographed).

situation further was the fact that these favourable conditions disappeared in the course of a few years. The severance of the customs union, for example, hurt some industries — especially cotton yarn, tanning, chemicals and beer — which sold large proportions of their output in the Syrian market. The already small local market began to face stiff competition from foreign goods, which increased after 1953. Overseas markets for Lebanese products proved, at best, to be precarious.

The scarcity of raw materials in the country was a major factor that had favoured certain industries over others. In 1950 the three most important industries mentioned above accounted for 60% of the labour employed in all industry, 62% of the capital invested and 58% of the value of gross net output.[15]

Table 3 shows the small size of Lebanese industrial firms, a further indicator of industry's weakness.

Table 3
Lebanon: Number of Industrial Firms in Terms of Size of Capital Invested, 1950

| Number of Firms | Capital Investment (LL) |
|---|---|
| 25 | 1 million or over |
| 29 | ½–1 million |
| 45 | ¼–½ million |
| 381 | 10,000–25,000 |
| 249 | 5,000–10,000 |

Source: Ministry of National Economy, *Bulletin Statistique Trimestriel*, October 1951.

It is important to bear in mind that these economic structural problems were the direct result of the political fragmentation of the Arab East during colonial times. These political and economic structures clearly favour (in their fragmentation) certain types of economic development patterns and reinforce the dominance of a certain social class on the political scene. This dominance, in turn, reinforces the economic dominant position of this social class.

The political clout of the comprador fraction of the dominant class has been reflected in liberal trade policies and reluctance to protect local industry.[16] Any protection granted local industry primarily had in mind those industries whose owners mustered enough political power to legislate or decree protection for big industries. Be that as it may, protective measures had offset some of the effects of the onslaught of foreign competition. Furthermore, bilateral or inter-Arab trade agreements had somewhat offset the fragmentation of the market.

What was more, the government had extended tax credits to industrial establishments with a capital of over one million LL. The Agricultural and

Industrial Bank provided scarce industrial credit which went to industrialists with political clout. In 1953, an industrial institute was established with US aid; it carried out production and marketing studies for prospective enterprises. The institute also assisted existing enterprises to modernize and optimize production factors (land, labour, capital) utilization.

Another assistance which the government extended to industry was the reduction it effected in the cost of electricity. When the electric company refused to expand its plant, the government intervened and took over company administration and reduced costs to consumers by 22%. In 1954 the government bought out the company and expanded output through publicly-financed new projects.

Despite government assistance to agriculture and industry, agriculture, the chief economic sector at independence, quickly lost its position to the services and other related sectors within a period not exceeding four years.[17] Furthermore, Table 4 shows the trade picture from 1950 to 1954.

Table 4
Lebanon: Foreign Trade and Transit Trade, 1950 to 1954
(Millions of Lebanese Pounds)

| Item | 1950 [a] | 1951 | 1952 | 1953 | 1954 [b] |
|---|---|---|---|---|---|
| Foreign Trade: | | | | | |
| Special Imports | 183.6 | 298.4 | 308.5 | 314.3 | 262.3 |
| Special Exports | 51.9 | 89.7 | 77.4 | 87.5 | 57.5 |
| Re-Exports | 1.9 | 1.6 | 3.9 | 3.0 | 1.8 |
| Import Surplus | 129.3 | 207.1 | 227.2 | 223.8 | 203.0 |
| Transit Trade: | | | | | |
| Re-Exports | 1.5 | 6.6 | 15.6 | 9.2 | 8.0 |
| Merchandise | | | | | |
| Transit | 222.2 | 323.1 | 327.6 | 304.8 | 259.9 |
| Petroleum | 111.1 | 459.1 | 471.2 | 472.8 | 349.3 |
| *Total* | *334.8* | *778.8* | *814.6* | *786.8* | *617.2* |
| Trade in Gold | | | | | |
| Special Trade | | | | | |
| Imports | 61.2 | 22.2 | 38.6 | 47.7 | 52.4 |
| Exports | 15.2 | 8.0 | — | 0.2 | 9.1 |
| Transit Trade | 177.3 | 354.6 | 239.9 | 285.3 | 147.3 |

a  14 March to 31 December
b  Nine months

Source: Ministry of National Economy, *Bulletin Statistique Trimestriel.*

Table 4 shows that Lebanon was a net importer in these years and was heavily dependent upon transit trade. For the sake of illustration, notice that the 'other' category for 1950 in Table 1 made up over one-third of NNI (Net National Income).

The main markets for Lebanese exports by order of importance were: Syria, Saudi Arabia, France, Egypt and the USA. Imports were chiefly brought from Syria, followed by the USA, the UK, France and the Netherlands.

A brief discussion of the major economic sectors is warranted here to appreciate Lebanon's heavy and precarious dependence upon the international capitalist market and upon political events in the region.

The opening of Beirut International Airport was a boost to transit trade, tourism and the services industry in general. Transit trade was also facilitated by the abolishment, in 1954, of port dues on goods in transit and through transit agreements that were reached mainly with Syria, Iraq and Jordan.[18] Income from transit in 1951 and 1952 was estimated at 36.9 and 46.8 million LL respectively. If gold in transit profits are added to these figures, the amounts are 113.1 and 95.4 million LL in 1951 and 1952, respectively. To encourage the gold trade, the government (in 1949) permitted gold to be kept in transit in the country for up to two months, after which it could be shipped to a country other than that to which it was originally destined. The following are figures of gold passed in transit (in tons): 1950 — 44; 1951 — 89; 1952 — 67; 1953 — 73; and 1954 (first six months) — 30.[19]

Along with a liberal gold policy, Lebanon had relaxed controls over the foreign-exchange market; these were later abolished altogether on 17 May 1952.[20] Although businesses were not affected by the official exchange rate, which was reserved for governmental transactions, the Exchange Stabilization Fund (established in 1949) attempted to prevent the appreciation of the Lebanese pound vis-à-vis the dollar. These attempts were not systematic, however, and were small in volume compared to the great volume of exchange operations taking place in the Beirut market. Consequently, this move could not very well protect Lebanon's competitive position.[21]

As mentioned earlier, tourism was another service that received a boost after independence. Capital investment in hotels was 145 million LL in 1952 (not including restaurants, cafés, etc.). In the same year there were 585 hotels with 14,350 beds (253 hotels with 4,960 beds in Beirut).[22] Table 5 presents an indicator of tourist development.

Table 5
Lebanon: Tourist Arrivals: 1949 to 1953

| Year | Number of Tourists |
|------|--------------------|
| 1949 | 60,000 |
| 1950 | 67,000 |
| 1951 | 127,000 |
| 1952 | 216,000 |
| 1953 | 285,000 |

Source: Michel Touma, 'Al-hurria al-Khamisa', *Muhadarat al-Nudwa* (Beirut, 1953).

Table 5 shows that the number of tourists increased by more than 400% in less than five years. Most of these were summer tourists from Arab countries.

Table 6 shows visitor expenditures for two years.

Table 6

Lebanon: Breakdown of Visitor Expenditure by Category: 1951 and 1952
(Millions of Lebanese Pounds)

| Category | 1951 | 1952 |
|---|---|---|
| Summer Tourists | 12.2 | 10.8 |
| Other Tourists | 17.8 | 30.2 |
| Transit Visitors | 1.6 | 2.1 |
| Foreign Students and Patients | 5.3 | 6.0 |

Source: Edward Fei and Paul J. Klat, *The Balance of Payments of Lebanon, 1951 and 1952* (Beirut, 1954).

A source of government income was payments by Iraqi Petroleum (IPC) and Trans-Arabian Pipe Line (Tapline) companies. These payments amounted to 5.5 million LL, and Tapline had local expenditures of 17.6 million LL, while IPC's expenditures totalled around 10 million LL yearly.

Lebanon was dependent upon capital movements, which show a positive balance in Table 7. Although information is scarce on this item, it is commonly assumed that, due to political conditions in the neighbouring Arab countries, capital came from Syria, Palestine and Egypt. Furthermore, capital from Kuwait and Saudi Arabia was either invested in real estate or deposited in Lebanese banks. Concomitant with this development, and as a complement to it, the banking system developed considerably. Consequently the number of banks increased from seven to 21 in 1954. Although 'national' banks increased in number, their role remained a minor one in the financial structure of the country.[23] In 1939 bank deposits were 27.5 million LL; in 1945 they increased to 227.1 million; in 1949 they declined to 180.6 million and increased to 392.2 million LL in 1954. The increase in deposits was mainly due to foreign capital seeking greater security and/or investing in short-term commercial and financial transactions, especially gold and transit. In addition, many foreign firms had located their Middle East headquarters in Beirut.[24]

A cursory look at the government budget shows the importance of the contribution of services to the budget. Table 7 shows that the greatest share of revenue came from customs duties and taxes on consumption. Although direct taxes had risen appreciably over the years, they still remained a minor part of revenue.

Expenditures for education had increased from 1.8% in 1946 to 12.6% in 1954 of total expenditures. Defence expenditure in 1954 was double that of 1946, but its share fell from 21.7% to 17%. Expenditure for public works also increased in the same period but its share fell from 19.8% in 1946 to

**Table 7**
Lebanon: Principal Items in Government Budgets: 1939 and 1948 to 1954 (Millions of Lebanese Pounds)

| Item | 1939 | 1948 | 1949 | 1950 | 1951 | 1952 | 1953[a] | 1954[a] |
|---|---|---|---|---|---|---|---|---|
| **Revenue:** | | | | | | | | |
| Direct Tax on Income/Wealth | 1.20 | 9.73 | 12.93 | 12.89 | 14.46 | 17.27 | 15.20 | — |
| Tax on Land and Animals | — | 1.28 | 1.09 | 1.09 | 1.01 | 0.63 | 0.65 | — |
| Registration Duties | | 6.41 | 7.00 | 7.66 | 8.77 | 10.48 | 10.48 | — |
| Customs Duties | 4.35 | 23.38 | 26.09 | 20.51 | 33.53 | 36.77 | 34.30 | 38.75 |
| Other Indirect Tax | — | 29.09 | 32.77 | 33.97 | 37.60 | 42.57 | 37.58 | — |
| Other Receipts | 1.65 | 6.77 | 7.24 | 7.09 | 9.73 | 17.04 | 14.47 | — |
| *Total* | 7.20 | 78.66 | 87.12 | 83.21 | 105.10 | 124.76 | 112.68 | 123.40 |
| **Expenditures:** | | | | | | | | |
| Education | 0.05 | 5.69 | 6.77 | 7.86 | 9.56 | 9.96 | 13.55 | 15.51 |
| Health | 0.28 | 3.73 | 4.82 | 4.82 | 4.56 | 4.66 | 5.81 | 6.27 |
| Defence | — | 13.31 | 17.32 | 14.56 | 17.08 | 17.42 | 19.06 | 20.92 |
| Public Works | 1.14 | 17.70 | 17.56 | 20.33 | 17.95 | 14.77 | 15.82 | 19.06 |
| Other Expenditure | 4.45 | 29.64 | 36.93 | 36.93 | 40.90 | 41.70 | 58.60 | 61.64 |
| *Total* | 6.73 | 70.07 | 83.40 | 84.52 | 90.05 | 88.51 | 112.84 | 123.40 |
| Balance | 0.83 | 8.50 | 8.59 | −1.31 | 15.05 | 36.25 | −0.16 | — |

[a] Estimates.

Source: United Nations Bureau of Economic Affairs, Fiscal Branch.

15.4% in 1954. The development projects were mainly irrigation works, power roads and communications. Ordinary budget funds for infrastructure projects totalled 173 million LL, 113 million of which was spent on roads, ports, buildings and other works. Of the 113 million spent between 1944 and 1953, 43 million were spent on roads.

State intervention was apparent at another level as well. In 1955 the Industrial, Agricultural and Real Estate Bank was established, with two million LL of state funds and three million of private funds. Also, under a Point Four General Agreement in 1951, a programme agreement was signed in 1952 by which the USA assisted in agricultural, forestry, irrigation, industrial and other projects. To assist new business, the government passed a law, in June 1954, exempting new enterprises from income tax for a period of six years.

The previous discussion of Lebanon's economy during the first decade of independence clearly shows the uneven development of the various economic sectors and sub-sectors. It also shows that Lebanon's 'prosperity' depended a great deal upon Middle East business: oil, transit, customs duties, capital movements and so on. It also depended to a great extent upon the vicissitudes of international economic trends.

Uneven development was also present among the geographic regions of the country. The share of each region of the services, industrial and agricultural sectors had clearly been uneven. The services sector, for instance, was concentrated in Beirut and Mount Lebanon. The same was true of the industrial sector, as Table 8 shows.

Table 8
Lebanon: Geographic Distribution of Industrial Activity

| Region | Value Added | Sales | Workers | Wages |
|---|---|---|---|---|
| 1954: | | | | |
| Beirut | 38 | 38 | 43 | 45 |
| Mount Lebanon | 32 | 30 | 36 | 32 |
| North Lebanon | 22 | 23 | 14 | 17 |
| Bekaa | 2 | 2 | 3 | 2 |
| South Lebanon | 5 | 7 | 3 | 4 |
| 1964: | | | | |
| Beirut | 25.4 | 25.5 | 29.8 | 27.4 |
| Mount Lebanon | 52.3 | 35.7 | 50.4 | 50.8 |
| North Lebanon | 14.6 | 18.0 | 14.0 | 16.4 |
| Bekaa | 3.2 | 3.2 | 3.5 | 2.3 |
| South Lebanon | 4.5 | 6.6 | 2.0 | 3.1 |

Source: A. Atallah and S. Khalat, *The Lebanese Industrial Sector: Its Growth and Development*. A Study for the Ministry of National Economy, Bureau of Industrial Development (Beirut, 1969).

The area of Mount Lebanon, where most of this region's industry is located, actually comprises greater Beirut. Seventy per cent of industrial activity (measured by value added) was concentrated in greater Beirut in 1954. This figure jumped to 77.7% 10 years later.[25]

Table 9
Lebanon: Share of Various Industries of Industrial Establishments over Different Periods (Per cent)

| Period | Food, Shoes and Clothing | Non-Metal Mining | Mining and Engineering | Chemical | Other |
|--------|--------------------------|------------------|------------------------|----------|-------|
| 1918 | 75 | 5 | 2 | 1 | 13 |
| 1919–28 | 68 | 13 | 7 | 1 | 11 |
| 1929–39 | 50 | 17 | 16 | 2 | 15 |
| 1940–45 | 47 | 25 | 11 | 3 | 15 |
| 1946–50 | 45 | 28 | 9 | 4 | 14 |
| 1951–55 | 46 | 28 | 9 | 2 | 15 |
| 1954 | 54 | 21 | 8 | 2 | 15 |
| 1964 | 44 | 29 | 7 | 3 | 27 |

Source: A. Atallah and S. Khalat (Beirut, 1969).

Structural changes that occurred within the Lebanese industry are shown in Table 9. The average number of new industrial establishments between 1918 and 1964 was 40. The period 1945 to 1955 witnessed the creation of above-average number of establishments, whereas the opposite was true in the period 1954 to 1964.

It is regrettable that statistics on value added, number of workers, sales value and so on are lacking for the periods under consideration.[26] However, the industrial establishment ratio in each industrial sub-sector remains a very good indicator of structural change. It is obvious from the above table that Lebanon lacked heavy industry and that most of its industry was concentrated in food, shoes, clothing and non-metal mining. Although some changes occurred, these were not enough to be counted as fundamental.

For geographic distribution of industrial establishments see Table 10.

Table 10
Lebanon: Share of Industrial Establishments in the Various Regions: 1954 and 1964 (Per cent) .

| Year | Beirut and Mount Lebanon | North | Bekaa | South |
|------|--------------------------|-------|-------|-------|
| 1954 | 78 | 12 | 5 | 5 |
| 1964 | 83.3 | 10.1 | 3.5 | 3.1 |

Source: A. Atallah and S. Khalat (Beirut, 1969).

It could be argued that many economic benefits to the country accrued because of concentration. This might be true if such efforts were planned and related to other sectors of the economy by either complementing or reinforcing other activities in the rest of the economic sectors and geographic regions. Undoubtedly, such elegant theories on concentration do not hold in the case of Lebanon. Whatever the theoretical advantages of concentration, they must have evaporated due to high production costs, brought about by wage increases and high land and plant values and rent, brought about in great part by concentration itself. Perhaps the worst problems of concentration are depicted by differentiation in income levels among individuals and groups inhabiting different geographic regions. Furthermore, migration to industrial areas brings about higher transport and housing costs.[27]

The record of the industrial sector was not encouraging and, as the various tables show, it lagged structurally behind services. This was also reflected in the yearly growth in production (3.75%).[28] Individual industries had registered negative growth; for example, food and textiles. Other industries had registered high growth; for example, paper, wood, printing and publishing. In general, industries that are more related to services grew more rapidly.

The structure of the economy did not encourage the entry of people into the industrial workforce. The average growth of employment was 1.84% between 1954 and 1964.[29] Food and textiles had in fact laid off many workers and employment growth was −1.33% and −1.84% respectively in the same period. Workers' productivity was 1.7% but it was mostly due to a declining rate of employment compared to the rate of production in most industries.[30]

Whatever indicator one uses to talk about industrial development and/or the industry's share of the GNP, each clearly points out the secondary nature of industry in the Lebanese economy. The study that this discussion is based upon puts the yearly average growth of capital (1954 to 1964) at 4.55%. The study concludes that 'this rate is considered insignificant and not encouraging to make the industrial sector increase its share of the GNP.'[31]

Data on capital-to-production ratios for the different industries show that the higher the ratio, the lower the rate of industrial growth, especially if the production volume is limited.[32] This is true in the case of Lebanon, whose industrial market was small and which needed the regional Middle East market and other outlets, especially if industry were to grow at all. For industry to grow, it would have to compete with foreign goods domestically, regionally and internationally. Needless to say, this was a difficult proposition for small industries that were threatened by big competition. Competition probably had been the major reason for low capital-to-production ratios compared to other industrial countries.[33]

To guarantee the domestic market for its products, Lebanese industry would have had to resort to protectionism. This could not have been done effectively because of the economy's bias towards the services sector. To keep a strong regional market, Lebanon would have had to control the political process in the region so that it could prevent legislation in neighbouring countries from encouraging their respective local industry. This absurd condition for protecting the regional market only demonstrates the constraints within which Lebanese industry had been operating. The best thing Lebanese industry was able to do was to go for bilateral agreements with separate Arab countries. These agreements, however, had been dependent upon the vagaries of the international capitalist market and the political (in)stability of the region as a whole.

All these problems — market size, political instability, the strong services industry and the fact that the political process was dominated by mercantilist interests — argued that Lebanon's industry would remain weak. In fact, industry's share of GNP up until 1974 remained almost the same.[34] The share of industrial salaries and wages grew at the expense of capital's share. That is, it was a zero-sum game reflecting no growth. In 1954 the share of wages and salaries was 31%, while capital's share was 69%. In 1964 the share of salaries and wages went up by 7% to 38%, while capital's share went down by the same amount (7%) to 62%.[35]

At the same time the average worker's real income increased from 1,409 LL in 1954 to 1,842 LL in 1964 (based on 1954 prices); this comprised a 2.66% increase measured against workers' productivity of 1.7% per year.[36] It is obvious that even this modest increase in the wage rate was inflationary due to the economic structure that Lebanon had been locked into even before independence.[37]

It would be somewhat misleading while discussing Lebanese industry not to bring forward data on value added. If one realizes that the valued added declined between 1954 and 1964, one begins to ask certain questions about Lebanon's economy.[38] Such questions deal with the mercantilist nature of the country's industry. It becomes clear that industry played a 'middle-man' role for foreign industry. Semi-finished goods were brought in, their manufacture was completed, then they were re-exported to the regional market. This meant that Lebanon did not initiate raw materials, technology, expertise and so on. While this practice was an 'ingenious' way of 'making a buck', it left Lebanon exposed to the unpleasant winds of international political and economic crises.

Between 1957 and 1965, about one-third of Lebanon's imports were for industrial needs. These imports registered a 12% yearly growth rate. Industrial imports were distributed as follows: capital goods 15%, intermediate goods 61%, raw material 24%. The data in Table 11 would confirm this view.

Value added for all industry had dropped from 38% in 1954 to 36% in 1964. Although some industries had shown an increase in value added, most were modest, except for machinery. Be that as it may, the basic problem remains: industry is weak, is geared for export, is mainly a consumer-goods industry, and is a 'middle-man' industry.

Table 12 gives data on imported industrial goods.

Table 11
Lebanon: Rate of Value Added for Various Industries (Per cent)

| Year | Food Products | Alcoholic Beverages | Tobacco | Textiles | Shoes and Clothing | Wood and Cork |
|------|------|------|------|------|------|------|
| 1954 | 30 | 61 | 79 | 39 | 43 | 50 |
| 1964 | 21 | 51 | 56 | 40 | 44 | 32 |

| Year | Furniture | Paper | Printing & Publishing | Leather | Rubber | Chemicals |
|------|------|------|------|------|------|------|
| 1954 | 42 | 36 | 55 | 23 | 43 | 35 |
| 1964 | 46 | 33 | 60 | 25 | 40 | 36 |

| Year | Petroleum Products | Metallic | Machinery | Transport Equipment | Appliances & Equipment | Other |
|------|------|------|------|------|------|------|
| 1954 | 18 | 28 | 28 | 35 | 50 | 35 |
| 1964 | 18 | 21 | 51 | 30 | 50 | 41 |

Source: A. Atallah and S. Khalat (Beirut, 1969).

Table 12
Lebanon: Value of Imported Industrial Goods Between 1957 to 1965 with Rates of Each (Value in Millions of Lebanese Pounds)

| Year | Industrial Capital Goods | | Intermediate Industrial Goods | | Raw Materials | | Total | | Total Imports |
|------|------|------|------|------|------|------|------|------|------|
| | value | % | value | % | value | % | value | % | value |
| 1957 | 25 | 5 | 102 | 19 | 45 | 8 | 172 | 32 | 542 |
| 1958 | 28 | 6 | 80 | 17 | 30 | 6 | 138 | 32 | 461 |
| 1959 | 24 | 4 | 98 | 18 | 41 | 8 | 138 | 30 | 555 |
| 1960 | 26 | 4 | 125 | 19 | 41 | 6 | 192 | 29 | 669 |
| 1961 | 33 | 5 | 124 | 17 | 43 | 6 | 221 | 28 | 725 |
| 1962 | 24 | 3 | 135 | 17 | 64 | 8 | 205 | 29 | 779 |
| 1963 | 30 | 4 | 150 | 18 | 59 | 7 | 329 | 29 | 837 |
| 1964 | 54 | 4 | 228 | 19 | 81 | 7 | 363 | 29 | 927 |
| 1965 | 66 | 5 | 256 | 19 | 86 | 6 | 308 | 30 | 1481 |

Source: A. Atallah and S. Khalat (Beirut, 1969).

Exported industrial products comprised 15.5% of Lebanese exports in 1957. The figure went up to 23.3% in 1965. In 1961 the value of these exports was 18.5 million LL; it increased to 129 million LL in 1968.[39] The Arab market was the natural market for Lebanese exports in general.

Between 1967 and 1970 a balance-of-trade surplus existed only with the Arab countries. Lebanon's largest balance-of-trade deficit was with the capitalist countries; this deficit has been increasing.[40] The table does not show that the largest deficit existed with the EEC countries, followed by the USA. In the early seventies Lebanon experienced a trade surplus with the Eastern-bloc nations while it maintained a deficit with the Western capitalist countries.[41]

Eighty-four per cent of Lebanon's industrial exports in 1967 went to Arab countries.[42] The structure of industrial exports is depicted by the following figures (1967): metallic products 13.5%; food products 16%; chemicals 10%; and non-metallic mining products 10%. These comprise the main industrial exports.[43]

The discussion on industry shows that uneven development existed among regions as it did among the economic sectors. The discussion shows that the regions' share of industry was uneven, and that the position of the industrial sector vis-à-vis the services sector was precarious. Table 13 shows that no change had really occurred since the early 1950s in the share of each economic sector and sub-sector of the GNP.

Table 13
Lebanon: Share of Economic Sectors of GNP

| Sector | 1957 % | 1964 % | 1965 % |
|---|---|---|---|
| Agriculture | 15.8 | 11.46 | 15 |
| Industry | 12.6 | 14.70 | 12 |
| Construction | 2.7 | 5.43 | 5 |
| Trade | 31.2 | 32.30 | 26 |
| Finance | 6.1 | 3.00 | 8 |
| Transportation | 5.3 | 6.80 | 7 |
| Housing | 9.3 | 7.74 | 10 |
| Services | 9.8 | 8.40 | 8 |
| Administration | 7.2 | 7.50 | 9 |
| Other | — | 2.50 | — |
| *Total* | *100.0* | *100.0* | *100* |

Source: Kuwait Fund for Arab Economic Development: *Report on the Lebanese Economy and its Developmental Projects* (June 1967).

Table 13 clearly shows the existence of a chronic tilt toward the services and other related sectors and especially trade. To continue our discussion, Table 14 shows figures on the labour force.

No wonder, then, that as early as 1959 the income distribution profile was as shown in Table 15.

This poignant portrayal of the miserable economic plight of the masses is compounded when one realizes that the share of each region of the various

Table 14
Lebanon: Distribution of Labour Force on the Various Economic Sectors in
1967 (in Thousands)

| Sector | Number | % |
|---|---|---|
| Agriculture | 300 | 49 |
| Industry | 60 | 9.75 |
| Construction | 20 | 3.25 |
| Trade and Finance | 153 | 24.5 |
| Transport and Communication | 30 | 4.9 |
| Administration | 17 | 2.7 |
| Armed Forces | 10 | 1.6 |
| Unemployed | 20 | 3.25 |

Source: Kuwait Fund for Arab Economic Development, (June 1967).

Table 15
Lebanon: Income Distribution

| Category | Per cent of Population | Level of Family Income (LL) |
|---|---|---|
| Destitute | 9 | 1,200 or less ($0–400) |
| Poor | 40 | 1,200–2,500 ($400–830) |
| Average | 30 | 2,500–5,000 ($830–1,660) |
| Well-Off | 14 | 5,000–15,000 ($1,660–5,000) |
| Rich | 4 | 15,000 or more ($5,000+) |

Source: Income Distribution Table, 1959 IRFED (Beirut, 1960–1961).

sectors has been uneven. What this means is that some regions have been more
depressed than others in terms of wealth and income distribution, and share
the minimum amount of public services. These are facts that cannot be
ignored in any study of Lebanon's economic development.[44] A readily-
available example may be helpful in this regard. Because agriculture is geared
to export and because fruit is the most important product, one sees that
Mount Lebanon is more affluent than the other regions. Although there are
no statistics available on the geographic distribution of agricultural workers,
it is well known in Lebanon that most of these workers are in the depressed
areas. This leaves most of the income from agriculture to a few people in the
Mountain. What confirms this observation is the pattern of small land
holdings in the Mountain. Most of the large landholdings are owned by
*zuama* in the plains, mostly in the depressed areas.

The lack of statistics and other relevant information, such as is normally
provided by national income accounting, frustrates research of the economy
even up to the late 1960s. In 1967, for instance, only an elementary attempt
at national income accounting existed. Its results remained tentative and
lacked internal consistency.[45] The available statistics, however, show that

not only did agriculture and industry lag behind services, but they were tied to export trade to a great extent. And in agriculture, Lebanon has been a deficit country in all products except fruit, as Table 16 shows.

Table 17 shows that cereal production declined or remained largely static in the years 1956 to 1966. The same was true of areas planted. The highest yield per hectare was achieved in 1962, while the lowest was in 1965. The average was just below one ton per hectare during the period in question. What we see is that an important agricultural product was allowed to stagnate at a time when there was a need for cereals to satisfy local demand, as depicted in Table 17. This situation was obviously beneficial to trade.

Table 16
Lebanon: Production, Import and Export of Agricultural Products in 1964
(In Millions of Lebanese Pounds)

| Products | Production | Imports | Exports | Deficit/Surplus |
|---|---|---|---|---|
| Cereals | 21.1 | 77.7 | 1.4 | − 76.3 |
| Fruits | 177.0 | 14.3 | 46.9 | 32.6 |
| Industrial | 34.0 | 51.3 | 13.9 | − 37.2 |
| Vegetables/Flowers | 64.4 | 21.9 | 16.1 | − 5.8 |
| Forestry Products | 0.5 | 6.3 | 0.2 | − 6.1 |
| *Total* | *297.1* | *171.5* | *78.5* | *− 93.0* |

Source: Kuwait Fund for Arab Economic Development (June 1967).

Table 17
Lebanon: Cereal Production 1956 to 1966

| Year | Production (1,000 tons) | Area Planted (1,000 hectares) | Yield/hectare (tons) |
|---|---|---|---|
| 1956 | 102.8 | 102.5 | 1.00 |
| 1957 | 115.5 | 106.0 | 1.08 |
| 1958 | 84.0 | 98.5 | .85 |
| 1959 | 107.4 | 104.2 | 1.03 |
| 1960 | 66.3 | 91.5 | .72 |
| 1961 | 94.6 | 89.1 | 1.06 |
| 1962 | 104.6 | 90.3 | 1.15 |
| 1963 | 82.9 | 71.8 | 1.03 |
| 1964 | 100.0 | 91.7 | 1.09 |
| 1965 | 78.9 | 96.2 | .82 |
| 1966 | 92.9 | 88.4 | 1.05 |

Source: Kuwait Fund for Arab Economic Development (June 1967).

Cultivable land area had not really changed from the 1950s to the 1960s. In 1967, for instance, it was estimated at between 256,000 and 310,000 hectares. Land tenure remained almost the same: prevalence of weak small holdings, 44% of which were owner-exploited, 55% owner- and farmer-exploited, while agricultural labourers worked for a few big landowners.[46] IRFED distinguished among the following:[47]

1. Fruits and vineyard lands: large investments, some of which belong to traders and capitalists.
2. Most of the countryside population have lands in non-irrigated areas. small units are prevalent, with low technical and living standards. The main source of migration to the city came from this group.
3. Very small investments in irrigated areas.

Agriculture had always suffered from distinct problems which had been detrimental to its development. To begin with, fruit and vegetables (export products) depend heavily upon export market conditions, which have often been insecure. Income generated from export trade was not enough to pay for imports of agricultural products, especially cereals. Although the Lebanese government had spent 25 million LL from 1961 to 1965, and 123 million LL from 1965 to 1969 on irrigation projects, 'no doubt this amount is modest compared to what the Lebanese countryside needs in investment.'[48] Once an area became irrigated, however, land values increased some four- to five-fold. Capital went to buy land for speculation. Because speculation did not need expertise in farming, speculators could not use the land efficiently during the waiting period between buying and selling. This practice put a heavy burden on the already non-competitive agricultural products vis-à-vis foreign ones.

Also in the late 1960s, financial aid was still ineffective in rendering the small landowners able, over short- or long-range periods, to service their debts and pay the principal while realizing some profits (interest rates were six to 10 per cent per month!). To try to meet their financial obligations, small landowners had to cut down on costs, which affected their work methods and resulted in low productivity and soil deterioration. Unable to meet their obligations, they were forced to go deeper into debt or sell the land, a practice that did not help productivity at all. Because of these practices, out-migration became a problem. In 1967, 80% of those who depended solely upon the land as a source of income were over 50 years of age. Furthermore, the standard of living declined and cooperatives became weaker. In 1959 there were 150 cooperatives, while in 1967 the number dropped to 27. Also, the laws pertaining to ownership were not conducive for cooperative formation or for efficient land utilization. Technical assistance was also denied those who did not seek out immediate financial loans. In this way, technical assistance and loans became structurally legislated for rich peasants and for agricultural business.[49]

Whatever 'development' was carried out in agriculture and industry did not change the picture of uneven development of the economy and did not change its structure from that obtaining in the 1940s and 1950s.

While a strict comparative analysis is almost impossible between the economy in these decades and in the 1960s (due to non-comparable statistical data of the different periods and other inconsistencies of the data pertaining to the same period),[50] it can be shown that the state of the economy in the two periods indicates that Lebanon had done little to alleviate the effects of uneven development of its economic sectors and geographic regions.

To corroborate the picture drawn earlier of the economy in the 1950s, and to complement the discussion on industry and agriculture in the 1960s, we now turn to a discussion of the principal items in the balance of payments for the years 1961 to 1965 (wherever possible comparison will be made with the figures for the 1951–1952 period, which give a picture of the balance of payments in the 1950s in general).

Commodity trade had three distinguishing features: (1) a big deficit; (2) a relatively great number of products (imports and exports), although fruit and vegetables were the major items; and (3) exports were mainly with the Arab countries, while imports were mainly from Europe. This was the same picture presented for this item on the balance of payments in the 1950s. Non-monetary gold sustained a deficit of seven million LL.[51] In the early 1950s this item registered a small surplus: 0.9 million in 1951 but −11.5 million in 1952. This represented, at least in theory, domestic consumption or savings of this item.[52]

The yearly growth of income from tourism had been estimated at 14% in the period under question. Income had risen from 147 million LL to 248 million, and tourism increased from 331,600 in 1962 to 601,500 in 1965.[53] The largest number were Arabs (40%) followed by 20% Western Europeans, and 15% Australians and North Americans.

Transport and insurance figures did not indicate reinsurance (local companies insuring in foreign ones). This sub-category is included in the 'other' category. Various studies of the Lebanese economy point to the poor commercial fleet of Lebanon. These studies further point out the need to find the reasons behind such a phenomenon. It was clear, however, that Lebanon did not have the capital to build a commercial fleet which was capable of competing with the world fleets.[54] As long as Lebanon kept depending upon the services sector to cover its balance-of-payments deficit, it could never build a commercial fleet of its own.

Investment income was in surplus to the tune of approximately 70 million LL, about one-third of which came from real-estate investments (buildings).[55]

Government operations included the UN and foreign embassies' and consulates' expenditure in Lebanon.

Other services included transit income, foreign-exchange income, financial, commercial and investment services, expenditure of foreign companies and so on. This 'other' category was very substantial and came close (on the credit side) to the comparable item of commodity trade.

The significant feature of Lebanon's foreign trade for the period in question was represented by the deficit in the goods and services account.

As shown here, in the period 1961 to 1965, the deficit was as follows: 240, 190, 129, 219, 259, and 349 million LL, respectively. The moving three-year average from 1953 to 1965 depicted a spiralling deficit: 90, 110, 135, 168, 196, 235, 246, 281, 267, 230, 200, 199, 272. Although the average fell from 281 in 1960 to 267, etc. in 1961 to 1964, we see that it rose again in 1965. The trend is clear: the deficit was rising and it remained a significant feature of the goods and services account.[56]

The deficit was covered by the following items on the balance of payments: remittances and donations, which had been a precarious and unpredictable item.

*Long-Term Private Capital:* The major sub-item was foreign investment and real estate, which in 1962 amounted to 90 million LL and in 1963 to 86 million LL; 54.2 and 52.2 million LL for the respective years reflects real-estate (other than buildings) investment. Not all foreign investments are reflected in this category.[57] As an example, foreign investments of 17 and 18 million LL for 1964 and 1965, respectively, were invested in trade at 35%, industry at 25% and finance at 13%. The Kuwait Fund Study reports that this item is expected to diminish because 'Lebanon does not offer an encouraging financial market for long-term investment.'[58]

*Short-Term Private Capital:* This item is the critical point in the structure of the external accounts for the period under consideration. The deficit in the balance of payments was covered by this item. But a deficit in current transactions cannot be considered covered by short-term capital due to the precarious nature of this item. With this in mind, Table 18 depicts a significant feature of the balance of payments.

Table 18
Lebanon: Balance of Payments Deficit, 1961 to 1965
(Millions of Lebanese Pounds)

| Category | 1961 | 1962 | 1963 | 1964 | 1965 |
|---|---|---|---|---|---|
| Current Deficit | −119.8 | −31.7 | −110.4 | −130.3 | −228.4 |
| Long-Term Capital | 44.0 | 52.4 | 50.1 | 63.1 | 74.3 |
| Long-Term Public Capital | 18.3 | 11.0 | 7.2 | 20.5 | 4.8 |
| *Total* | −57.5 | +31.7 | −53.1 | −46.7 | −143.3 |

Source: Kuwait Fund for Arab Economic Development (June 1967).

It was unrealistic to imagine that this deficit could be covered by increasing the country's exports of goods and services. This move was impossible without a structural change in the Lebanese economy which, needless to say, was not forthcoming: the mercantilists were in dominant control of the political process and of state power. Instead of this dramatic change, Lebanon had been relying upon financial transactions as indicated by the increase in the number of local and foreign banks (Table 19).

Most of these banks were owned or controlled by foreign interests, mainly

Table 19
Lebanon: Banks Development in Selected Years

|  | 1945 | 1954 | 1959 | 1963 | 1965 | 1966 |
|---|---|---|---|---|---|---|
| Number of Banks | 7 | 21 | 29 | 70 | 80 | 99 |

Source: Kuwait Fund for Arab Economic Development (June 1967); and
F. Qubain, *Crisis in Lebanon* (Washington DC, Middle East Institute, 1961), 5.

European but also US: Chase Manhattan (1950), First National City Bank
(1955) and Bank of America (1956).[59]

In 1966, 82 banks were headquartered in Beirut. All banks had 232
branches. However, most of these banks were small. Less than 10 'local'
banks were considered important in 1965. They are listed in Table 20.

Table 20
Lebanon: Top 'Local' Banks (In Millions of Lebanese Pounds)

| Bank | Capital | Reserve | Other Income |
|---|---|---|---|
| Intra | 60 | 10.5 | 766 |
| Beirut-Riadh | 25 | 1.3 | 68.5 |
| Leb. and the ME | 15 | 1.4 | 147.7 |
| Alahli | 10 | 4.2 | 152 |
| Leb. Union | 10 | 2.2 | 26.6 |
| Development | 8 | 0.11 | 34.6 |
| Commerce | 5 | 1.9 | 157.5 |
| Belgian Lebanese | 5 | 2.7 | 62 |
| Leb. and Overseas | 5 | 1.4 | 60.2 |

Source: Kuwait Fund for Arab Economic Development (June 1967).

Table 21 shows the aggregate financial structure of the commercial banks.
Despite the abundance of 'local' banks, most of the deposits were in the
Lebanese branches of foreign banks, 20 branches of which had in the summer
of 1965 about 75% of local deposits and 85% of deposits of non-residents.[60]
Added to the problem of foreign financial control or perhaps as a result of
it, financial markets were virtually non-existent to attract long-term deposits
to balance short-term deposits. In this respect one could talk of a chronic
structural weakness in the Lebanese banking system — a weakness in the
strongest economic sector of Lebanon!

In 1955 the Industrial, Agricultural and Real Estate Bank was founded in
an attempt to alleviate some of the effects of the structural weakness of the
economy. By the late 1950s and early 1960s, however, it was clear that this
institution was incapable of achieving its goals. This was witnessed by the fact
that the authorities, in recognition of the problem, had proposed in 1962 to
establish a bank for industrial development with the participation of the

Table 21
Lebanon: Commercial Banks, 1964, 1965, 1966
   (In Millions of Lebanese Pounds)

| Item | 1964 | 1965 | 1966 |
|---|---|---|---|
| Reserves | 100 | 108 | 188 |
| Foreign Capital | 1,460 | 1,848 | 1,584 |
| Claims on Private Sector | 1,945 | 2,310 | 2,336 |
| *Total:* | *3,505* | *4,266* | *4,108* |
| Demand Deposits | 890 | 962 | 894 |
| Term Deposits in Foreign Currency | 1,271 | 1,705 | 1,891 |
| Foreign Commitments | 1,023 | 1,156 | 820 |
| Other Items | 322 | 443 | 503 |
| *Total:* | *3,506* | *4,266* | *4,108* |

Source: Kuwait Fund for Arab Economic Development (June 1967).

International Finance Corporation.[61]

One policy which, in the opinion of the Kuwait Fund Study, contributed greatly to uneven development was the fiscal policy of the state. A surplus in the budget existed from 1943 to 1962. This was a conservative policy which was a hurdle to the rate of growth of GNP. The study implies that government intervention was needed to alleviate uneven development in the economic sectors. Although a slight deficit obtained each year after 1962, government policy remained conservative. In 1964, for instance, government spending was only 16% of the national income. This policy financed yearly expenditures by ordinary income and financed developmental projects through new income or loans.[62]

Lebanon, it seemed, had been caught in a general contradiction: on the one hand its economic policy contributed greatly to uneven development; on the other it had to have this policy to protect its domestic monetary position and to try to avoid whatever threatened the monetary value and purchasing power of the Lebanese pound. However, these fiscal and monetary policies were conscious decisions by the state. Given the fact that Lebanon's foreign-exchange market had been free from all restrictions since May 1952, and since short-term capital had played an important part in covering the balance-of-payments deficit, the state had to have a conservative policy. The alternative would have been an inflationary fiscal policy under conditions of lack of state control over foreign transactions which would — sooner or later — have driven away much-needed short-term foreign capital from Lebanon.

But this was not all in terms of the general contradiction. Despite this conscious conservative fiscal policy, Lebanon did not escape the economic problems brought about by total monetary integration into the capitalist market. What fiscal policy tried to avoid, Lebanon began to experience (recession and inflation) by 1965–66. Like most countries' economies that have been caught in the grip of capital, Lebanon's characteristic features had become inflation and recession.

On the eve of the conflict of 1975, these economic ills contributed greatly to the conflagration.

So far we have argued that the period 1943 to 1965[63] had been one that plunged Lebanon deeper into uneven development and had created heavy dependence upon external political and economic forces. We have also argued that the political set-up had reinforced the services sector at the expense of other sectors, and that the structural set-up of the economy had in turn reinforced the political set-up.

The period beginning in 1964–65* was not much better. The late sixties experienced slow economic growth and nothing of significance happened until 1972 in terms of development projects.[64] Due to internal and external disturbances, and because Lebanon depended heavily on the services sector, long-term private capital inflows decreased rapidly. The Intra Bank crisis of 1966, the 1967 war and the 1969 Lebanese army clashes with the Palestinian guerrillas all contributed to slow growth.[65]

Agriculture kept showing an increasing deficit while having a 20% share of exports. Local production covered 70% of domestic consumption. The share of agriculture in the GDP declined from 20% in 1950 to 10% in 1968 and 9% in 1973. The services sector increased from 63% to 70% in the same years. The share of manufacturing of GDP increased from 14% to 17% in 1974. Export-oriented manufacturing led to this growth.[66] At the same time the labour force was distributed as in Table 22.

Table 22 is a glaring portrayal of the inequities of income distribution due to the economic structure. What the table does not show, however, is the breakdown of who gets what and how much in each sub-sector of the services. For example, the category of white-collar workers includes managers and clerks, two categories that do not have equal wages and benefits. In fact, the effects of the inequities are more devastating than the table seems to suggest.

The IBRD reported, 'Concerned with growing imbalances between sectors and income groups, the government decided in 1970 to go forward with five

---

* 1964–65 may be considered as the beginning of a new period for the following reasons: (1) For the first time in Lebanon both a recession and inflation occurred about the same time. (2) This stagflation, as it is called, had set the stage for unparalleled economic dislocations in the period ahead. Most notably, the Intra Bank collapse of 1966 shook the foundations of Lebanon's financial and banking system and economy. (3) On the basis of blatant uneven development which was a result of Lebanon's full integration into the international capitalist market, mass political and economic challenge to the system (through strikes, demonstrations, etc.) began to show a marked increase in 1964–65. This challenge reached its peak in the 1970s (before the civil war). For the first time this challenge assumed a broad-based organized form in the Lebanese National Movement. Unlike the previous period, this challenge was consistent and able to pose a threat to the capitalist economy.

Table 22
Lebanon: Distribution of Labour Force Among the Economic Sectors, 1974
(Per cent)

| Labour Force | Economic Sector | GDP |
|---|---|---|
| 50% | Agriculture | 9 |
| 20% | Industry | 17 |
| 30% | Services | 74 |

Source: International Bank for Reconstruction and Development (IBRD).

irrigation schemes that could . . . start in 1975.'[67] Nineteen seventy-five was the year the civil war began.

The Intra Bank collapse of 1966 had discouraged foreign capital from investing in Lebanon (mostly in Beirut). An important part of this capital was invested in real estate. Construction funds became more difficult to come by: 'Present [1969] political uncertainties are not, however, likely to be favourable to fast growth in this sector.'[68]

The reliance of Lebanon on the services sector had devastating effects on the economy, due to the political and economic disturbances of the 1966–70 period. Although exports picked up fast in 1967, mainly due to the closing of the Suez Canal (a temporary phenomenon and not a healthy factor upon which to build economic policy), it was clear that the situation was not conducive to the political and economic development of the country. A few had benefited at the expense of the rest of the population and even at the expense of some of the élite in the agricultural sector. The economic 'recovery' of 1968 witnessed a fast rise in imports which, despite a 14% export growth, had widened the trade deficit by 150 million LL. This was offset by growth in tourism and other receipts, however. Again we see that the services had kept the balance of payments in surplus. That is to say, this sector was shoring up the precarious economy. This practice did not prevent the impoverishment of the population, especially those in agriculture (50% of the labour force), who did not share in the benefits derived from the services.

The 1970s also reconfirmed the precariousness of the whole situation. To appreciate fully the precarious position of Lebanon economically and politically, we will have to begin with the agricultural sector, then go to industry and finally to services. Before presenting any statistics on the various sectors, see Table 23 — a profile of Lebanon's population at the beginning of the decade.

The first thing to notice about the figures in Table 23 is that the population lived mostly in the big cities and towns. This means that most jobs existed in non-rural areas. This is confirmed by the figures on manpower, labour force and employment. Employment figures, and especially the rate of unemployment, are relatively low. This is so because these figures do not take into consideration under-employment or hidden unemployment, and

Table 23
Lebanon: Population, Education Enrolment, Labour Force and Employment,
1970 (In Thousands)

| Designation | Beirut | Beirut Suburban | Other Towns | Rural Areas | Total Lebanon |
|---|---|---|---|---|---|
| Population | 474.9 | 464.1 | 339.0 | 848.3 | 2,126.3 |
| Education Enrolment | 160.7 | 154.7 | 126.4 | 272.5 | 714.3 |
| % of Population | 33.8 | 33.3 | 37.3 | 32.1 | 33.6 |
| Manpower | 275.7 | 242.1 | 173.4 | 420.8 | 1,112.0 |
| % of Population | 58.1 | 52.2 | 51.2 | 49.6 | 52.3 |
| Labour Force | 142.0 | 123.7 | 77.9 | 212.4 | 556.1 |
| % of Manpower | 51.5 | 51.1 | 44.9 | 50.5 | 50.0 |
| Employment | 136.6 | 118.9 | 75.5 | 207.4 | 538.4 |
| Rate of Unemployment | 3.8 | 3.9 | 3.1 | 2.4 | 3.2 |

Source: Ministry of Planning; Central Statistical Office: Employment Survey,
November 1970.

also because it has been difficult to collect employment statistics in Lebanon.
Nevertheless, one can see the gap between 'manpower' and 'labour force'
statistics. This is so for two major reasons: (1) many had given up looking for
jobs; and (2) many worked outside Lebanon. Also conveniently excluded are
the Syrian labourers (a backbone of the economy) and the Palestinian population of Lebanon, who contributed much to the economy.

To go a step further and show uneven development in terms of employment, Table 24 shows interesting statistics about the labour force. They
basically show that the structure of the economy on the eve of the 1975
conflict had been the same since independence.

GDP figures further show uneven development in the economy on the
eve of the conflict; it is clear from Table 25 that agriculture was the least
important sector, especially when a sub-sector of the services (namely,
transport and communication) was two-thirds as large as agriculture in 1972
and almost equal to it in 1971. As a percentage of GDP in 1971, agriculture
was 8.6 and transport 8.1.

The International Monetary Fund (IMF) study of 21 January 1975
entitled 'Lebanon — Recent Economic Developments' corroborates the
picture of the Lebanese economy presented in Table 25. Although agricultural
exports increased in absolute terms in the 1970s, their relative share of total
exports had declined from one-third in the late 1960s to 18% in 1973.[69]
Lebanon in the 1970s remained a net exporter of fruit, vegetables and
poultry products and a net importer of cereals, dairy products, livestock and
animal feed. The average annual growth rate of agricultural exports in the
period 1970–73 was 13%, while the rate of imports was 9%. In 1973 the
export growth rate slowed down to 5%.[70]

Lebanon's agricultural policy was to encourage diversified agriculture

Table 24
Lebanon: Employment by Sector, 1970[a]
   (In Thousands)

| Sector | Beirut | Beirut Suburban | Other Towns | Rural Areas | Total Lebanon |
|---|---|---|---|---|---|
| Agriculture[a] | 0.6 | 1.6 | 5.5 | 94.1 | 101.8 |
| Industry | 23.4 | 33.4 | 16.1 | 22.6 | 95.5 |
| Power and Water | 1.1 | 1.1 | 0.9 | 2.5 | 5.6 |
| Construction[a] | 6.0 | 8.5 | 5.3 | 15.3 | 35.5 |
| Commerce and Hotels | 34.4 | 24.3 | 14.9 | 18.0 | 91.6 |
| Transport and Communication | 11.0 | 11.0 | 5.9 | 10.3 | 38.2 |
| Finance and Services to Enterprises | 10.2 | 4.4 | 1.8 | 2.0 | 18.4 |
| Other Services[a] | 49.5 | 34.1 | 24.8 | 41.4 | 149.8 |
| Not Allocated | 0.4 | 0.5 | 0.3 | 1.2 | 2.4 |
| *Total Employment* | *136.6* | *118.9* | *75.5* | *207.4* | *538.4* |
| Unemployed | 5.4 | 4.8 | 2.4 | 5.0 | 17.7 |
| *Total Labour Force* | *142.0* | *123.7* | *77.9* | *212.4* | *556.1* |

Source: Ministry of Planning: Central Statistical Office: Employment Survey, November 1970.

a   Excludes temporary, seasonal labour and Palestinians in camps.

and to improve farmers' income. However, the semi-public Agricultural, Industrial and Real Estate Credit Bank (BCAIF) had strict lending policies that precluded lending to farmers with less than five hectares of land. Moreover, the bank's loans to agriculture were very limited. Since commercial banks extended credit mostly to large farmers, small farmers were forced to rely on the exorbitant interest rates of private moneylenders. To alleviate the problem the government extended credit to the National Union for Cooperative Credit (UNCC).[71]

Agricultural production was further supported by tariffs and import licensing and price supports were extended for tobacco, cereals and sugar. The ensemble of agricultural policies was designed to benefit big farmers and did little to help small farmers.

Industrial activity in the 1970s remained geared to light industries such as textiles and food processing.[72] The Arab market was of benefit to industry, which was geared toward export. Industrial exports increased from 87 million LL in 1967 to 800 million LL in the first nine months of 1974.[73]

Of 6,500 industrial establishments in 1971, about 140 employed 50 or more workers. These 'large' firms accounted for over 30% of value added. Industry's share of GDP was about 16% in the 1970s. Between 1970 and 1973 industrial exports grew to an average annual rate of 29%. Over 80% of

Table 25
Lebanon: Gross Domestic Product by Origin 1966–73
  (In Millions of Current Lebanese Pounds)

| Origin | 1966 | 1967 | 1968 | 1969 | 1970 | 1971 | 1972 | 1973[a] |
|---|---|---|---|---|---|---|---|---|
| Agriculture, Live-stock & Fisheries | 442 | 426 | 436 | 432 | 445 | 466 | 631[b] | 675 |
| Energy & Water | 88 | 93 | 99 | 104 | 113 | 118 | 129 | 140 |
| Industry & Handicrafts | 512 | 492 | 552 | 610 | 661 | 750 | 884 | 1,038 |
| Construction | 231 | 196 | 194 | 216 | 218 | 239 | 290 | 300 |
| Transport & Communication | 310 | 329 | 380 | 383 | 401 | 438 | 478 | 513 |
| Housing | 284 | 300 | 335 | 385 | 430 | 495 | 558 | 610 |
| Financial Services & Insurance | 141 | 149 | 164 | 146 | 165 | 197 | 235 | 285 |
| Other Services | 357 | 337 | 397 | 461 | 482 | 522 | 676 | 791 |
| Trade | 1,183 | 1,160 | 1,359 | 1,435 | 1,527 | 1,723 | 2,007 | 2,241 |
| Government | 319 | 337 | 357 | 393 | 424 | 451 | 477 | 507 |
| GDP at Market Price | 3,867 | 3,820 | 4,273 | 4,565 | 4,866 | 5,399 | 6,365[b] | 7,100 |
| Less: Indirect Taxes Less Subsidies | 300 | 267 | 303 | 342 | 345 | 412 | 489[b] | 562 |
| GDP at Factor Cost | 3,567 | 3,553 | 3,970 | 4,223 | 4,521 | 4,987 | 5,876 | 6,538 |
| *(As Percentage of Total)* | | | | | | | | |
| Agriculture | 11.4 | 11.2 | 10.2 | 9.5 | 9.1 | 8.6 | 9.9[b] | 9.5 |
| Power, Industry | 15.5 | 15.3 | 15.3 | 15.7 | 15.9 | 16.1 | 15.9 | 16.6 |
| Construction | 6.0 | 5.1 | 4.5 | 4.7 | 4.5 | 4.4 | 4.6 | 4.2 |
| Transport & Communication | 8.0 | 8.6 | 8.9 | 8.4 | 8.2 | 8.1 | 7.5 | 7.2 |
| Services & Trade | 50.8 | 51.0 | 52.8 | 53.1 | 53.6 | 54.4 | 54.6 | 55.3 |
| Government | 8.3 | 8.8 | 8.3 | 8.6 | 8.7 | 8.4 | 7.5 | 7.2 |
| GDP at Market Prices | 100.0 | 100.0 | 100.0 | 100.0 | 100.0 | 100.0 | 100.0 | 100.0 |

a  Estimates.
b  In 1972 the statistical base of agriculture was revised, adding about 150
   million LL to the production figures.

Source: Ministry of Planning; Central Statistical Office, Beirut.

industrial exports went to the Arab market.

To a great extent, industry financed its own expansion through retained
earning. Commercial banks which preferred to extend short-term credit to

commercial transactions had, in 1973, extended only 16% of their loans to industry. BCAIF had a limited capability to finance industry. In 1973 the government-controlled National Bank for the Development of Industry and Tourism was established. It increased the available medium- and long-term credit to industry.[74]

In the 1970s the government felt compelled to intervene directly in economic development. To encourage industry, the government gave tax holidays for six years to firms that had an annual wage bill of 200,000 LL and an investment exceeding one million LL. The tax holiday was extended to 10 years for industrial establishments outside Beirut.

In the 1970s the services sector was still the most important. This was indicated by the receipts categories of the general budget, which showed that services were the main contributors. Indirect taxes, of which 'customs duties' was the major item, were the largest in the budget from 1969 to 1975.[75]

In 1973 tourism accounted for 8% of GDP. Tourist receipts also accounted for 16% of receipts from goods and services. A major services sub-sector, banking, consisted of the Bank of Lebanon, 74 commercial banks and four medium- and long-term credit institutions. The IMF study contends:

> Commercial banking in Lebanon is characterized by the large number of heterogeneity of banks and by the degree of foreign ownership. Over half of the commercial banks are foreign controlled and these banks account for about three-quarters of total deposits. In terms of deposits, the largest Lebanese-controlled bank ranked eighth at the end of 1973 . . .The number of foreign banks has risen significantly in the last two years as a result of the purchases by foreigners of small Lebanese banks. These acquisitions have been motivated by the desire to establish a market presence and thus, hopefully, benefit from the large volume of petrodollars expected to flow through Beirut.[76]

Table 25 sums up the story of development in Lebanon under a system which is widely recognized as the epitome of free enterprise. One could present additional data on investment, agricultural production and industry. However, they are superfluous at this point and would only corroborate the pattern of the sectors depicted in Table 25. They would also show that in industry as well as in agriculture those conditions oriented towards export trade took priority over others. At this point, it will be more useful to sum up the effects of economic development in Lebanon.

In 1975 the IBRD contended:

> One of Lebanon's main development problems continues to be the slow rate of execution of public investment programs. The growing imbalances between the private sector and public facilities may not only slow down economic growth, but is likely to undermine the delicate political balances on which the system has been established.[77]

This is a development problem that, at a more basic level, is the result of an anarchic and chaotic economic policy that could not have been otherwise, given the control over the economy by international economic forces operating in the world market.

The IBRD contention is significant in another respect, because it points to the interconnection of politics and economics; namely, how chaotic economic planning can undermine 'the delicate political balances...'. The IBRD suggests, however, that Lebanon could have solved the problems it faced in 1974 by increasing government spending and by planning to cope with the growth of the private sector. Consequently, it suggests borrowing from international finance through international organizations for that purpose.[78]

The IBRD did not mention uneven development, inequities of income and wealth distribution as problems in Lebanon's development. In fact, it contends:

> However, in view of Lebanon's unique position in the Arab World, the rising level of income and consumption in the Middle East and the dynamics of the Lebanese private sector, medium term prospects for the economy are good.[79]

The IBRD was basing its judgement upon aggregate figures, and its problematic is not the welfare of Lebanon but the opening of the country further to international finance: 'Lebanon remains credit-worthy for borrowing substantial amounts on conventional terms.'[80] However, the IBRD report contradicts its recommendation on borrowing for public investment when it contends:

> However, government investments have declined in real terms since 1969, and their share of GDP went down from 3.8 per cent to 2.8 per cent in 1973, as compared to almost 19 per cent for private investment. The low level of public investment may have helped to avoid overheating of the economy and more in particular the construction sector.[81]

Clearly, according to the IBRD, Lebanon was caught in a double bind: on the one hand, the slow rate of execution of public investments was not conducive to growth; on the other, higher rates would have overheated the economy (causing more inflation which would have had serious political repercussions).

Furthermore, the 'relatively low foreign debt' that the IBRD refers to ($56 million) which 'is negligible compared to the size of export earnings and foreign reserves'[82] is not relatively low at all if the IBRD recognizes that Lebanon has unstable foreign investments and an unstable economy.

The picture is completed when one considers capital movements and foreign reserves. Because of bank secrecy laws, knowledge of these flows is limited. In 1973, net capital inflows — which had quadrupled since 1969 —

reached 725 million LL. The Lebanese banking system exported capital so that net deposits abroad grew from 1,179 million LL at the end of 1970 to 2,105 million LL in August 1974. Large parts of this capital inflow went into construction and real-estate speculation; most of the 1.5 billion LL of foreign deposits in Lebanon were short-term.[83] In the 1970s, as it was earlier, this was the critical point in the structure of foreign investment in Lebanon, a point that rendered the economy shakier than it might have appeared at first sight.

In 1973 and 1974, the government was trying to appease the population with some reforms in an attempt to keep uneven development within limits 'comfortable' to the system. We now know that these efforts were undertaken at an extremely late stage of the game. As the foreign investment picture presented here shows, the myriad problems of the economy were not alleviated by it. Rather, the structure of foreign investment was a major factor in further disrupting the economy which, along with other domestic, regional and international factors, resulted in the conflagration of 1975.

## Conclusion

Since independence, Lebanon's economy has displayed a bias toward the services sector, which developed at the expense of agriculture. Capitalist relations penetrated agriculture as commercial profits and income gains in the services sector were invested in the production of fruit and vegetables. These two agricultural products were in surplus and geared towards export. Other agricultural products have been in deficit since independence. These developments in agriculture favoured the comprador bourgeoisie which had a vested interest in keeping Lebanon a deficit country in agriculture.

The primacy of the services sector of the economy was a result of the strong linkages that colonialists had established between Lebanon and the international capitalist market. The 'infrastructure of dependence' was created for the most part by these colonialists. Tourism, trade and finance helped build the Mountain areas into summer and winter resorts and Beirut into a bustling centre for Arab East business activity. The rest of the geographic regions were, for the most part, left undeveloped or became underdeveloped.

During the first several years after independence, industry also had a small share of the net national income. Since the early 1950s food processing and textiles showed a marked development compared to other industries, such as chemicals.

Uneven development also manifested itself within each of the economic sectors. This is indicated in agriculture, for example, where growing of fruit and vegetables was preferred to cereals and other agricultural products. Lebanon's regions also developed unevenly because industry was concentrated mainly in Beirut and its vicinities. Foreign and transit trade, banking and other services were also concentrated in Beirut. This type of development primarily favoured Christian and especially Maronite areas in the Mountain and Beirut. For the most part, the rest of the country was neglected.

In its public policies, the Lebanese state favoured the development of the services sector. This was evidenced by liberal trade policies and by state expenditure on such projects as the construction of Beirut's airport. The state also encouraged banking through the Bank Secrecy Law, which mainly facilitated foreign capital to invest in real estate (chiefly in the Mountain and Beirut) or short-term deposits. In so far as the state assisted industry and agriculture, this was beneficial mainly to those people who already had political clout and/or to those industries and agricultural products that were geared toward export.

The lack of consistent statistics for the 30-year period before 1975 makes it difficult to make any comparative analysis for the whole period. Table 26, however, adapted from Tables 13, 22 and 25, provides a good picture of Lebanon's economic development.

Table 26
Lebanon: Distribution of the Labour Force Among the Economic Sectors and its Share of the GDP[a] by Sector (per cent)

| Labour Force | Sector | 1957 | 1964 | 1965 | 1966 | 1967 | 1968 | 1969 | 1970 | 1971 | 1972 | 1973[b] |
|---|---|---|---|---|---|---|---|---|---|---|---|---|
| 50 | Agriculture | 15.8 | 11.64 | 15 | 11.4 | 11.2 | 10.2 | 9.5 | 9.1 | 8.6 | 9.9 | 9.5 |
| 30 | Industry[c] | 15.3 | 20.13 | 17 | 21.5 | 20.4 | 19.8 | 20.4 | 20.4 | 20.5 | 20.6 | 20.8 |
| 30 | Services[d] | 68.9 | 68.1 | 68 | 67.1 | 68.4 | 70.0 | 70.1 | 70.5 | 70.9 | 69.5 | 69.7 |

a   Per cent of GNP is used for 1957, 1964 and 1965.
b   Estimates.
c   Industry includes power and construction.
d   Services include transport and communication, trade, finance and government.

This table shows a steady decline in agriculture's share of the GDP over the years. This declining share was distributed among 50 per cent of the labour force.

Industry (which included power and construction) had a steady share of GDP, especially in the 1970s. This share was distributed among 20 per cent of the labour force. The statistics are somewhat distorted because power is a state sector and its employees are state employees who could be included under services.

The services sector's share of GDP was distributed among 30 per cent of the labour force. Services' share of GDP was more or less steady during the 1970s.

Inequities in income distribution were also reflected among the populations of the various regions. This is evidenced, for example, if one looks at Lebanon's pattern of land holdings, which is mainly characterized by small land holdings in the Mountain and large land holdings (owned by *zuama*) in the under-developed areas. Middle and rich farmers mainly concentrated in the Mountain and were tied to export of fruit. Because tourism also favoured the Mountain, one sees that its population was much better off than that of the rest of Lebanon. Most of the population in the other areas of Lebanon were either agricultural labourers or poor peasants subsisting on the land. One finds that the 'destitute' and the 'poor' (Table 15) lived in these areas and in the slums of Beirut.

This conclusion is also supported by the statistics given in Table 24, where the majority (94.1%) of those employed in agriculture reside in rural areas, which mostly are located in the Bekaa, the south and the north. In these areas the overwhelming majority of the population are Sunni and Shiite Muslims.

Table 24 also shows that those employed in industry resided mostly in Beirut and its suburbs. The same occurred in terms of employment in 'commerce and hotels' and 'finance and services to enterprises'.

Finally, this kind of uneven development among the economic sectors, the regions and the populations provided the Maronite right wing with a mass base mainly in the Mountain and Beirut. The mass base of the progressive parties was mainly in the Bekaa, the south, the north, parts of Beirut and some parts of the Mountain.

# Notes

1. K.S. Salibi, *The Modern History of Lebanon* (New York, Praeger, 1965), 167, 171, 178.
2. A.H. Hourani, *Minorities in the Arab World* (London, Oxford University Press, 1947).
3. In 1949, 1952 and the civil war of 1958.
4. H. Bassat, 'The Lebanese Economy: Problems and Solutions', *Arab Studies* (March 1972), p. 39.
5. See Chapter Two.
6. International Monetary Fund, *First Annual Report on Exchange Restrictions* (Washington, DC, 1959), p. 129.
7. H. Bassat, op. cit., p. 43.
8. See pp. 71–73.
9. Lebanese delegation to the Fourth Regional Conference of the Food and Agricultural Organization (FAO) of the United Nations, Beirut, 13–16 September 1954. 'Le développement de l'alimentation et de agriculture au Liban' (Mimeographed).
10. 'Proceedings of the Agricultural Credit Conference' (Beirut, 12–14 October 1953).
11. Ibid.
12. Ministry of Agriculture, 1950.
13. Lebanese delegation to the Fourth Regional Conference of the FAO op. cit.
14. Ministry of National Economy, *Bulletin Statistique Trimestriel*, Beirut,

for oil and textiles, *Le Commerce du Levant* (3 July 1954); for construction, A. Badre and A. Altounian, 'National Income of Lebanon', Monograph 2, 'Income Arising in the Construction Sector', (Beirut, November 1951).

15. A. Badre, op. cit. See also Table 3.
16. R. Himadeh, *The Fiscal System of Lebanon* (Unpublished MA thesis, AUB, Beirut, 1953).
17. See Table 1.
18. Baron Maxime de Dumast, 'Le Transit, Vocation du Liban', *Les Conferences du Cenacle* (Beirut, 1953).
19. *Le Commerce du Levant* (9 February 1952).
20. International Monetary Fund, *Fourth Annual Report on Exchange Restrictions* (Washington DC, 1953), 221.
21. International Monetary Fund, *International Financial Statistics* (Washington, DC, 195?).
22. M. Toum, 'Al-Hurria Al-Khamisa', *Muhadarat Alnudwa* (Beirut, 1953).
23. *Le Commerce du Levant* (7 July 1954).
24. F. Qubain, *Crisis in Lebanon* (Washington, DC, Middle East Institute, 1961), 5.
25. A. Atallah and S. Khlat, *The Lebanese Industrial Sector: Its Growth and Problems*, Ministry of National Economy, Bureau of Industrial Development (Beirut, August 1969), 20.
26. Ibid., p. 10.
27. Ibid., p. 22.
28. Ibid., p. 32.
29. Ibid., p. 36.
30. Ibid., p. 34.
31. Ibid., p. 2 (my translation).
32. Ibid., p. 48.
33. Ibid.
34. International Monetary Fund, *Lebanon — Recent Economic Developments, SM/75/18* (21 January 1975). The report indicates an increase of industry's share of GDP from 13% to almost 15% between 1969–1973; this is a growth rate of 14% (pp. 2, 7). This, however, does not indicate a structural change in the economy.
35. A. Atallah, op. cit., p. 51.
36. Ibid., p. 54.
37. Ibid., p. 56.
38. Ibid., p. 63; see also Table 11.
39. Ibid., p. 73.
40. H. Bassat, 'The Lebanese Economy: Problems and Solutions', *Arab Studies* (Beirut, March 1972), 45.
41. I. Dik, *A Survey of the Economic Potential for Industrialization of Lebanon* (Unpublished MA thesis, University of Utah, 1975), 110.
42. A. Atallah, op. cit., p. 73.
43. Ibid.
44. See Kuwait Fund for Arab Economic Development, *Report on the Lebanese Economy and its Development Projects* (June 1969); see also A. Atallah, op. cit.
45. Kuwait Fund, op. cit., pp. 5, 11.

46. Ibid., p. 19.
47. IRFED, vol. II, chapter 4.
48. Kuwait Fund, op. cit., p. 24.
49. Ibid., pp. 24–26.
50. Invariably every study on Lebanon's economy points out the lack of comparable and consistent statistics over the range of 30 years. See Kuwait Fund, op. cit., A. Atallah, op. cit., IMF reports and Sayigh, *The Economics of the Arab World: Development Since 1945* (New York, St Martin's Press, 1978).
51. Kuwait Fund, op. cit., p. 55.
52. Edward Fei and Paul J. Klat, *The Balance of Payments in Lebanon, 1951 and 1952* (Beirut, 1954).
53. Kuwait Fund, op. cit., p. 55.
54. Ibid., p. 56.
55. Ibid.
56. Ibid., p. 58.
57. Ibid., p. 59.
58. Ibid.
59. Qubain, op. cit.
60. Kuwait Fund, op. cit., p. 62.
61. Ibid., p. 68.
62. Ibid., p. 73–74.
63. Sayigh, op. cit., divides the period as such: pre-1950, 1950–1958, 1958–1964. In 1958 the statistical base had changed from the previous periods. This does not change the fact, however, that in these subperiods uneven development had been developing.
64. IBRD (20 May 1975).
65. IBRD (11 September 1970), pp. 1, 2.
66. Ibid., summary ii, p. i.
67. IBRD (20 May 1975), pp. iii, viii.
68. Ibid., p. 3.
69. IMF (21 January 1975), p. 5.
70. Ibid.
71. Ibid.
72. Ibid., p. 6.
73. Ibid.
74. Ibid., p. 9.
75. Ibid.
76. Ibid.
77. IBRD (20 May 1975), p. ii.
78. Ibid.
79. Ibid., p. iii.
80. Ibid.
81. Ibid., p. 2.
82. Ibid., p. 8.
83. Ibid.

# 5. Politics in the Confessional State: 1943-1974

Two general periods of economic development may be identified in Lebanon's history between political independence and the conflict of 1975. The first period stretches from 1945-64 and the second from 1965-75.[1] Each period may be sub-divided to coincide more or less with different regimes. This coincidence was not accidental. It was rather a reflection of the form that the organic link between politics and economics assumed in Lebanon and of shifting alliances among the various capitalist class fractions in the power bloc (landlords, high finance and so on).

In the first period, three regimes may be identified: Khoury (1941-52), Chamoun (1952-58) and Chehab (1958-64). The first regime was overthrown through mass action in the form of pressure from capitalist class fractions that were not dominant in the power bloc, with other classes acting as supporting classes (workers, peasants and petty bourgeoisie). The second regime fought a civil war against opposition that perceived Chamoun to be working to undermine its political and economic interests. The Chehab regime allowed space for the old Chamoun opposition to develop some strength. For the first time in Lebanon's history certain kinds of political and economic reforms were attempted under Chehab. These attempts strengthened the position of the progressive[2] forces within the opposition on the mass level.

The second period includes two regimes: Helou (1964-70) and Franjieh (1970-75). Helou's regime witnessed economic dislocations and political upheavals that anticipated the 1975 conflict. This regime and Franjieh's are particularly important to study in order to determine the relations of forces at the conjuncture on the eve of the 1975 conflict.

It was stated earlier that the political and economic structures in Lebanon developed to such an extent that they became conducive to the ascendancy of the comprador bourgeoisie at the expense of the other classes in the Lebanese social formation.[3] The political economy of Lebanon also shows that the services sector was dominant and that even the industrial and agricultural sectors were mainly geared towards exports.

The class alliances and the supporting classes of the power bloc during the fight for and at the dawn of independence reflected the hegemony of the Christian (mostly non-Maronite) high-finance grouping, supported mainly by the landlords. Further, the political scene was dominated by pro-system classes whose various fractions were in competition with each other to become members of the power bloc.

Khoury's overthrow and Chamoun's subsequent election were the result of other classes and fractions of classes vying for more political power in an attempt to legitimize and advance their economic interests. This power struggle within the power bloc and on the political scene reflected the development of the Lebanese economy. This development shows that agriculture (the main sector before independence) rapidly lost ground to other sectors, especially services. Capital outlay to increase production of fruit and vegetables came from 'commercial profits and income gained in the services sector'. This development showed that the comprador were penetrating agriculture and developing those crops which were most profitable for export. By and large, fruit and vegetables were grown in the Mountain and along the coastal area south of Beirut.[4]

It is important to discuss the way in which the first regime gave way to Chamoun's to gain a better insight into the conflict among the various class fractions and groupings on the political scene. To do so, one needs to identify, by way of introduction, the various forces in the power bloc and the supporting classes during Khoury's regime.

Initially, the main figures in this regime came from the major families that were dominant in their respective capitalist class fractions. These families through their patriarchs constituted the regime and provided it with its power base. These were the dominant personalities in the initial stages of the regime: Riad al-Solh, Henri Pharaon, Sabri Hamadeh, Majeed Arslan, Ahmad al-Asaad and Abdul-Hamid Karami.[5] Solh, the Sunni Prime Minister, had his power base in the south of Lebanon among the urban and semi-urban Sunni petty bourgeoisie.[6] The Sunni zuama of Beirut (such as Salam, Yafi and others) saw in him a powerful rival who had undercut their political power in the confessional system (by virtue of his being the Prime Minister, the post was not available to them).

Ahmad al-Asaad (a Shiite) was the most powerful landlord in the south of Lebanon. He, in fact, controlled the south and wielded more political power than anyone else in the regime. Pharaon, the wealthy Greek Catholic, provided the regime with a power base in Beirut and the Bekaa region. And along with Habib Abu-Chahla (Greek Orthodox), Phillippe Taqla and Michel Chiha (both Greek Catholic), Pharaon provided the regime with the support of the trade and financial groupings of Beirut.[7]

In the Bekaa region, Pharaon secured the backing of the dominant Shiite landlord Sabri Hamadeh. Furthermore, financial circles were responsive to the regime to such an extent that Pharaon acted as the coordinator of a grand coalition that also included Karami (the Sunni zaim of Tripoli in the north) and Arslan (the powerful Druze lord in the Chouf area of Mount Lebanon).[8]

The power bloc that emerged from this grand coalition displayed the comprador fraction of the bourgeoisie as hegemonic. This bloc was capable of giving polity cohesion and relative stability during the first several years of the regime, and in this way the bloc served the common interests of the dominant class in the Lebanese social formation.

While the regime was capable of regenerating itself in two elections which took place in 1947 and 1951, there were already signs of change almost immediately after independence. These signs came mainly from two quarters: a power struggle within the power bloc and among different fractions and groupings within the dominant class which was reflected in the 1947 and 1951 elections. The struggle within the power bloc originated mainly from the tension between the regime's need to broaden the grand coalition in each area by appealing to more zuama families and the internal conflicts among these various families that belonged to the same class fraction. In the north, for example, the most powerful urban zaim, Karami, was alienated from the regime by Khoury when the latter sought alliances with the former's rivals, the Muqaddam, Al-Ali, Abboud, Jisr (all Sunni) and Franjieh (Maronite) families. These policies prompted Karami to leave the power bloc in 1947.[9]

In the south, Al-Asaad was opposed to lesser zuama families: the Osseirans and Al-Khalils. In the Bekaa, Hamadeh threatened to withdraw support for the regime unless the Greek Catholic zaim, Joseph Skaf of the Bekaa, was allowed to run in the 1947 elections as a candidate from the south.[10] The stiffest resistance to the regime, however, came from the Patriarch of the Maronite church and from Emile Eddé of the National Bloc (NB). This resistance in Mount Lebanon grew in intensity after the 1947 elections, when two of Khoury's Constitutional Bloc (CB) candidates, Jumblatt and Chamoun, accused the regime of corruption. As early as 1946 Jumblatt was a critic of the regime pushing for political and economic reforms. In an attempt to co-opt Jumblatt, Khoury gave him two ministerial portfolios, those of the national economy and agriculture, in 1946.[11] After the elections, however, Jumblatt began to think seriously of replacing the regime with one that was more responsive to his reforms.

In Beirut the regime won the opposition over by allying with Abdallah al-Yafi, Sami al-Solh and Hussein al-Oueini (all Sunni). Despite countrywide opposition, the power bloc was capable of dominating the election results. This was made possible through the 'grand list' system, whereby the country was divided into five electoral districts (south, north, Bekaa, Akkar, Mount Lebanon). In this way, the most powerful in each class was able to dominate the entire region during elections.[12] Al-Asaad, for instance, was able to spread his power over the south by striking alliances with zuama who belonged to other confessions. All ran in one 'grand list' and Al-Asaad was guaranteed the votes of other confessions while he reciprocated by guaranteeing 'his' votes to the other zuama. In most cases, this practice eliminated all opposition in the region from entering the parliament.

As a result of the 1947 elections, which excluded many urban and 'feudal' zuama and which alienated such people as Jumblatt, the opposition to the regime increased. The regime, however, was strong in parliament, where it introduced and passed a constitutional amendment which allowed Khoury to renew his presidential term in 1949.[13]

To further ensure the regime's victory in the 1951 elections, Khoury re-arranged the electoral districts and increased the parliamentary seats from 55 to 77. These tactics served to split the votes of his opposition and, although some of the opposition won seats in the elections, he was guaranteed a strong majority in parliament.[14]

Those members of the opposition who lost in the elections were extremely strong competitors of the pro-regime candidates. This was evident by the smaller number of votes which the winners gained in the 1951 elections as compared to the previous 1947 elections.[15] Despite Khoury's opposition to his candidacy, Pierre Eddé, Emile's son, the National Bloc candidate, was elected in the Matn district of Mount Lebanon. The Socialist National Front, whose declared aim was to root out corruption by reforming the government, was also able to win five of the nine seats in the Chouf district of Mount Lebanon. Jumblatt, the head of the SNF, was elected along with Camille Chamoun, Emile Bustani, Ghassan Tueini and Anwar al-Khatib.[16]

## The Lebanese Communist Party

The only party that was anti-system and which scored votes in the elections was the communist party, in whose name the candidate Mustafa al-Ariss ran and lost.[17] This party's early origins may be traced to utopian Lebanese communists such as Iskandar al-Riyashi, Yousuf Ibrahim Yazbek and the renowned poet Elias Abu Shabaka. Riyashi's paper, *The Roaming Journalist* (Al-Sahafi al-Taeh) was used by these utopians to support trade-union organizing and to preach equality among classes in opposition to oppression and injustice.

Yazbek, Fuad al-Shamali (a worker, Elias Sroor and others then formed the 'Party of the Lebanese People'. *Al-Insaaniyya* (Humanity), Yazbek's newspaper, was the party's organ. The party's activity in support of the 1925 anti-French nationalist rebellion in Syria increased its support among the masses. In that year the party and a group of Armenian communists in Lebanon (the Spartacus League) decided to form the Communist Party of Syria and Lebanon. The CP's Central Committee included Arteen Madoyan, Fuad al-Shamali (party chief), Ibrahim Yazbek and Elias Abu Nadher. Within a few years the party was able to spread to the various Syrian and Lebanese regions, but was especially strong among the workers in Damascus, Tripoli and Beirut. In 1932 a new Central Committee was elected, which included the 12-year-old Khaled Bakdash (who joined the Damascus party organization in 1930) as party chief, Arteen Madoyan, Rafeek Daya, Farajalla al-Hilu and Nicola al-Shawi.

The declaration of Lebanon's independence from France prompted the party to hold a congress in Beirut, at which it agreed to form two communist parties, one Lebanese (with Al-Hilu as General Secretary), the other Syrian (with Bakdash as General Secretary).[18]

By the time of the 1951 elections, the Lebanese Communist Party (LCP) had a substantial base of support among workers, professional and petty-bourgeois elements and among the various strata such as students and the intelligentsia. The LCP was able to develop a substantial base among the Christians, especially in Al-Koura in the north and in Beirut and some of its suburbs. It was unable, however, at this early stage of independence to successfully challenge confessionalism or Khoury's regime.

Other problems compounded the regime's troubles and weakened it in the the face of growing opposition. Palestinian refugees entered Lebanon in 1948 at a time when the war boom was all but over. In addition, the regime was destabilized by the 1949 attempted coup by the Syrian Nationalist Party (SNP). This party was founded in 1932 as a clandestine insurrectionist organization by the Lebanese Antoine Saadeh (born in 1904 in Shwere). In 1935 Saadeh was arrested by the French for his political activities. While in jail, he developed the party's ideology in his sociological work *The Rise of Nations*. The party believes that

> the Syrian homeland is the natural environment in which the Syrian nation was born. It has geographic boundaries that distinguish it from others [homelands], and extends from the Taurus mountains in the north-east to the Suez Canal and the Red Sea in the south, including the Sinai Peninsula and the Gulf of Aqaba, and from the Syrian [Mediterranean] Sea in the West, including the island of Cyprus, to the arc of the Arabian desert and the Persian Gulf in the East . . . It [the homeland] is expressed commonly by: the Syrian Fertile Crescent and its star Cyprus.[19]

The party spread in Syria, Lebanon, Palestine and Jordan, but was unable to spread to Iraq and Kuwait, which, according to Saadeh, are part of the Fertile Crescent. The rapid spread of the party among the Lebanese in 1948–49 led the Lebanese government to repress it by jailing its members and harassing them. The party reacted in 1949 but was unable to seize power. Consequently, Saadeh fled to Syria. He was later extradited to Lebanon, where he was tried and executed (within 24 hours of his capture) on 8 July 1949.[20] The party was anti-Arab-nationalist and primarily appealed to the petty bourgeoisie (professionals, peasants, shopkeepers, etc.). It had a strong base among the Christians in the Mountain and in Al-Koura in the north. It had followers in all the Lebanese regions and its members came from all the religious sects.

Saadeh's execution led the party to strike back at the regime by assassinating Riad al-Solh, the Prime Minister. This action weakened the regime further as it lost support among the Sunni zuama.[21] In addition, the severance of the customs union by the protectionist Syrian bourgeoisie in 1950 put substantial strain on the teetering Lebanese economy.

The deteriorating economic situation (high unemployment, increases in the wholesale price index and cost of living index) guaranteed the opposition mass support. The regime was overwhelmed by demonstrations, rallies and strikes called by the Socialist National Front (SNF).[22] The regime retaliated by closing down the opposition's newspapers. This led to more strikes by the opposition, which at that time was aided by the resignation of Sami al-Solh (Riad's brother) as Prime Minister. What had aggravated the situation for the regime was that the army remained neutral. All these developments rendered the regime's position untenable.

The élite political actors who formed the opposition were, as mentioned earlier, organized in the SNF, which was a parliamentary grouping that included the Socialist Progressive Party (SPP) headed by Jumblatt, the National Bloc (Eddé), the National Call Party, as well as deputies such as Hamid Franjieh and Chamoun. Workers and peasants were organized as supporting classes for the élite opposition by the Popular Front, which included such organizations as the National Organization, the National Congress and Al-Hayat al-Wataniya. These organizations were mostly comprised of Muslim professionals and businessmen who saw that Khoury's regime was denying them full economic and political opportunity. The Popular Front also included the LKP (Phalangists) and the Najjadah Party (both of which were founded in 1936).[23]

The main party in the SNF was the SPP, which was founded by Kamal Jumblatt on 17 March 1947. The party included Sheikh Abdallah al-Alaili (Muslim), George Hanna, Albert Adib, Fuad Rizk and Farid Jubran (all Christians). All of these were prominent people in their communities. The party's objectives were to build a society based on 'true' democracy where social justice, freedom and peace would be supreme. The party was also pan-Arab in that it regarded Lebanon as part of the Arab nation.

Since its inception the party had called for the abolition of feudal and class titles, freedom of the press, nationalized health care, agricultural co-operatives, unemployment insurance and free education. Its electoral programme was summed up in the slogan: 'Bread for all. Jobs, education and freedom for all.' Due to its platform the party was able to spread to all Lebanese areas and among all religious sects.[24] However, the party's strongest base of support was in the Chouf among the Druze, primarily due to Jumblatt's popularity among his co-religionists, who were mostly from the petty bourgeoisie. It was to Jumblatt's credit that he was able to utilize traditional allegiances in the service of progressive social and political goals that would benefit the majority of the Lebanese.

The broad-based alliances that were represented by the SNF and the Popular Front compelled the regime to hand over power to General Chehab on 19 September 1952. On 23 September the parliament elected Chamoun (of the SNF) President.[25] Two days before his election Chamoun signed a pledge, witnessed by the SNF leaders, to respect the Constitution and the National Pact and to reform the administration.[26]

One significant aspect of the Khoury episode was that, despite a majority in parliament (66 out of 77 deputies), his regime was regarded as illegitimate by the masses and the other pro-system (but anti-regime) forces. These pro-system forces had to resort to extra-systemic methods to achieve their political goals. This shows that the system had no mechanisms to integrate the demands of even the pro-system forces. More important, however, the absence of these mechanisms was not an oversight on the part of the dominant class. The nature of the system (confessional and zuama-oriented), plus the country's small size and her extremely limited resources, militated against the system's responsiveness to the needs of all of these competing classes inside and outside the power bloc.

On another level, a cursory look at the composition of the opposition would show that most of its components were urban-based (businessmen, lawyers and merchants) or came from Mount Lebanon and were mainly represented by the NB, the LKP and the SPP. The NB, the LKP and Chamoun wanted a bigger share of Lebanon's economic development and/or hegemony over the power bloc.

From the outset, Chamoun began to solidify his regime's control over the polity. Within the context of confessionalism, he set out to curb the power of the landlords and of his opponents in general. The 1953 parliamentary election results illustrate what happened. In Beirut and Mount Lebanon the NB defeated the CB. In the north the regime's opponents were re-elected by slim margins. Rashid Karami was also re-elected in Tripoli as was Hamid Franjieh of Zgharta. In the south, Al-Asaad and his son Kamel were re-elected but the family's power was weakened. For the first time the Osseirans and Khalils won parliamentary seats. While these were landlords, they supported the regime against Al-Asaad.

Another important development during the Chamoun period was that the SNF began to falter when the President rejected Jumblatt's proposals for land reform and nationalization of business. Two members of the SNF, Tueini and Bustani, were not interested in Jumblatt's reforms and had joined the SNF earlier to improve their positions in the system. The Chamoun regime gave them that opportunity. Chamoun wanted Jumblatt to be defeated in the 1953 elections. He was unable to secure this goal, however, but was able to curb Jumblatt's influence somewhat when Anwar al-Khatib, the SPP candidate, lost to Bustani.[27]

While the 1953 elections were a reflection of intra-class struggle within the dominant class, they also reflected the efforts of the comprador bourgeoisie (especially its Maronite sector) to consolidate its power at the expense of other classes within Lebanon. Within the confines of confessionalism, however, alliances had to be sought between this Maronite sector and non-dominant groupings of the bourgeoisie (for example, the Khalil and Osseiran landlord families that had been excluded from the Khoury regime).

Other developments helped sharpen the tensions within the dominant class. The confessional arrangement and the National Pact provided the parameters for the rules of the game in Lebanese politics. What this meant in practice was that the various bourgeois fractions had to compete with each other for hegemony in the power bloc. In the case of the various bourgeois sectors and groupings, they had to compete with each other for dominance in the Lebanese social formation in order to become part of the regime. At the same time, the confessional arrangement safeguarded the common interests of the dominant class. Given the general dynamic of economic development in Lebanon which favoured the services sector, however, it was tempting to certain bourgeois factions to dishonour this arrangement. In an attempt to strengthen their political power and break the power of the land-lords and other bourgeois fractions and groupings, the comprador in the regime had no other option but to pursue this policy.

The moves on the part of the regime that took advantage of the inter-national situation (characterized by a US-dominated international capitalist market that was supportive of comprador class development in the neo-colonies) to effect its policy were not without great risk. Chamoun faced resistance from an opposition that was riding high on a wave of mass protest against the regime. He manipulated the 1957 parliamentary election in an attempt to unseat his opponents and help his supporters to parliament.[28] In the north and the Bekaa his major opponents could not be unseated. Rashid Karami, Hamid Franjieh and Kahtan Hamadeh won in their races. The regime's supporter, Charles Malik, however, won in the Koura district in the north. In Beirut, Chamoun's opponents Salam and Al-Yafi lost to Sami al-Solh's list. Jumblatt also lost in the Chouf. The pro-regime deputies were distributed as follows: Beirut 10 out of 11; Mount Lebanon, 18 out of 20; Bekaa, six out of 10; the south, six out of 11:and the north, eight out of 14.[29]

Despite the fact that these results were an improvement upon the 1953 elections for Chamoun, they did not reflect the regime's popularity. It was only a numbers game that allowed the regime to consider amending the Constitution and pass certain legislation that was favourable to Chamoun. In point of fact, that was precisely what the opposition accused him of doing.

## The Rise of Nasserism in the Region

These domestic events were not isolated from others in the region. The Egyptian Free Officers' coup of 23 July 1952 (led by Nagib and Nasser) came at a time when the cold war was on the ascendant. The coup was a response to the corrupt Egyptian regime of King Farouk. The July coup also signified a triumph for the ideology of Arab nationalism.[30]

The Egyptian and Syrian Arab nationalist regimes were both committed to fighting imperialism in the region. The Egyptians, for instance, were negotiating British withdrawal from the Suez Canal zone. In addition, US policies were in direct conflict with the aspirations of the nationalist regimes and the Arab masses in general. The masses rallied to Nasser's call for Arab nationalism and unity. Against this rising tide of Arab nationalism and unity stood Iraq, Iran and Saudi Arabia, whose interests were tied to neocolonialism. When the Baghdad Pact was formed in 1955, Iraq, Iran and Turkey were its principal parties in the area. Their interests coincided to a large degree with those of US policies in the region.[31]

Under the guise of serving Arabism, Chamoun started to strengthen his ties with Iraq, Jordan and Saudi Arabia. He also made moves that were interpreted by the Arab nationalists as attempts to join the Baghdad Pact. In that same year he invited the Turkish President to Lebanon. This move raised havoc in Lebanon, Syria and Egypt. The intensity of the public uproar forced Chamoun to declare that he had no intention of joining the pact.[32]

What aggravated the situation further was Chamoun's stance during the 1956 Suez war. He did not sever relations with the aggressors, Britain and France, to show solidarity with the Arab world, nor did he recall his ambassador from London as a sign of protest. To do that was to invite major economic dislocations that would have compromised comprador bourgeois interests and threatened that class fraction vis-à-vis other dominant classes and class fractions in Lebanon. In other words, the interests of this bourgeois fraction were not congruent with those of the Arab masses inside and outside Lebanon.

During this period of mass resurgence and anti-imperialism, US imperialist interests and policies within the region appeared to be in trouble. To contain these developments, Eisenhower, the US president, announced his doctrine to 'protect' the region from the amorphous 'threat' of communism. On 5 January 1957, he asked Congress to approve the following:[33]

1. Co-operate with and assist any nation or group of nations in the general area of the Middle East in the development of economic strength dedicated to the maintenance of national independence;
2. Undertake in the same region programmes of military assistance and co-operation with any nation or group of nations which desired such aid; and
3. Employ the armed forces of the United States to secure and protect the territorial integrity and political independence of nations in the area requesting such aid against overt armed aggression from any nation controlled by international communism.

On 16 March 1957, Chamoun accepted the Eisenhower Doctrine. This was a move that brought further denunciation from the Arab nationalists. Other members of Lebanon's dominant class saw a clear violation of the National Pact being committed by Chamoun. This was interpreted as a curtailment of their power. On 1 April 1957, 20 Lebanese political leaders from the United National Front (UNF) submitted a memorandum to Chamoun demanding the following:[34]

1. The next Chamber should consist of 88 members, not 66 as the President was reported to want;
2. The present cabinet should resign in favour of a 'neutral' cabinet to supervise the forthcoming parliamentary election (due in June);
3. The immediate cancelling of the state of emergency and of press

censorship, both imposed in November 1956, during the Suez crisis;
4. The present cabinet should not enter into agreement with any foreign power until the election of a new Chamber.

The memorandum also warned that if Chamoun did not comply, the 20 political leaders would 'feel compelled to take practical steps as dictated by the interests of the country'.

On 3 May 1957, the government lifted the emergency regulations and press censorship in preparations for 'free' elections. The election programme of the UNF essentially called for social and political reforms. It was also anti-imperialist. The elections took place on 9 June 1957, after the cabinet was forced to resign under popular pressure. When the election returns came in, however, they were a victory for Chamoun. He was able to secure more than two-thirds of the parliamentary seats for his protégés. The opposition accused him of rigging the elections.[35]

The outcome of these new elections widened the gap between the Lebanese regime and the Arab nationalist regimes of Syria and Egypt. These regimes perceived that Chamoun was consolidating his power to quickly and openly join imperialist designs against Arab nationalism.

When union between Egypt and Syria was declared on 1 February 1958 (which was perceived as the first step towards uniting the entire Arab world), delegations from the UNF in Lebanon went to congratulate the officials there on this momentous occasion. Furthermore, popular celebrations were held in all Lebanese cities. These celebrations were also used to denounce imperialist designs against Arab nationalism. Anti-Arab-nationalists in Lebanon, who now had a majority in parliament, began to agitate among the Maronites to create a mass base which would support Chamoun's re-election and thwart the spontaneous upsurge of Arab nationalism.

To broaden its support among the masses, the opposition relied upon Arab nationalism as an ideology, traditional support (zaim power) and a call to institute social reforms.[36] It is important to note that traditional support alone would have been incapable of defeating Chamoun. It was for this reason that traditional forces allied themselves with Arab nationalist forces in the area. To those in Lebanon who had social democratic and/or Arab nationalist tendencies, Chamoun's defeat was seen as a way of strengthening their position on social reforms and pan-Arabism. To the landlords and other zuama, the UNF was a tool by which they were able to defend their economic and political interests and blame all the social ills their districts suffered from on Chamoun.

The opposition was multi-confessional. The Lebanese Communist Party, the Arab Baath Socialist Party and the Arab Nationalist Movement, all of which comprised both Christian and Muslim members, were cases in point. The Arab Baath Socialist Party was formed in Syria on 7 April 1947 under the initial name of the Arab Baath Party. Its two founders, Michel Aflaq (Christian) and Salah al-Din al-Bitar (Muslim), were anti-communist Arab nationalists who called for Arab unity. In 1952 the party merged with the Arab Socialist Party of Akram al-Hourani in Syria, to form the Arab Baath Socialist Party (ABSP). The merger gave the original Baath Party a solid peasant base.[37] The party quickly spread in most Arab countries including Lebanon, where it recruited members from all the religious sects. As in the rest of the Arab countries it spread to, its power base in Lebanon was primarily among the urban and rural petty bourgeoisie.

The Arab Nationalist Movement (ANM) was formed in the early 1950s by the Palestinian George Habash and others who subscribed to Arab nationalist thought. The ANM also followed Nasser faithfully through the 1950s. As an anti-communist, pro-nationalist organization, it appealed primarily to the petty bourgeoisie and operated mostly in Lebanon, Jordan, Syria and Iraq.[38]

The UNF also included the Third Force, which was the organization of the liberal bourgeoisie who believed Chamoun was violating both the democratic process and the National Pact. This coalition was also multi-confessional. It included the Maronite Patriarch, Charles Helou, Henri Pharaon and other Christian and Muslim businessmen and financiers.[39]

Chamoun could not count on widespread backing except from the Syrian Nationalist Party (SNP), the LKP (Phalangists) and a few traditional leaders such as Sami al-Solh, the Prime Minister, Kazem al-Khalil (Shiite), Fawzi al-Hoss (Christian) and Kahtan Hamadeh (Druze). This alliance, needless to say, was anti-Arab-nationalist, anti-reform and openly for alliances with the United States. The only significant force which remained 'neutral' was the Lebanese army. This was possible for two reasons: (1) General Chehab, the Army Commander, was a Maronite who was sympathetic to the opposition; and (2) Chehab was afraid the army might split along sectarian lines if he decided to get involved.

Given this state of affairs, hostilities between the government and the opposition took an ugly turn when the anti-Chamoun Maronite journalist Naseeb al-Matni was assassinated. This incident precipitated the civil war on 8 May 1958. In view of the forces arrayed against Chamoun, it is difficult to characterize the war, as some do, as a conflict between Muslims and Christians.

## The Class Nature of the 1958 Conflict

Lebanon's political economy provides much evidence to support the argument that one of the basic problems of the country was its uneven development. The comprador fraction of the bourgeoisie, which had been heavily represented in the state, supported the development of the services sector and mainly opposed the development of industry and agriculture. This kind of political and economic development resulted in a cost-of-living index increase of 75 points between 1955 and 1957. This increase struck where it hurt most – at the poor and the middle class.[40]

Another illustration of some of the effects of uneven development that revealed its intensity, even at this early stage in the life of the polity, was the Doxiadis Associates' study of 1957, which estimated that 3% of the workforce (14,000) earned $3,300 annually, while 51% earned $500 or less.[41] Furthermore, the United Nations Food and Agricultural Organization (FAO) study of 1959 indicated that per capita income in Lebanon was $147 among low-income groups, while the national average was $327. While this study was conducted several months after the civil war, it could be viewed as an indicator of the situation on the eve of the war.

IRFED's study of 1960–61 may also be taken as an indicator of uneven development and the plight of the masses in general. Among other things, IRFED reported the following: the agricultural workforce (50% of Lebanon's total) accounted for 15.8% of the GNP. The ratio of percentage of national product and percentage of workforce in agriculture was 0.324. The financial sector workforce amounted to 0.44% of Lebanon's total and accounted for 6% of the GNP (a ratio of 13,623 as opposed to 0.324 for agriculture).[42]

Another indicator of the class nature of the conflict was the fact that the areas which were held by the pro-Chamoun forces during the conflict were the most affluent, while the opposition were, for the most part, in control of severely underdeveloped areas of the country.[43] The previous chapter, on Lebanon's political economy, clearly shows that the development of the economic sectors mainly benefited Beirut and the Mountain.[44]

The conjuncture on the eve of the civil war was shaped by the events that have been discussed thus far. The relation of forces obtaining at the conjuncture, in turn, conditioned the outcome of the war. It is perhaps appropriate at this point to look more closely at these forces before discussing foreign intervention in the civil war.

It was clear that those who allied themselves with Chamoun were class fractions or groupings that benefited from the regime at the expense of other fractions or groupings in their respective classes. The alliance of the Syrian Nationalist Party with Chamoun was prompted by SNP enmity towards the United Arab Republic (UAR – Syria's union with Egypt). The LKP, despite its secondary differences with Chamoun, allied itself with the regime because of overriding factors such as its perception that the anti-Chamoun movement was against Maronite interests and hegemony over their power bloc.[45] Just before the civil war Pierre Gemayel, the LKP chief, toured Mexico and the United States to drum up support for the regime among the Lebanese émigrés (mostly Maronite) and to secure a guarantee from the United States for the 'protection' of Lebanon (i.e. protection of Maronite and US interests in the region). The LKP's support of the Eisenhower Doctrine must be seen in this light.[46]

The financial interests in the Third Force, such as Pharaon, Abu-Chahla and Taqla, actually attacked the LKP for its support of Chamoun.[47] The perceptions and the actual stances of the two groupings of the financial bourgeoisie indicate that the character of the conflict was not along confessional lines, as is strongly asserted by many writers such as Entelis and Salibi. In the first place, the two groupings were, for the most part, Christian.

In the second place, the two groupings' perceptions were shaped by their material conditions of life. In Chamoun's case, he felt the need to transcend the National Pact (which emphasized that no alliances could be sought with foreign powers and that Lebanon's 'neutrality' must be maintained) by seeking foreign alliances to increase the power of his regime.

As was mentioned earlier, Chamoun's bourgeois grouping allied itself with the SNP, the LKP and other zuama. Of these the LKP was the most significant because of its class make-up. The mass base of this party, as mentioned earlier, was mostly in the Mount Lebanon area. It was mainly comprised of small and rich peasants and urban petty-bourgeois elements who enjoyed a higher standard of living than their respective counterparts in other areas of Lebanon. As suggested earlier, this was one of the main reasons that the party supported Chamoun and could not get over its sectarianism. It is clear that the party had deeply-rooted confessional characteristics. These characteristics have been a main component of the LKP's ideology, which rationalized its stance on the 6:5 Christian–Muslim ratio in Lebanon's political representation. The LKP's sectarianism rendered the class basis of the conflict nebulous. For the most part, this sectarianism was reinforced by the fact that, by and large, Maronite areas were developed and non-Maronite areas were not. The development of underdevelopment assumed in large measure a confessional facade.

While the pro-regime alliance took the form described above, the opposition alliance was prompted by many factors which have been alluded to earlier. The alliance was possible for the following reasons: (1) zuama such as Rashid Karami, Saeb Salam and Abdullah al-Yafi were against the Baghdad Pact and the Eisenhower Doctrine because they violated the National Pact, thus upsetting the balance among the factions and groupings of the dominant class; (2) they also were against Chamoun's attempt to change the Constitution because that would have undercut their power in the system; and (3) the masses were anti-Baghdad Pact. They also felt that Chamoun wanted to ally Lebanon with Iraq, Jordan and Saudi Arabia to enhance the US position in the area and open up the country further to Western capitalist interests. This was diametrically opposed to the interests of the great majority of the Arab masses. Those interests expressed themselves in Arab unity and independent political and economic development.

Zuama and mass interests converged. However, the traditional zuama were capable of leading the struggle against imperialism because the political parties which then existed among the masses were incapable of articulating their interests in a comprehensive political and economic programme. The lack of leadership from these parties can be ascribed to the following reasons.

(1) Among the Arab nationalist masses, Nasserism as an ideology was supreme. Among other things, Nasserism did not believe in the need to have political parties to lead the masses in the fight against imperialism and for socialism. It only believed in having a leader at the head of the masses.[48] Within this political environment, pan-Arab organizations such as the Baath Party or the Arab Nationalist Movement (ANM) could not hope to mobilize

the already-politicized masses. Furthermore, these parties were operating mainly in the cities, largely because of their class composition, which was petty-bourgeois.[49]

(2) The Lebanese Communist Party (LCP) had an unpopular position on Arab unity.[50] As a pro-Moscow party, it interpreted Arab politics in much the same way as Moscow did. It saw, quite correctly, that the main contradiction was between the nationalist forces in the area and the imperialist alliances. Given this, the party had no choice but to trail after Nasser, who was leading the fight against imperialism in the region.

(3) Nasser's alliance with the Lebanese opposition zuama gave them more credibility with the Lebanese masses. The Arab nationalist parties had no choice but to follow Nasser's wishes on the subject of the zuama.

(4) The masses did not see any qualitative difference between the nationalist parties and Nasserism. In point of fact, Nasserism, with its political and economic clout, had more appeal than the parties. Nasserism was also capable of articulating their interests (anti-Baghdad Pact, pro-Arab unity, etc.) much better than the parties could.

## US Intervention

The basis for US intervention in Lebanon had been secured by the Eisenhower Doctrine. Prior to that, Lebanon had received US aid through an agreement signed in 1954 (the Point Four). Six days after the civil war started, the United States airlifted arms to Lebanon. Robert McLintock, the US Ambassador, declared, 'We are determined to help this government to maintain internal security.'[51] Meanwhile, the size of American amphibious forces in the area was being doubled. On 17 May, the United States declared its intention to send tanks to the Lebanese government, and on the 18th it was considering sending American troops to Lebanon.

Chamoun accused the UAR of stirring up trouble in Lebanon. Given what had transpired already, the accusation could be seen as a justification for turning to the United States for help. While the insurgents were receiving arms, and probably men and money, from across the border, the fact that Chamoun's domestic and foreign policies had precipitated the crisis could not be dismissed or argued against rationally.

In a violent coup on 14 July 1958, the Iraqi monarchy was deposed. The imperialist pact automatically collapsed. The new Baghdad regime boosted the nationalist forces in the area. On the next day US marines landed in Lebanon and British commandos landed in Jordan.[52] Clearly, this massive intervention was designed to contain the revolutionary situation in the area. Immediately the United States started assessing the damage to its position and attempted to salvage as much of its prestige and its interests as possible. To do this, Eisenhower sent his special emissary, Robert Murphy, to Lebanon to negotiate a settlement. Domestically, the Third Force was the group best equipped to achieve a compromise solution. The effect was that Chamoun was not re-elected, the National Pact remained intact and socio-economic reforms were agreed upon, in principle, to accommodate some of the demands of the masses.[53]

The 'no-victor-no-vanquished' settlement appeared to benefit the anti-Chamoun forces.[54] The LKP, however, seized this opportunity to enhance its position in the system. Consequently, it called for a general strike in its areas. Kidnappings and killings along religious lines became common occurrences, initiated by the LKP members.[55] These moves were designed to limit any significant shifts in the polity towards sweeping reforms.[56] What appeared to be a personality clash on representation in the new government of Rashid Karami was in fact a clash over the share of each bourgeois fraction or grouping in the new cabinet. The crisis that the LKP precipitated lasted for 22 days, a period characterized by the party as the '22 journées glorieuses'.[57]

The crisis ended on 14 October 1958, when Karami as Prime Minister formed a cabinet that included three other members: Oueini (Sunni), Gemayel (LKP) and Eddé (NB). When the crisis was over, the US marines left Lebanon the same month. The newly-elected president, General Fuad Chehab, the Maronite Army Commander, had the blessings of all parties concerned in the conflict, including the UAR and the United States.

## Chehab's Reforms, and Mounting Opposition

Chehab's election reflected the need for reforms if the confessional system were to function without major dislocation. One of the reforms the new regime called for was expenditure on an irrigation and land-reclamation project to alleviate some of the consequences of uneven development. The project was initially conceived to allow southern farmers to own a few acres of land. Other reforms concerned universal and free education, health insurance, the social security code and administrative reforms. All of these were demands put forward by the progressive forces (communist, socialist and nationalist) in the country over a span of several years. These forces, however, were not part of the capitalist state. As such, they were unable to share in the implementation of these programmes. They were forced to operate through zuama such as Jumblatt and Karami.

The LKP, a conservative force, was also for these reforms. It espoused them, however, for sectarian reasons. Hudson contends:[58]

> To counter demands from non-Christian socialists for significant income-redistribution policies, Pierre Gemayel has suggested that, because Christians pay about 80 percent of the taxes (his figure), they are theoretically entitled to 80 percent of the services. Although the Kataeb [the LKP] does not advocate strict adherence to such an allocation, Gemayel's statement is a reminder of how the party views social progress. Within this framework there is nevertheless unquestionably a realization that the stability of the Lebanese entity depends

increasingly on 'social justice' as well as a 'free economic system'.

To effect any of these reforms meant an impingement upon traditional zuama power. It also meant the creation of a new mechanism to replace this power, to the extent to which it was to be curtailed. In a polity such as Lebanon, power[59]

... is monopolized by an establishment of clerics, semifeudal political bosses, bankers, businessmen and lawyers. The members of the establishment come from fewer than fifty prominent families. The establishment derives its influence partly from economic success, and Lebanese politics today is still essentially the competition among its members to advance their various parochial interests — sectarian prerogatives, commercial privileges, and pork-barrel benefits.

As Chehab himself found out, curtailing zuama power was an extremely difficult task. Even while attempting to do it, Chehab had, to some extent, to rely on the establishment. This inherent constraint in the confessional system could not be removed without undermining the foundations of the system itself.

Consequently, for the first time in Lebanon's political development, a major contention arose within the dominant class and its zuama institution. Despite the fact that more contending zuama were elected in the 1960 parliamentary elections, this did not lead to an increase in zuama representation within the power bloc, even though parliamentary seats had increased to 99. Nor did this representation reflect, as readily as it usually had in past elections, the composition of the power bloc. This was because the location of decision-making had shifted within the state itself. Technocrats and the army were responsible for important state decisions, while parliament was left to its internal bickering. In this way, the regime maintained a semblance of tolerance towards the traditional political game.[60]

Realizing that these moves by the regime were designed to 'rob' them of their power, various traditional zuama, both Muslim and Christian, started to come together in opposition. These major rivals, who represented the dominant class fractions in the various regions, were Al-Asaad, Chamoun, Salam, Eddé and the Maronite Patriarch. All of these figures (except Al-Asaad) formulated a semi-formal coalition against the regime.

The major pro-regime forces were Jumblatt and his SPP, the LKP and Karami. Other figures who had won in the 1960 and/or 1964 parliamentary elections were also pro-regime (the Deuxième Bureau — military intelligence — helped pro-regime zuama succeed in the elections). These included deputies such as Marouf Sa'd of the southern city of Sidon, who played a major role in the 1958 civil war against Chamoun. And, for the first time in Lebanon, non-traditional leaders such as the Arab nationalist Ali Bazzi (who had been an interior minister before the 1960 elections) were able to win seats in the parliamentary elections.

The new hegemonic fraction in the power bloc was a curious animal — combining the technocracy and the army — both of which represented a Lebanonist 'modernizing' trend. Given the social and political pressure exerted by the masses, this fraction was willing, up to a point, to reform the state institutions and effect other social reforms in order to maintain its control and power.

The reformist trend was able to develop due to the relative calm of regional politics in the first three years of Chehab's regime (1958–64). It was briefly interrupted by an attempted coup against Chehab, instigated in December 1961 by the SNP, and by the earlier coup in Syria, in September 1961, led by anti-nationalist forces opposed to Syria's unity with Egypt in the UAR.[61] These events, however, did not result in serious dislocations in Lebanon. Furthermore, the anti-imperialist trend in the area still maintained momentum, as exemplified by another coup in Syria against the earlier anti-Nasser coup of September 1961. This Baathist coup of March 1963 came hard on the heels of another Baathist coup in Iraq, which took place in February of the same year against the Qassem regime.

The significance of these Arab events to Lebanon lay in the fact that Chehab did not have to make any serious decisions on formal alliances or affiliations with Lebanon's Arab neighbours. He was able to keep Lebanon on a neutral course and on friendly terms with all of them. He was, therefore, able to spend most of the regime's energies dealing with the domestic situation. As mentioned earlier, the hegemonic fraction in the new power bloc allied itself with other progressive political figures and with those traditional zuama who were more inclined towards reforms than the majority of zuama. In the absence of strong independent political organizations that were capable of representing the peasants and workers, these groups remained supporting classes of the reformist figures of the power bloc. This position vis-à-vis the reformists was rational and was reinforced by the ability of the zuama to act as brokers between the masses and the state. The legitimacy of the zuama role was assisted by the ideological conviction of the lower classes, reinforced by concrete everyday events, that as Muslims or non-Christians they were discriminated against by the state. They saw in these zuama the capability of ameliorating this discrimination.

The anti-system political parties were incapable of doing much for the masses other than providing them with Arab nationalist slogans. As was the case in the 1958 civil war in Lebanon, however, these slogans were easily adopted by self-seeking zuama in opposition against Chamoun. The Lebanese Communist Party (LCP) and the Arab Baath Socialist Party (ABSP), despite their more coherent and consistent philosophies, were also unable for the most part to represent the interests of the workers, peasants and the petty bourgeoisie. In the case of the LCP this was so because the party, as mentioned earlier, had a negative position on Arab nationalism and, at any rate, supported Nasser's anti-imperialist policies. The LCP found itself trailing behind the nationalists and allied with traditional pro-Nasser or pro-reform zuama. With regard to the ABSP, it was rather difficult for it to represent the majority of the Arab nationalist masses in Lebanon who already had given their allegiance to Nasser. For one thing, Nasser had been at odds with the ABSP since the 1958 union of Syria and Egypt.

Despite these drawbacks in terms of workers' and peasants' political organizations, the spontaneous mass movement that carried the brunt of the fighting in 1958 was politicized as never before. In addition, Jumblatt and his SPP became strong advocates of Arab nationalism. As a member of the power bloc, Jumblatt was able to articulate the interests of the progressive movement in the state. In this sense, this may be regarded as a step forward for the mass movement. For one thing, it had more freedom of movement inside and outside the state machinery. This did not change the fact, however, that the classes which comprised the mass movement remained supporting classes. The mass movement's gains, along with Sa'd's election in Sidon and the strong showing in the 1960 parliamentary elections of the ABSP's candidate Rafi'i in Tripoli, indicated that important changes had occurred on the political scene.

## The Helou Period: Economic Crisis

The relative calm of the Chehab regime began to wither away during Charles Helou's presidential term. In many respects the Helou regime was supposed to be a continuation of Chehab's. Political, social and economic reforms were to be carried out as specified under the Chehab regime. More important, the role of the army in decision-making remained intact. It was clear, in fact, that Elias Sarkis, a Chehabist, wielded great power as the head of the presidential bureau.

Helou's regime provided a convincing argument that not even Chehabist policies were capable of ameliorating Lebanon's inherent problems. These problems were structural, which reforms were unable to resolve. Furthermore, these reforms interfered with the confessional arrangements in the polity and were not easy to implement at a time of relative calm in the region. When major dislocations, such as the 1967 war, began to occur in the area, even these innocuous reforms became unacceptable to the traditional and sectarian forces in the country.[62]

The Helou period was witness to an economic crisis and to more uneven development of the country. The economic crisis was mainly characterized by a steep recession that reached its peak with the Intra Bank collapse. A tight money market and political animosity between rival banking groups who shared interests with differing foreign financial groupings led to the collapse of one of the main pillars of the economy in October 1966.[63] Saudi Arabia was also pressuring Lebanon to modify what it regarded as its pro-Nasser stand. Saudi and other Arab oil money was quickly withdrawn from Intra Bank, thus precipitating the crisis.

The Bank of Lebanon did not come to the aid of Intra. This probably was a conscious effort on the part of the state to undermine the bank on behalf of rival banking groups that were represented in the new power bloc (Taqla, Pharaon and others were old friends of Helou and were members of the Third Force).

Despite attempts to ameliorate uneven development during the Chehab and Helou periods, the services sector developed at a much faster rate than other sectors of the economy. Lebanon also remained a deficit country in all agricultural products except fruit, which was geared towards export (in 1964 vegetables, which were earlier in surplus, recorded a deficit).

Concomitant with the development of this economic crisis, the Israeli decision to divert the waters of the Jordan River (whose sources were in Lebanon, with tributaries in Syria and Jordan) brought about a major political crisis in the country. Lebanon was once more put before the mirror, thus revealing her schizophrenic character: without the Arab world Lebanon was unable to survive economically. The dominant class was able to maintain a relatively high standard of living for the middle class, because of the profitable economic arrangement with the Arab world. While over half of Lebanon's population identified with the Arab world on various levels, the dominant class did not feel obliged to share in the problems that affected the area. Specifically, the crisis manifested itself in Lebanon's unwillingness to assume her responsibilities as a part of the Arab League, of which it was a member, to defend the common interest of the Arabs vis-à-vis Israel in protecting the waters of the Jordan River.

Lebanon offered its traditional answer: it wished to remain 'neutral' in the dispute lest Israel would attack. When the Arabs offered Egyptian and Syrian troops to defend Lebanon's southern border, Lebanon emphatically rejected the offer on the grounds that such Arab military presence on her territory would compromise her sovereignty.[64]

On the ideological level, the crisis manifested itself between 'Lebanonism' and 'Arabism'. These two categories assumed clear religious overtones in the presentation of the question by the main representatives of the Maronite bourgeoisie and the Maronite church.[65] Although the crisis began to take shape in 1962, it was the first Arab summit meeting of October 1964 that marked the qualitative shift in the crisis.[66] While none of the summit's participants were willing to face Israel militarily, each felt obliged to respond to the collective Arab crisis in an attempt to pacify, at least for a while, the Arab masses. To this effort two steps were taken: (1) The Palestine Liberation Organization (PLO) was formed with a pro-Saudi Palestinian at its helm (Ahmad al-Shuqairy).[67] (2) A unified Arab military command, comprising Egypt, Syria, Lebanon and Jordan, was set up.

Lebanon reluctantly agreed to this arrangement, which also stipulated that no Arab troops were to enter Lebanon except at the request of the Lebanese authorities. Furthermore, Palestinians in Lebanon who wanted to seek military training were to go to PLO bases in other Arab countries and had no right to return to Lebanon.[68]

Aside from the PLO, which the Palestinians perceived (quite correctly) as ineffective in the fight against Israel, the first Palestinian military operation inside Israel was conducted by a new organization. Al-Fateh issued its first communiqué describing the 31 December 1964 operation in Israeli territory. They even captured the imagination of the Arab masses and signalled a qualitative shift in the response of the Palestinians to their plight.

This event, however, was a cause of concern to the Lebanese state. Lebanon was presented with the almost impossible task of keeping the Palestinians in the country away from the influence of Fateh. The Chehabist Deuxième Bureau (military intelligence) kept the Palestinian refugee camps under close surveillance and especially terrorized Palestinian youth.[69]

The opposition to Chehabism was aided by the death of Jalal Kawash, a Palestinian guerrilla fighter, under torture by the Deuxième Bureau. The anti-Chehabists, those who genuinely supported the guerrilla movement and those who did not, seized upon the opportunity to attack the power base of Chehabism. The Deuxième Bureau survived these attacks, however, and kept its grip on Lebanese politics and on the Palestinian refugee camps.[70]

## The Defeat of 1967 and its Aftermath

Not until the Arab defeat on 5 June 1967 in the Arab-Israeli war did politics in Lebanon and in the Arab world in general take a sharp turn towards the development of a revolutionary mass movement. The humiliating defeat was an unequivocal proof that all the Arab regimes, including Nasser's Egypt and Baathist Syria, were unreliable in the face of Israeli power. This perception by the Arab masses was in one sense liberating. The conclusion — that they must take a direct role in politics — was extremely clear to them. To the Palestinians, who were by and large followers of Nasser, the vehicle for direct participation was already present: the guerrilla movement was almost overnight catapulted into prominence. Fateh, the Popular Front for the Liberation of Palestine (PFLP) and Saiqa were the major guerrilla organizations to whom the Arab masses lent allegiance and legitimacy.[71]

Soon afterwards, the innocuous PLO, with its helpless chairman Shuqairy, was taken over by the guerrilla movement, which comprised the core of what came to be known as the Palestinian Resistance (or Revolutionary) Movement. Yasser Arafat, the Fateh chief, was elected PLO chairman in 1968.

The turning point for the guerrilla movement came on 21 March 1968, when at least 6,000 Israeli troops, supported by helicopters and armoured vehicles, attacked the village of Karameh on the east bank of the Jordan River. The roughly 400 guerrillas there, along with the villagers, took to mobile warfare in a battle that lasted for about 20 hours.[72] In the last few hours of the battle, a nearby Jordanian army artillery unit, defying orders from headquarters, entered the battle. The unit's role was decisive in turning away a defeated Israeli invasion force. The fact that the guerrillas, despite heavy losses, were capable of successfully handling a much superior force was cogent proof that a people's war was the method best suited for the liberation of the occupied territories. The battle was also significant in that it gave more power to the Resistance, which was able to spread its legitimate control over all areas of the Arab world where Palestinians resided.[73]

Lebanon, with about 300,000 Palestinians and a history of popular support for the Palestinian cause, was a logical place for political activities by the Resistance. The Palestinians were a living proof of the organic link between Lebanon and the Arab world. They contributed heavily to Lebanon's economic development (cheap skilled labour, remittances from abroad and the establishment of the Intra Bank) yet, for the most part, they did not share in its gains. Their lot was comparable to that of the majority of the Lebanese population who lived in the extremely underdeveloped areas of the country. The Palestinian Resistance was already an ally of the Lebanese deprived classes. The alliance developed at a rapid rate under pressure of regional and international developments.[74]

At this point, it is perhaps appropriate to discuss the response of the right-wing forces to this developing mass movement in Lebanon.

If 'Lebanonism' (or, as some call it, 'Lebanism') was not easy to create in times of relative stability (Chehab's regime), it was impossible during periods of upheaval, as witnessed in the Arab world since 1967. Chehabism during the Helou regime was increasingly working itself into a double bind. On the one hand, it wanted to accommodate the pan-Arab forces within the limits that the system allowed; on the other, the system itself was incapable of handling the legitimate demands forced upon it by regional and domestic developments (such as the 1967 war, the rise of the PLO and worsening economic performance).

The pro-system forces articulated their interests in terms of extreme 'Lebanonism'. They rejected any compromise with those demands which Chehabism had, to a certain extent, been willing to accommodate. This extreme 'Lebanonism' manifested itself in 'Maronitism', the representatives of which were Chamoun and his Party of Free Nationalists (PFN), Eddé with his NB and Gemayel with his LKP. These forces formed the Tripartite Alliance, or the Hilf.[75] Although the PFN (which Chamoun formed a few years after leaving the presidency) included Catholics and some Shiites (primarily those that had allegiance to the Khalil family), the party's 'Maronitism' was indisputable. It was also strong in the Chouf area among the Maronites.

Despite what authors such as Entelis claim, the LKP cannot be regarded as qualitatively different from the other parties in the Hilf, whom Entelis quite correctly perceives as reactionary, sectarian and dogmatic in terms of a 'Christian Lebanon'.[76] As Hudson contends, 'As long as "Lebanon first" continued to be interpreted by Muslims as "Christian first" . . . the Kataeb (LKP) will not become an integrating national party.'[77] One would have to refer to Gemayel's conception of reforms in Lebanon and his famous '80% argument' to realize that the 'Muslims' that Hudson talks about had a well-found concern that the LKP was sectarian 'Lebanonist'. Furthermore, Entelis himself concedes 'the fact that it [the LKP] decided to join the LNP [PFN] and NB indicated that the systematic pressure had exceeded its capacities to control or direct them.[78] But the Chehabists were espousing 'Lebanon first' as well. If the LKP were different from the PFN and the NB, it had the option to ally with the Chehabists as it did during the Chehab regime. That the LKP did not was a telling criticism that it was not amenable to an alliance with a trend that was coming under attack from all quarters. The LKP had to become part of the Hilf. Otherwise it would have lost much of its mass base among the Maronites to the other Hilf parties.[79] It is the opportunism of the LKP and its sectarianism, rather than what Entelis contends, that explains the party positions during this period of instability in Lebanon.

More important, perhaps, is the fact that the LKP's philosophy was not very different from Chamoun's or Eddé's. In an article published in *L'Orient* on 11 July 1967, 'the Hilf called for the continuation of all forms of relations with the West since the Western world has the same faith as we do, in one God, in a parliamentary democratic system, in the rights of man, his liberty and dignity, as well as in economic liberalism.'[80] This quotation actually reflects one of the major ideological components of 'Lebanon first'. Viewed in a historical context, this category becomes a defence of capitalist interests in general and Maronite capitalist interests in particular. The Hilf becomes the mechanism by which 'Maronitism' reared its head in an attempt to become the hegemonic force within a new power bloc in the state. In point of fact, the Hilf was a formidable force that eventually helped unseat Chehabism and elect a president who was to become a major ally of the PFN and LKP during the conflict of 1975.

As mentioned earlier, the power bloc and its hegemonic fraction during the Helou regime were not representative of the political forces on the political scene. To begin with, the hegemonic fraction was under constant challenge from new forces in the power bloc. Furthermore, Chehabism as a phenomenon was incapable of resolving Lebanon's inherent problems. As such, it had to attack the nascent Lebanese National Movement (LNM), which, in turn, had to protect itself from Chehabism.

The Israeli commando raid on Beirut International Airport on 28 December 1968 brought about the resignation of the Yafi cabinet, which was accused by the people of incompetence.[81] Karami was able to form a new cabinet on 15 January 1969, and pledged to meet the demands of the masses, which were expressed during the strikes and demonstrations that took place all over Lebanon. These demands were for: (1) military conscription; (2) fortification and defence of border villages; and (3) co-ordination of Lebanon's foreign policy with the rest of the Arab world through the Arab League and Arab summit conference.

Chamoun boycotted the cabinet since it did not include him but included the two Hilf leaders, Gemayel and Eddé. The latter two, along with two other allies, resigned their cabinet posts in support of Chamoun. As a response to this challenge, Karami simply appointed four other people to the vacant cabinet posts. The Hilf responded with a strike on 30 January 1969. Gemayel declared that 'the street would be more effective than the Chamber.'[82] The main objective of the strike was 'not the toppling of the present government but the restoration of democratic principles . . . the secondary aim of this campaign is to make the extremists understand that the Lebanese cannot and will not kneel down to their demands . . .'; according to Gemayel the strike was to counter the 'communist peril'.[83]

At any rate, the strike was a fiasco: the Karami cabinet 'received parliamentary confirmation (60-30-8 absent)'. Nevertheless, the Hilf declared that the strike 'confirmed the opposition of a large majority of Lebanese to demagogic tendencies'.[84] What the strike confirmed, however, was the fragility of the confessional arrangement and the weakness of the Hilf vis-à-vis the nascent LNM, the Palestinian Resistance and those of the Muslim élite who chose to ally themselves with the LNM against the exclusive Maronite parties.

The Chehabists naturally came up against the Hilf in parliament by giving confirmation to the Karami cabinet. The Hilf's defeat was a victory not only for the Chehabists but also for the LNM. To arrest any further development of LNM power, the LKP opened dialogue with the sectarian Muslims such as the Najjadah and the National Committee (Al-Hay'at al-Watiniya, an organization of Muslim businessmen who wanted more representation within the confines of confessionalism and 'Lebanonism'). These two groups did not have any mass following to speak of. The masses were gravitating toward the LNM and its main figure, Jumblatt (who since independence had identified with social and political reform). The motive of the LKP was obvious: it wanted to present itself as a party concerned about national unity, which was supposedly being undermined by the LNM. Needless to say, the LKP's conception of national unity was that it comprised two poles, Muslim and Christian, which remained non-antagonistic. This conception, of course, dodged the issue of dealing with the main adversary, the LNM.

The LKP tactics also reflected the fact that, while the party was challenging the regime, it did not want to challenge the confessional system. These tactics were designed to enhance the Hilf and the LKP positions in the system; however, they backfired. This was evident when Gemayel clearly stated the Hilf's position that 'the only solution to the crisis is the cabinet's resignation; no other alternative is possible.'[85] When it was incapable of doing so, however, the Hilf retracted its position and held a conference in Brummana (near Beirut) on 7, 8 and 9 March 1969. There it stated that 'it was no longer a question of participation in the government, but one of political programme.'[86]

Entelis is correct when he states that 'the objective was to arouse national consciousness against what the Hilf perceived as a developing socialist-revolutionary trend among Muslim forces in Lebanon.'[87] Except, of course, that this national consciousness was 'Lebanonism' and the socialist-revolutionary forces were not Muslim but of various religious backgrounds. The fact that writers like Entelis choose to categorize the conflict as Christian-versus-Muslim attests to the weakness of their analyses and their inability to understand politics in Lebanon beyond its superficial manifestations.

In its description of the problems in Lebanon, the Hilf's conference never mentioned that Lebanon's economic development had anything to do with the crisis at hand. Instead, the Hilf simply pointed out that the current political problems were due to:

> (1) disequilibrium in the delegation of constitutional powers; (2) paralysis of democratic institutions; (3) administrative corruption; (4) exploitation of government for personal ends; and (5) oligarchical rule.[88]

But these were the symptoms of the underlying reasons, about which the Hilf kept silent. It was clear that the Hilf was agitating against any reform the LNM wanted to achieve in the system. Furthermore, the Hilf wanted to impose its will upon the regime in an effort to become the hegemonic force in a new power bloc. Such a position, it hoped, would enable it to deal with the LNM from a position of strength, so as to nip it in the bud.

The Brummana conference was a strategic undertaking in this effort. Other representatives of the dominant class, however, declared that the conference 'purposely exaggerated the communist threat'. Furthermore, the Muslim sector of the dominant bourgeois class stated that the conference resolutions were a 'denunciation of the Mithaq [National Pact] by its call for foreign protection' and that the Palestinian cause should be supported.[89] In response to these developments the Hilf threatened to resort to extra-legal means. This, of course, prompted President Helou to remind the Hilf to 'respect the rules of the game'.[90] The Hilf's tactics prompted Jumblatt to declare that 'the Alliance [Hilf] aimed at instigating some sects in the country, strengthening the confessional schism, and causing internal divisions.'[91] The Hilf was incapable of confronting the LNM head-on. In fact, its strategy called for agitation to create conditions of polarization that would in turn rationalize its sectarian stance and its defence of the system against those who called for its reform.

The inconsistencies of the Hilf's position were, in fact, deliberate tactics to bring about a dangerous polarization in the country. The Hilf sought to strengthen its position among the Maronites through drumming up their fears of 'Arabism' and 'communism'. Having succeeded in elevating this sectarian conflict to the level it desired, the Hilf opted to end the crisis without achieving any of the aims it had ostensibly been seeking.

Another major reason for the Hilf's decision to end the crisis was the fact that the Lebanese presidential elections were less than two years away. The Hilf zuama were each eyeing the presidency. The Hilf enhanced its position within the Maronite community, and also struck an alliance with the Central Bloc (founded in 1969) which included Salam, Asaad and Suleiman Franjieh.[92]

## Clashes between the Army and the PLO

As mentioned earlier, the Palestinian Resistance in Lebanon was perceived as a threat to the Lebanonists, especially by the Maronites. Not only did the Resistance provide a model for the oppressed Lebanese to follow, it was their only natural ally in the face of the state. These long-neglected Lebanese masses, especially in the south, believed the state should protect their villages from Israeli raids and give support to the Resistance in its struggle against the Zionist entity.

The state and the army, however, saw things differently. They proceeded to prepare to end the PLO threat. The army sought to assert its role through a series of clashes with the Palestinian Resistance forces between May and October 1969. The polarization of Lebanon assumed dangerous proportions. Many of the Muslim élite, such as Prime Minister Karami, had no choice but to side with the Resistance. This was so mainly because the power base of such zuama rested upon people who were also pro-Resistance. The Prime Minister had to come up with a compromise solution which he found in the concept of 'co-ordination'. This concept referred to co-ordination of activities against Israel between the army and the Resistance.

'Co-ordination' found its official expression in the Cairo Agreement, which was signed on 3 November 1969 by Arafat and the Lebanese Army Chief General Bustani. The agreement, in effect, was a concession that legalized the presence of the Resistance on Lebanese soil; but constrained its activities somewhat, in terms spelled out in the actual agreement.[93]

The Hilf supported the President and the army against the Resistance. However, it did not dare go public against the Resistance, since to do so would have jeopardized the credibility of each of the Hilf's members, who were already eyeing the presidency. In Lebanon the presidency could not have been won by any candidate who did not have substantial support from the Muslim sector of the bourgeoisie. This sector had to maintain a semblance of support for the Resistance to appease its overwhelmingly pro-Resistance constituency.

In dealing with the Resistance, therefore, the Hilf had to resort to trickery. It tried to drive a wedge into the popular support of the Resistance, by blaming communists and Baathists in the Resistance for the troubles that Lebanon then faced, and praising Fateh and the Palestinian cause. The Hilf declared that it was not against the Palestinian revolution, but did not want any guerrilla bases in the country. Furthermore, the Hilf was of the opinion that 'co-ordination' was not a workable concept and, as such, was unacceptable to the Hilf.[94]

The Hilf, however, had to agree, unwillingly, to the Cairo Agreement. The popular pressure and the pressure of radical and conservative Arab states alike convinced Chamoun and other Hilf zuama of the futility of their position. The LKP and Chamoun were not ready to clash militarily with the Resistance. Eddé, who dissented at first, was convinced by the Maronite Patriarch to agree to Chamoun's and Gemayel's position on the Cairo Agreement.

In essence, the Resistance was becoming deeply rooted among the masses, and the LNM (formed in 1969) was in full support of the Resistance. The Hilf was unable to undo what had transpired historically in terms of this revolutionary development. Such a development was not only a threat to the Maronite bourgeoisie but also to the Muslim sector of the bourgeoisie.

However, because the latter relied primarily upon a mass base supportive of the Resistance, it had to become a moderating force between the Hilf and Resistance while paying lip service to the Resistance and the LNM.

This moderating force had the main function of attempting to keep the system intact at a time of grave dangers to confessionalism. With the rise of the LNM, this moderating function assumed greater importance. These moderating forces were able officially to represent the Lebanese masses, who did not subscribe to the Hilf's position. In a major way this sector of the bourgeoisie prevented the development of the revolutionary situation to the point of rupture. Events, however, kept pushing the social formation toward rupture; this meant that the moderating elements were losing their grip on the masses, who were not satisfied with partial responses to the crisis within the country. They gravitated towards the LNM because it was capable of articulating their interests.

The Hilf had so far been dealing mainly with the Resistance and blaming it for the troubles of the polity. The LNM, in turn, accused the Hilf of using the Resistance as a scapegoat because it did not want to deal with the problems of Lebanese development and underdevelopment.

Following its earlier tactic of escalation, the Hilf (and specifically the LKP) opted to clash with the Resistance. On 25 March 1970, it instigated clashes with the Resistance which lasted until 29 March. The Kahala incident soon spread to Beirut, where guerrillas from the Resistance clashed with LKP militia in refugee camps and in major parts of the city proper. What started as an attack at a guerrilla funeral procession threatened to become a fully-fledged war capable of encompassing all of Lebanon.[95] However, that was to come later, when other requirements of the regional and international level were ripe for the 'great event'. Internally, Lebanon was sitting on a powder-keg; the various political forces were primarily engaged in fine tuning of their political and military power, while waiting for the right cue to achieve rupture in the system.

Clashes stopped on 31 March after mediation by the Libyan foreign minister. The March attack on the Resistance had another important cause. The LKP was eyeing the presidency in the August 1970 elections. The party wanted to project itself as the group capable of dealing with the guerrilla movement. In fact, many Muslim members of the bourgeoisie did not protest at the LKP's clashes with the Resistance because they saw the Palestinians as a destabilizing force which worked against their capitalist interests. These clashes rendered Gemayel more attractive as a presidential candidate to most bourgeois sectors and fractions than either Eddé or Chamoun. It looked as if the competition was going to be between Gemayel and a Chehabist candidate. With the prevalent anti-Chehabist trend in the country, Gemayel had a good chance of being elected.

Two major problems, however, militated against the prospect of Gemayel for President. The first was the association of the LKP with Maronite bourgeois interests. This meant that the party, if it assumed the presidency, would have had to work for this bourgeois sector, to the detriment of most of the other bourgeois sectors and fractions. The second was that, as early as 1969, another Maronite personality had been working with the presidency in mind. Suleiman Franjieh entered into an alliance (the Central Bloc) with Salam and Asaad. Franjieh became more attractive than Gemayel to the majority of the anti-Chehabist bourgeois groupings. Franjieh too had a tough stand on the Resistance, and yet was acceptable to some groups within the LNM such as Jumblatt's.[96]

When the elections were finally held, the race was between Elias Sarkis, a Chehabist, and Franjieh. On 17 August 1970 the latter was elected by parliament with a majority of one.[97] The election results were good news for the Arab conservative regimes (Saudi Arabia, etc.), who began to grow more wary of the Resistance and its influence on the Arab masses, and who welcomed a tough president they thought capable of dealing with the issue. The United States was also pleased by the Chehabist defeat because of the Chehabists' traditional closeness to France and Nasser.[98]

## Franjieh Takes on the Resistance

The defeat of the Resistance in Jordan, in what came to be known as 'Black September' of 1970, put more stress on the Lebanese system. Lebanon was the only place in the Arab world contiguous to Israel where the Resistance had the power to move freely and where it enjoyed a common tradition of struggle with the Lebanese masses, especially in the south. For this reason the Resistance increased its activities in Lebanon after Black September.

Franjieh was determined to play tough with the Resistance. This was evident during his first month in office, when he refused to allow into Lebanon a plane-load of Palestinian guerrillas from the Arab Liberation Front (ALF − Iraqi-sponsored). This act consolidated his position with the anti-Resistance political forces inside and outside Lebanon. Conveniently, he did not damage his reputation with the pro-Resistance forces since he was abiding by the letter of the Cairo Agreement. The agreement had made no stipulation allowing guerrillas to arrive in Lebanon by air.[99]

The three Central Bloc (CB) allies were now the President, the Prime Minister (Salam) and the speaker of parliament (Asaad). In parliament Tony Franjieh, the President's son, organized a new pro-regime alliance, the New Central Bloc (NCB).[100]

As an anti-Chehabist, Salam's main function was to form a cabinet, which was called the 'youth cabinet' (in Lebanon most of the politicians who were cabinet members were old zuama and mostly members of parliament). This 'youth cabinet', which was formed from outside parliament, was supposed to dismantle Chehabist institutions in the army and the bureaucracy. The cabinet, however, was unable to accomplish any reforms because of the stiff resistance from groupings of the dominant class who insisted that the cabinet must be formed from members of parliament.[101] The failure of this maverick cabinet prompted Salam's resignation. However, he at once formed another cabinet made up of traditional politicians selected from within the newly-elected 1972 parliament, in the best tradition of confessional politics.[102]

No sooner was the cabinet issue resolved than the regime began to be accused of nepotism, corruption and alliances with special interests (businessmen and traditional politicians). These accusations became more acute and intense as inflation and unemployment started to climb. Most of these accusations came from the progressive parties, such as the SPP, the LCP, the Baathists, etc. The President's son and close associates were openly accused of rigging the prices of pharmaceuticals and other commodities and services. These and similar accusations, coming from all levels of society, indicated growing dissatisfaction among the masses.

Two events in the 1972 parliamentary elections indicated the development of the mass movement. The first was the victory of Dr Rafi'i, the Baath Party candidate from Tripoli; the second the victory of Najah Wakim, an Arab nationalist from Beirut. Both candidates ran against pro-Chehabists. These events showed the lack of confidence of two major urban concentrations in the traditional leaders, and the willingness of the population to elect those who could be more responsive to their needs.

Salibi claims that Wakim's victory 'appeared as a spontaneous expression of the political and social frustrations and anxieties of the Sunnite Muslim masses, whose sentiments were pan-Arab rather than radical, and who continued to regard the figure of the late President Nasser of Egypt as a symbol of their cause.'[103] This contention, however, is misleading. The separation between 'pan-Arab' and 'radical' — whatever Salibi means by this second term — is a false one. If by 'radical' he means anti-imperialist, surely 'pan-Arabism' had a history of this at least since the 1950s. If, on the other hand, by 'radical' he means comprehensive social reforms and major restructuring of the economy and politics, then indeed 'pan-Arabism' qualified on this score decades ago: Nasser's mottos were 'Freedom, Socialism, Unity'. The Lebanese masses who gave their allegiance to Nasser were at the same time 'radical' in terms of Lebanese politics. Their objective was to restructure the Lebanese polity and do away with confessionalism. And that certainly was not simply 'pan-Arab'.

The formation of the LNM in 1969 brought together a large coalition of anti-confessional parties which included Arab nationalists and Marxists.[104] These parties and organizations formulated a common programme.[105] A civil war was fought in an attempt to implement this programme. To separate 'radical' and 'pan-Arab' in the context of Lebanon in the period under question is to display one's misunderstanding of the Lebanese situation. Furthermore, if one were to accept such a separation of categories, one would be hard put to categorize, for example, the Arab Baath Socialist Party. Is the ABSP 'pan-Arab', or socialist and hence 'radical'?

Moreover, it is abundantly clear, although Salibi and others completely ignore it, that 'pan-Arabism' or Arab nationalism and socialism cannot be identified with the Muslim masses or with Islam.[106] This is so despite the fact that the majority of the Lebanese masses are Muslim. The motive force behind events in Lebanon has been the methods by which the dominant class elected to run the country, and the responses these methods engendered from the masses. The interaction between these two forces basically defined a whole historic epoch.

## A New Shiite Movement

The LNM's ability to articulate the plight of the masses posed a threat to the powers-that-be, as well as to the religious establishments of the various sects. The Shiite landlord class (the Asaads, etc.) in the south, for example, was already losing its grip on the predominantly Shiite masses in the region. The Communist Party, the ABSP (Baath) and others were gaining more popularity, especially in the border villages where the parties' cadres were defending the villages against Israeli raids.[107]

In an attempt to counter this development, the Shiite religious establishment, in the person of its Imam Musa al-Sadr, began to take a different position from the Shiite landlord class. It stood to reason that Musa Sadr had to have a progressive position vis-à-vis the Shiite masses if he were to remain influential among them. At a time of mass impoverishment, continual Israeli raids and strong allegiance by the Shiite masses to the Palestinian cause, religion alone would have been unable to satisfy the needs of the population. Sadr, therefore, had to support what the LNM had already articulated, and what the masses believed should take place on the political and economic levels: specifically, sweeping reforms in the administration and the economy, the arming of the people in the border villages, and unconditional support of official Lebanon for the Palestinian Resistance.

Sadr, however, differed from the LNM in one major respect: he articulated the above changes in the social order along confessional lines: i.e. he wanted more participation for the Shiite sect in the affairs of the confessional state. Further, his demand for the defence of the border villages 'placed him ahead of the radical parties which were active in south Lebanon, and were eager to reap political advantage from the situation which had come to prevail there.'[108] Salibi suggests that Sadr knew that the Lebanese state could not agree to such a demand. The strike and other activities that the Imam engaged in catapulted him to the head of the Shiite movement (the Movement of the Deprived) which he 'saved' from the influence of the LNM.[109]

The power bloc consisted of a formidable alliance between Franjieh, Salam, Asaad, Chamoun, the LKP, the NBC and other individual deputies. The hegemonic fraction was the comprador bourgeoisie. The anti-regime opposition included the remnants of the Chehabist deputies, led by Karami, and Eddé with his NB. Other sources of opposition to the regime came from outside parliament. The most influential were Tueini and Imam Musa Sadr. While Jumblatt and his SPP were anti-Salam, until 1972 Jumblatt had no major quarrels with the President personally.

The increasing strength of the Palestinian Resistance and the increased frequency of Israeli raids further intensified the situation in Lebanon during the first two years of Franjieh's presidency. The scandal over the purchase of Crotale surface-to-air missiles for the defence of Lebanese territory confirmed to the masses that the Lebanese state was not serious about enhancing its defence capabilities. The money that was supposed to go for the purchase of these missiles was embezzled by the Army Commander. On 10 April 1973, Israeli commandos struck in the heart of Beirut. Their major targets were three top Fateh officials (Adwan, Najjar and Nasser) who were assassinated in their Beirut apartments.[110] Demonstrations in protest at the Israeli actions and at the lax security measures taken by the state, especially when the Israeli commandos left unscathed, brought down the cabinet. Before his resignation as Prime Minister, Salam asked for the dismissal of Army Chief Iskandar Ghanem. This demand was refused by the president.[111]

Franjieh called upon Amin al-Hafiz, a pro-Chehabist, to form a new cabinet. This was a clever move on the president's part to appease the pro-Resistance opposition, whom he thought would agree to have a pro-Chehabist Prime Minister and one who was also sympathetic to the Resistance. Furthermore, there was not one of the traditional zuama who was willing or able to form a cabinet under those circumstances. A new face for the premiership was the only choice that Franjieh had.

The frequency of crises increased after April 1973. As soon as Hafiz became Prime Minister, a group of five Popular Democratic Front for the Liberation of Palestine (PDFLP – an offshoot of the PFLP) guerrillas were arrested near the United States Embassy. The PDFLP countered by abducting three Lebanese soldiers in an attempt to secure the release of their comrades. This led, for the first time, to clashes with the Lebanese armed forces. On 18 May the clashes ended with both sides (the Resistance and the army) pledging to observe the Cairo Agreement.

After much pressure from the anti-regime forces, Hafiz finally resigned in June 1973.[112] A major consideration of the anti-regime forces was that the dominant Muslim class sectors in the social formation and the power bloc wanted stronger representation within the bloc, which they felt that Hafiz was not capable of providing, especially when he was known to be a pro-Chehabist. The Muslim sector of the dominant class sought to win stronger representation in the power bloc through appointing as Prime Minister a Sunni Muslim from a prominent family who was more amenable to the opposition. The Muslim sector saw this as a temporary solution until such time as they could actually strengthen the office of the Prime Minister by having that office assume more authority. To appease this dominant sector of Muslims, the president asked the Sunni Taqi al-Din al-Solh to form a cabinet.[113] The traditional Muslim zuama found this appointment to be in their interests for the time being.

Actually, Solh's cabinet was a token move on the part of the President to satisfy not only the traditional Muslim zuama but also most of the opposition. The cabinet included a progressive figure, Ali al-Khalil, who was mandated to study the ways in which administrative reforms were to be carried out. But the cabinet also included the President's son, traditional zuama and business-men who were not interested in reform.

While Solh's cabinet was capable of mending fences with Syria and the Palestinian Resistance, it was hardly successful in addressing the economic and political problems within Lebanon.[114] The continual Israeli raids and the political and economic demands of the masses exacerbated the situation. Demonstrations and strikes were driving the country deeper into crisis. The Muslim sector of the bourgeoisie seized upon this rising wave of popular de-mands to improve its position within the state machinery. They called for more Muslims to be represented at all levels of the state. These demands, as suggested earlier, also had the function of undercutting the LNM's anti-confessional stand, and were, therefore, a clever attempt to maintain the confessional system.

## The October War, and Lebanon's Gathering Storm

While the various fractions and sectors of the dominant class were bicker-ing among themselves over their respective shares within confessionalism, the October 1973 War (in which Egypt and Syria fought Israel) elevated the entire struggle to another plane. To begin with, Lebanon put her fuel supply and radar at the service of the Syrian armed forces. This move was primarily taken to appease the growing opposition within the country. Due to the October War, however, Lebanon once more faced a bitter choice on the Arab level: either to side with the advocates of a final peace settlement with the Israelis (who included Egypt and Saudi Arabia) or with those who were against the settlement (primarily Libya and Iraq). The first choice would have alienated the domestic opposition; the second was not possible for the con-fessional system, because it would have meant the straining of Lebanese relations with the West and especially with the United States. This was a step the confessional system was not prepared to take if it were to survive as a confessional capitalist system.

Two main components of the unrest in Lebanon at the end of 1973 were the domestic political and economic problems, and the larger regional issue (the Palestinian question).[115] These two components were inseparable: those Lebanese social forces that fought against Kissinger's Middle East policies were the same forces that fought to amend the Lebanese labour laws to make them more favourable to the workers. Labour unions, with heavy socialist and communist influence, along with nationalist parties were the main forces in this fight. The influence of these parties was also evident in a major stratum of the population (high-school and university students), most of whom fought for social and political reforms, supported the Palestinian Resis-tance and opposed the Kissinger-sponsored Middle East policies.[116]

Meanwhile, the November 1973 Arab summit meeting recognized that the PLO was the sole legitimate representative of the Palestinians. It further agreed that no peace would be negotiated with Israel unless the PLO were a direct party to it. The next Arab summit meeting, in October 1974, further strengthened the PLO's position when King Hussein of Jordan was prevailed upon to relinquish his claim to the West Bank in favour of the PLO.[117]

As early as 1970 Lebanon's right-wing parties and organizations such as the LKP (Phalangists), the PFN, Franjieh's private militia and other smaller groups, were arming themselves. By 1974 they were armed to the teeth in preparation for the conflict to come. With President Franjieh being part of the right wing, it was no secret that the state was providing the umbrella for right-wing military preparation. These forces were also getting aid from, and co-ordinating with, Israel for the selection of the most propitious moment to strike against the Resistance and the LNM.

The PLO's strength and prestige had allowed LNM groups to arm themselves under the PLO umbrella. Most of the LNM groups, however, neglected to arm themselves as independent organizations. They simply relied upon the PLO 'in case of fire'.[118] As we shall have occasion to see later, this policy was detrimental to the independent development of the Lebanese revolutionary forces and affected independent political and military decision-making by the LNM. This policy also reflected the LNM's erroneous assessment of the intentions of the right-wing and the methods they would use.

The targeting of the Resistance by the right-wing groups was no accident. The LKP, especially, resorted to time-honoured tactics of divide and rule. It tried to drive a wedge between the LNM and the Resistance by dividing the latter into what it called 'honourable guerrilla action' and non-honourable.[119] The right wing accused some guerrillas of dealing in hashish and contraband. The problem was exaggerated by the right wing for political reasons. These tactics were reminiscent of King Hussein's ploy to divide and rule the PLO in Jordan. This time, however, the majority of the masses did not accept this distinction.

In 1974 the right wing, in collusion with the Lebanese state, sought to escalate hostilities through major armed clashes with the Palestinian Resistance and the LNM. This was done in order to provoke a situation in which the state could assume a stronger role in crushing the emerging revolutionary forces that threatened the status quo. The most important clashes were: the 29–30 July fighting between the Resistance and the LKP; the 21 August Sidon incident, in which a policeman shot and killed a guerrilla; and the 22 September fighting between the LKP and the SPP in Tarshish, a village in the High Matn in Mount Lebanon.[120] The trend was obvious. The LKP and the state were aiming for a military solution that would do away with the Palestinian Resistance, which would in turn weaken the LNM and thus safeguard the confessional capitalist system.

It was also clear that the state and the Lebanese right wing were going for a comprehensive peace settlement in the region, one that did not favour the Palestinian revolution. For this reason the LKP (the largest and most powerful right-wing party) announced in late September 1974 that it sought to join mainstream Arab policies favouring a regional settlement. However, no one in Lebanon was impressed by this announcement, not even the traditional Muslim bourgeoisie. Mainstream Arab policies meant the acceptance of the US-sponsored policies for the region. The LKP's decision came hard on the heels of a tour by Gemayel to Egypt, Syria, Jordan and Saudi Arabia.[121] This policy pitted the LKP directly against the Palestinian Resistance and especially the Rejection Front, formed at the end of 1973.[122] The Rejection Front included all Palestinian groups that opposed imperialist-imposed regional settlements. This included the PFLP, the Arab Liberation Front (ALF), the National Struggle Front (NSF) and the PFLP-General Command (an offshoot of the PFLP). The LKP was also pitted against the LNM and most of the Muslim Sunni and Shiite traditional zuama, who saw in the LKP's Arab manoeuvring a threat to their own power in the system. The LKP became the strongest representative of Maronite bourgeois interests allied with Arab reactionary and imperialist interests in the region. As such, the LKP remained allied with the PFN, Franjieh and the Maronite Order of Monks.

After about 14 months in office Taqi al-Din al-Solh resigned the premiership in the face of the rapidly deteriorating situation. The LNM was quickly gaining grounds in terms of mass support, which allowed it to exercise a great deal of pressure on the state and to confront right-wing manoeuvring on the political level. President Franjieh was forced to ask Rashid al-Solh, a strong ally of Jumblatt, to form a cabinet. The new cabinet had 18 members, with strong representation of Jumblatt's SPP, the LKP (Gemayel) and the PFN (Chamoun). The cabinet appointments allowed the President to weaken the traditional Muslim zuama, since Rashid al-Solh was not a traditional zaim and was new to the premiership. At the same time, however, these appointments gave the LNM a strong voice in the power bloc. Yet this power bloc was a curious creation. The major adversaries in the social formation were now represented at the political level. For the first time in Lebanon's history, an anti-system coalition, the LNM, had been given a strong voice in the state. This power bloc, however, was formed as a last resort to avoid the breakdown of the system and maintain unity and cohesion. This new state of affairs, however, was unable to do anything but buy time for the system. All the parties within this curious arrangement were aware that such an unnatural and contradictory situation within the power bloc would be short-lived. All were jockeying for position; one group had to give way. The LKP (like the Hilf before it) was determined to settle accounts with the LNM and the Palestinian Resistance once and for all.

The approaching 1976 presidential elections prompted the formation of the Tahaluf (alliance) between Karami, Salam (both Sunni Muslims) and Eddé (Maronite). It was a desperate attempt on the part of a sector of the Lebanese bourgeoisie to save the system. The Tahaluf presented itself as an alternative to both the regime and the LNM. For this reason, Eddé attacked Franjieh, the LKP and Chamoun, charging them with corruption. The Tahaluf also blamed the regime for the chaos in Lebanon.

Meanwhile, on 28 February 1975 fishermen in Sidon demonstrated against the licensing of the Protein Company which allowed it to monopolize the fishing industry. The company was financed with Kuwaiti money and its chairman was no other than the 'anti-Arab' Chamoun. The army clashed with the demonstrators and shot and critically wounded Marouf Sa'd, the city's deputy in parliament who was at the head of the demonstration.[123] The traditional Sunni Muslim zuama seized upon this opportunity to call for the resignation of the Premier, Rashid al-Solh, and the dismissal of the Army Chief. They further called for the reorganization of the army command to reflect equitable representation of both Muslims and Christians. Jumblatt supported these demands, which were opposed by Chamoun and Gemayel. Jumblatt, however, backed Solh as Prime Minister in opposition to the traditional Muslim leaders. The LNM supported Jumblatt on this point. In backing the traditional zuama on the question of the reorganization of the army, Jumblatt wanted further to isolate the Maronite right wing and the President from all other forces in society. He also sought to out-manoeuvre the traditional zuama, who were trying to divert support from the LNM by posing as reformers of the state. Jumblatt demonstrated that the question of the reorganization of the army had been raised by the SPP and the LNM earlier.

Marouf Sa'd, the Sidon deputy in parliament, died on 6 March 1975.[124] His death made the reorganization of the army command a more pressing need. The Maronite right wing refused to budge. They were not in favour of relinquishing a major state position (the Commander of the Army was always a Maronite) or sharing it with any other sect in Lebanon. Having decided upon open conflict with the progressive forces in Lebanon, they needed all the state power they could muster against the opposition. Had they not decided on conflict, they could have reached a compromise settlement with the Muslim bourgeoisie which could have strengthened the Maronite right-wing position vis-à-vis the LNM.

Conditions were ripe, on all levels, for the apocalypse. Two major forces were already polarized: the LNM on the one hand and the Maronite right wing on the other. The other pro-system forces (such as the traditional Muslim zuama) stood at various points between the two major contenders.

## Conclusion

The institution of confessionalism helped to prevent serious challenges within the Lebanese power bloc where the comprador bourgeoisie (mostly Maronite) were hegemonic. The comprador, however, increasingly sought to improve their position (politically and economically) at the expense of the rest of the power bloc components. During the period 1943–75, several tenuous situations emerged that on a few occasions threatened the existence of the confessional arrangement. On two occasions (1958 and 1975) the consequences of the intra-power bloc conflict were two civil wars. This was proof that the political system was incapable of accommodating the varied interests of the dominant classes, let alone the interests of the population.

The confessional system allowed the dominant class in the social formation to practise policies inimical to the country's social and economic development. Through economic and other types of legislation, such as banking laws, election laws, and so on, the dominant class, and especially the hegemonic bourgeois class fraction in the power bloc, exacerbated Lebanon's economic ills. Inflation and recession worsened as the country was opened more to international finance.

Imperialist interests and those of the comprador were congruent, but diametrically opposed to those of the majority of the Lebanese. Ideologically and politically, these two interests expressed themselves as 'Lebanonism' for the comprador bourgeoisie and as 'Arab nationalism' for the majority of the Lebanese. The first major conflict between these two ideologies reached its peak in the 1958 civil war. Certain power bloc components and zuama rode a wave of Arab nationalism in an attempt to topple the Chamoun regime in 1958 and thus enhance their position in or enter into a newly formed power bloc. At that time the interests of these zuama were congruent with those of the majority of the masses. The masses, however, were not organized in political parties independent of these zuama, nor were they capable of articulating their interests on the level of the 'political'. Consequently, they were engaged in such political practices as supporting classes of the non-Maronite bourgeoisie or other zuama not in the power bloc.

The hegemonic class fraction (which, as I mentioned before, was predominantly Maronite) and its allies, relied on those fractions of the lower classes which belonged to their confessions and/or those who entered into a zaim-client relationship with their respective zuama. In the case of the majority of the Maronites, for instance, these kinds of relationships were possible due to the relatively higher incomes they enjoyed compared with the fractions of the lower classes of other confessions, or of those who lived in the other regions.

The demise of the Chamoun regime in 1958 dealt a heavy blow to the comprador bourgeoisie and to imperialism in the region. US military intervention at that point helped to preserve confessionalism and US interests in the area. Confessionalism also remained intact, since the zuama were not serious about changing the confessional system. Even with the ascendancy of Chehab, who was a reformer, the Lebanese political system was powerful enough to prevent any actual change in the mode of production. While Chehab did attempt economic planning, and some reforms were implemented, but these reforms did not challenge the existing economic structures.

Furthermore, the modernizing trend that Chehab represented failed to defeat the zuama institution. In fact, in his attempt to weaken this institution he was forced to rely on some zuama. Throughout his presidency, his attempts to shift the decision making process in the state in order to bypass the zuama backfired. He left the presidency in 1964 without implementing most of the reforms he had planned.

The supposedly Chehabist regime of succeeding President Helou did not accomplish much reform either. Despite the fact that industry was given more importance under Chehab and Helou, most of this industry was geared to export. As such it primarily benefited foreign trade, a major component of the services sector. This was especially the case since most raw materials were being imported or the value added was to imported semi-finished goods that were in turn exported. At any rate, when the Helou regime was finally over in 1970, the country was experiencing major economic dislocations.

On the ideological level, as mentioned before, the major contradictions within Lebanese society were being eulogized in 'Lebanonism' versus 'Arab Nationalism' and vice versa. Inevitably, however, given the interests of a certain sector of the ruling class, 'Lebanonism' was transformed into 'Maronitism'. This was evident on the level of the 'political' when the major defenders of confessionalism were the Lebanese Kataeb Party (Phalangists) or LKP, the Party of Free Nationalists (PFN) and the National Bloc (NB). These Maronite parties were firm believers in 'free enterprise' and were supported by the Maronite middle and working-class fractions. These parties, however, represented the exclusive interests of the Maronite bourgeoisie; Chamoun was a comprador capitalist and Eddé a banker. The LKP represented Maronite industrialists, and commercial and tourism interests.

The Maronite Order of Monks, Franijieh and lesser Maronite fractions obsessed with their exclusivist 'Maronitism', rendered it less palatable to the rest of the Lebanese. Non-Maronite Christians and Muslims in and out of the power bloc also recognized that 'Maronitism' was contradictory to the National Pact and, therefore, contrary to their confessional arrangement. This was one reason for their lack of support for the Hilf – the tripartite coalition between the Phalangists (Pierre Gemayel), the National Bloc (Eddé) and the PFN (Chamoun). Incidentally, the Maronite Chehabists were not in support of the Hilf. Although they were 'Lebanonists', they were also 'Modernists', and primordial themes such as 'Maronitism' were perceived to be backward and sectarian to them.

Under Chehabism (1958–70), Muslim 'modernizers' such as Karami could find 'Lebanonism' appealing since they were nationalists, and Chehabism enjoyed a friendly relationship to the Arab nationalist regimes. This 'Lebanonist' trend, however, was an aberration in the polity's development. It was partially viable in times of relative calm in the region, but as was said earlier, it came into conflict with the entrenched confessional zuama institution. More importantly, Chehabism was unable to develop a mass base that would have enabled it to become an alternative to 'Maronitism'.

During these times the Palestinians in Lebanon were contributing to Lebanon's economic development without receiving much in return; Palestinians were paid much less than their Lebanese counterparts for the same work. Also, tens of thousands of Palestinians working outside of Lebanon were sending money back to their families still residing there. This channelled capital certainly bolstered Lebanon's economy and contributed to its development. In addition, Palestinians contributed much in the way of skilled and highly skilled labour that helped the economic and social development of Lebanon and other Arab countries. Despite all of these factors, Palestinians who had been residing in Lebanon since they were exiled from their homeland in 1948 were still considered an alien problem and were persecuted and discriminated against by the Lebanese state and certain sectors of Lebanese society.

The Palestinian question is the focal point for the revolutionary movement, not only in Lebanon but throughout the Arab world, since their presence provides an 'organic link' between the Lebanese masses and those in the rest of the Arab world. Such a revolutionary force is contradictory to the interests of the dominant classes in any social formation; and it was certainly in conflict with 'Lebanonism'. The Palestinians were thrust on to the front line of battle against reaction, imperialism and Zionist encroachment in the Arab East. The conflict intensified after the Palestinians became an organized force that enjoyed the support of the majority of the Lebanese people.

The period after 1967 witnessed increased politicization of the masses. Economic conditions within Lebanon were deteriorating and more and more people were migrating to the cities in search of work. These problems were compounded by aggressive Israeli attacks that terrorized and bombed Lebanese villages in the South. The dynamics of the Palestinian question and the political situation in the Arab East further intensified the internal contradictions within the Lebanese polity. Anti-system political parties were on the ascendancy as more people retracted their allegiance from the zuama. This was an important step in revolutionary development. It signified the beginning of a shift in the class practices of the spontaneous mass movement; the masses were not content with their role as supporting classes and were, in fact, looking toward developing more independent political class practices in the field of the 'political' (the class struggle). Certainly the armed presence of the Palestinian Resistance contributed greatly to revolutionary development in Lebanon, and provided political, moral and military support in the interest of the Lebanese masses.

By 1969 the Lebanese National Movement (LNM) had established itself as the organized expression of the nascent mass movement. The LNM provided the Lebanese masses with the opportunity to be represented in the political field. This was possible because the LNM included 'working-class' parties such as the Communist Party (CP), the Arab Socialist Action Party (ASAP) and the Organization of Communist Action (OCA). More importantly, the 'minimum programme' of the LNM articulated the aspirations and needs of the Lebanese masses at a particular stage of revolutionary development. The programme was also capable of linking the short and long term goals of the revolutionary movement.

The LNM was a loose coalition of the progressive parties whose members came from all the religious sects (Muslims, Christians and Druze). These parties sought to institute reforms by utilizing the political process. They were significantly successful in mobilizing the already politicized masses in the struggle against confessionalism. In this conflict the LNM was capable of allying with the already alienated Muslim establishment, which was also seeking major changes in confessionalism. This, however, was a precarious tactical alliance, since the bourgeois and landlord Muslim establishment were naturally not in favour of a complete overthrow of the system. This Muslim sector was still hopeful of reaching an understanding with the Maronite right-wing to bring about a new form of confessionalism. It appears that this aspiration rested upon an idealized conviction that the Maronites would prefer to reach an agreement with their sector of the Muslim establishment rather than jeopardize confessionalism.

The class alliances that were struck between the LNM and Muslim sector of the bourgeoisie and other bourgeois fractions were brought about for a variety of reasons; for example, all those forces were in opposition to the methods the right-wing chose when settling accounts with their adversaries. There were also opportunist motivations behind these alliances. Some comprador bourgeoisie, such as Eddé, were willing to strike an alliance on a certain level but against changing the confessional arrangement. Eddé, in particular, had the procurement of the presidency in mind and so he was willing to make some concessions. Other bourgeois fractions were willing to settle for some reforms provided the confessional arrangements were not challenged. The Muslim sector of the bourgeoisie was willing to strike an alliance with the LNM since it perceived an opportunity of increasing its own political power through certain reforms.

Since the right wing was opposed to all reforms, these bourgeois forces mentioned above found it advantageous to ally with the anti-confessional LNM, even though they were pro-confessional. The Muslim establishment also opted for this alliance in an effort to keep its legitimacy among the masses who were increasingly shifting their support toward the LNM.

The LNM also included zuama such as Kamal Jumblatt. Jumblatt was anti-system but relied upon a confessional base, the Druze. His party, the Socialist Progressive Party (SPP), which also included a minority of Christians (including Maronites) and Muslims, was anti-imperialist, pan-Arab, anti-confessional, democratic and championed social and economic reform. Jumblatt played an important role in enabling the LNM to utilize the political process to press for reforms within the system.

The devastating aspect of this reliance on the political process was that, for the most part, the LNM found it neither important nor necessary to pursue other courses of action against the right wing. The Maronite right wing was arming itself to the teeth, while the LNM was content with the fact that its strategic ally, the Palestinian Resistance, was militarily strong. The LNM also relied heavily upon the assumption that it was politically effective and capable of instituting reforms through the system. It seemed that the LNM opted for reforming such state institutions as the army, not realizing that, although the Resistance was militarily strong, it was also crucial for the LNM to keep an independent political line and an independent military apparatus. This was important, because although the LNM and Resistance could unite for tactical purposes, ultimately, the strategic goals to which both organizations aspired were of a different nature; consequently, at times contradictions arose between the interests of both organizations. For instance, as will be shown in Chapter 7, the Resistance was unwilling to render massive support to the LNM during the Mountain offensive. The Resistance was pursuing a course of action at that time that the Palestinian leadership thought was most appropriate for the achievement of their goals under the circumstances. When the LNM cleared all right-wing positions south of Beirut, that offensive was successful because of heavy Palestinian and Syrian (Saiqa) commitment. During that offensive, however, on many occasions, the Syrians and the PLO bypassed the LNM political leadership in decisions of great importance. These problems hampered the revolutionary progress and success both of the LNM and the Resistance; at times they were actual setbacks. Without a strong military apparatus, the LNM found itself in compromising situations, not only in relation to the Resistance but more detrimentally in relation to Syria and the right wing.

## Notes

1. H. Bassatt, 'The Lebanese Economy — Problems and Solutions', *Arab Studies* (March 1972), 39–40. Bassatt deals with two periods: 1945–1965 and 1966–1972.
2. In general, 'progressive' forces are those which are anti-confessional.
3. Comprador is that fraction of the bourgeoisie that is tied directly or indirectly to foreign finance and industry. Bankers and agents of foreign products, such as cars, are comprador.
4. See Chapter Three, pp. 45–49 and pp. 54–59 for a discussion of the development of the services sector that favoured the comprador bourgeoisie in foreign and transit trade, banking and real estate that attracted foreign investments. These developments resulted in a coalition that included Jumblatt (the reformer) and Chamoun and Eddé (Maronite comprador) against the dominant landlord class fraction and the Khoury regime in general.
5. M.C. Hudson, *The Precarious Republic* (New York, Random House, 1968), 149.
6. Ibid.
7. Ibid., p. 150.
8. Ibid., p. 149.
9. Ibid., p. 151.
10. Ibid.
11. Ibid., p. 150.
12. Abdo Baaklini, *Legislative and Political Development: Lebanon 1842–1972* (Durham, Duke University Press, 1976), pp. 145–147. See also Hudson, op. cit., p. 163, fn. 18.
13. F. Qubain, *Crisis in Lebanon* (Middle East Institute, Washington DC, 1961), p. 22.
14. Hudson, op. cit., pp. 151–153.
15. Ibid., pp. 152–153.
16. Ibid., p. 153.

17. Ibid.
18. Sami Zubian, *The Lebanese National Movement* (Beirut, Dar-Al-Masseerah, 1977), 159–185.
19. Ibid., pp. 299–300. My translation.
20. Ibid., p. 301.
21. Solh was assassinated in Amman, Jordan, in 1951 by SNP members in retaliation for the execution of the SNP founder by Lebanese authorities.
22. Qubain, op. cit., p. 23.
23. Ibid., p. 22.
24. Zubian, op. cit., p. 137.
25. Ibid.
26. Ibid., p. 24.
27. Hudson, op. cit., p. 155.
28. Ibid., p. 156.
29. Ibid., pp. 152–153.
30. That the 1952 coup was a milestone in Arab politics is unquestionable. Nasserism emerged as the leading ideology in the Arab world. See, for instance, R.W. Baker, *Egypt's Uncertain Revolution under Nasser and Sadat* (Cambridge, Mass., Harvard University Press, 1978).
31. See, for instance, Qubain, op. cit., pp. 39–47.
32. Ibid., p. 37.
33. Leila Meo, *Lebanon: Improbable Nation* (Bloomington, Indiana University Press, 1965), 102–103.
34. Qubain, op. cit., p. 49.
35. Ibid., p. 57.
36. Hudson, op. cit., p. 114.
37. Zubian, op. cit., p. 193.
38. Ibid., p. 191.
39. Qubain, op. cit., p. 50.
40. Hudson, op. cit., p. 64.
41. Ibid.
42. Ibid.
43. Ibid., pp. 110–111.
44. See Chapter Three, pp. 59–62.
45. These Maronite interests were tied to the development of the services sector, especially foreign and transit trade, banking, real estate and tourism. This development accelerated under Chamoun, who took advantage of the economic structures that already favoured the comprador bourgeoisie.
46. J.P. Entelis, *Pluralism and Party Transformation in Lebanon: Al-Kata'ib, 1936–1970* (Leiden, R.J. Brill, 1974), 175–176.
47. Ibid., p. 176.
48. The Arab Socialist Union in the United Arab Republic (UAR) was an arm of the state which at best was a quasi-party. At any rate, the ASU did not exist outside of the UAR, where the pro-Nasser masses could gravitate towards it.
49. Beirut, Tripoli, Sidon and Tyre were the largest concentrations of the mass bases for the Communist Party, ABSP and the Arab Nationalist Movement (ANM). Their bases were comprised mainly of students,

professionals and small shopkeepers.

50. M. Suleiman, *Political Parties in Lebanon* (New York, Cornell University Press, 1967), 85–91.
51. Qubain, op. cit., p. 113.
52. Hudson, op. cit., p. 110.
53. Ibid., p. 155.
54. Ibid., p. 160.
55. Ibid., p. 145.
56. Ibid.
57. Ibid.
58. Ibid.
59. Ibid., p. 126.
60. Ibid., p. 161.
61. Baker, op. cit., p. 57.
62. See, for instance, E. Salam, *Modernization Without Revolution: Lebannon's Experience* (Bloomington, Indiana University Press, 1973).
63. Hudson, op. cit., p. 95.
64. K. Salibi, *Crossroads to Civil War: Lebanon 1958–1976* (New York, Caravan Books, 1976), 24.
65. Entelis, op. cit., pp. 159–173.
66. Salibi, op. cit., pp. 23–24.
67. Ibid., p. 26, pp. 24–25.
68. Ibid., p. 25.
69. Ibid., pp. 27–28.
70. Ibid., p. 28.
71. The Popular Front for the Liberation of Palestine (PFLP) is a Marxist-Leninist guerrilla group with a large mass following. The PDFLP (D for democratic) and the PFLP-General Command are offshoots of the main group with little or no mass base. The Saiqa is a Syrian-financed and controlled Palestinian guerrilla group.
72. The battle of Karameh was a turning-point in the history of the Palestinian revolutionary movement. Yearly celebrations are held on its occasion.
73. This explains the reasons behind the upsurge in popularity of the Resistance in Jordan, Lebanon and elsewhere in the Arab world.
74. Most Palestinians in Lebanon lived in refugee camps all over the country. Three of these camps were overrun by the right-wing forces and the Syrians.
75. Entelis, op. cit., pp. 161–162.
76. Ibid., p. 162.
77. Ibid., p. 146.
78. Ibid., p. 162.
79. This is reminiscent of the LKP's stance in defence of Maronite bourgeois interests. The party's base in the Matn and Kisrwan districts of Mount Lebanon.
80. Entelis, op. cit., p. 162.
81. Salibi, op. cit., p. 39.
82. Entelis, op. cit., p. 168.
83. Ibid.
84. Ibid.

85. Ibid., p. 169.
86. Ibid., p. 170.
87. Ibid.
88. Ibid.
89. Ibid., p. 171.
90. Ibid.
91. Ibid.
92. Salibi, op. cit., p. 49.
93. Ibid., pp. 42–43.
94. Ibid., p. 44.
95. Entelis, op. cit., p. 209, fn 1.
96. Salibi, op. cit., p. 50–51.
97. Ibid.
98. Ibid., p. 51.
99. Ibid., p. 55.
100. Ibid., p. 56.
101. Ibid., pp. 56–57.
102. Ibid., p. 61.
103. Ibid., p. 62.
104. INM, SPP, CP and OCA were major components of the LNM.
105. See Chapter 7 for discussion.
106. The ideology of the ABSP (an Arab Nationalist party) clearly distinguishes and separates between Islam and Arab nationalism. See, for instance, M. Aflaq, *Fee Sabeel Al-Baath*. It is significant to note that Aflaq, the founder-leader of the party, is a Christian. The party has many Christian cadres in all levels of leadership. Other nationalist parties, such as the ANM, have similar stances on the Islam question. Before the ANM's transformation into Marxist-Leninist groups all over the Arab world, George Habash (Christian), the PFLP leader, was its chairman.
107. K. Kahlil, 'South Lebanon Between the State and Revolution', *Arab Studies* (February, 1975), 32.
108. Salibi, op. cit., pp. 63–64.
109. Shiite merchants and businessmen were the chief supporters of Imam Musa Sadr and were heavily represented on the Shiite Religious Council, which was controlled by the Imam.
110. Salibi, op. cit., p. 66.
111. Ibid., p. 67.
112. Ibid., p. 70.
113. Ibid., p. 71.
114. Ibid., p. 72.
115. For a discussion of the economic situation in the years before 1975 see Chapter Three, pp. 81–226. This situation was one of the major causes for the heightening of class conflict. Under Helou and Franjieh problems of underdevelopment were compounded by regional problems. It is important to note that the LNM mass base was mainly in the underdeveloped areas of the Bekaa, the south and the north. The LNM had also a base in the slums of Beirut where migrants from the south resided. Traditional Muslim areas of Beirut also provided Arab nationalist components of the LNM (especially the INM) with a mass base.

The ABSP was particularly strong in Tripoli. In the deep south and in the slum areas of Beirut, the Marxist components of the LNM were especially strong.

116. H. Barakat, *Lebanon in Strife: Students Preludes to the Civil War* (Austin, University of Texas Press, 1977), 165–167.
117. Salibi, op. cit., p. 76.
118. Interview with PFLP official: 2 January 1979 (Kuwait).
119. Salibi, op. cit., p. 82.
120. Ibid., p. 80.
121. Ibid., p. 81.
122. Those Palestinian organizations that rejected the US 'solutions' to the Palestinian problem organized themselves in the Rejection Front. The PFLP and the ALF were its chief components.
123. Salibi, op. cit., p. 93.
124. Ibid., p. 95.

# 6. The Right-Wing Offensive: 1975

This chapter discusses the development of the right-wing offensive, attempting to provide a framework for evaluating the responses of the Lebanese National Movement and the Palestinian Resistance to this challenge. Strengths and weaknesses of the LNM will be assessed. This discussion will also consider the material conditions that led to the development of the LNM during the offensive and to its incorrect strategies in responding to this offensive.

Many changes occurred on the political scene in the Lebanese social formation between 1943 and 1975. During this period anti-system parties were becoming more successful in their challenges on the political level. In their efforts to transform the system these political parties were also utilizing the traditional political process. Since the state was a power centre of the dominant class, any erosion of this class's power was regarded as a threat to its state machinery. This meant that the class which stood to lose out from such threats, real or perceived, was compelled to oppose the LNM in a significant way. Given the Lebanese situation in early 1975, this meant nothing short of a calculated, full-scale military offensive against this nascent progressive movement (the LNM) to stop it dead in its tracks.

The calculations for such an offensive were well thought out, co-ordinated and acted upon by the various components of the right-wing Maronite alliance. By 1975 the alliance had completed its preparations domestically, regionally and internationally. This was evident from the quality of the arms with which the alliance equipped itself, as well as from the tour which its leader, Pierre Gemayel, undertook to reactionary Arab countries. It was no secret that the alliance supported the US-sponsored settlement in the region. Nor was it a secret that the interests of the LNM and the Palestinian Resistance ran counter to this alliance and to the pro-settlement regional and international forces (Saudi Arabia, Egypt, the United States . . .)

With these formidable forces aligned against the loose LNM coalition and the fragmented Resistance, it seemed as if the Maronite alliance would be assured of a swift and easy victory. At the propitious moment, extremist pro-system forces were transformed into agents of 'system explosion'. The natural consequence was the conflagration of 1975–76.

On 13 April 1975 LKP (Phalangist) members ambushed a busload of Palestinians and murdered everyone on board. The massacre took place in the suburb of Ayn al-Rummaneh, where Pierre Gemayel, the LKP boss, was attending the consecration of a Maronite church.[1]

Having heard of the massacre, Palestinian units of the Resistance engaged the enemy throughout Beirut and its suburbs. The result of the first three days of fighting was the complete military supremacy of the Resistance.

The massacre triggered Arafat's call for the diplomatic intervention of other Arab countries to resolve the deteriorating relations between Lebanon and the Palestinians. On the night of 13 April, the LNM met and decided to call for the expulsion of the LKP ministers from the cabinet and the banning of the LKP.[2] Due to the intervention of the Secretary-General of the Arab League, Mahmoud Riad, a cease-fire was arranged on 16 April. The next day, however, sniper fire emanating from LKP areas paralysed economic activity in the city.[3] It appeared that a concerted effort was being made to continue the discord in order to accomplish the political objectives of the LKP.

The Palestinian position on the bus massacre was clear. The Resistance wanted the LKP to hand in the seven members accused of the crime. The Resistance also aided the Lebanese security forces in eliminating the snipers, thus proving its willingness to search for a peaceful solution to the conflict.[4] Gemayel handed in two of the accused to the Lebanese state. He responded to the Resistance's demand that he deliver the others by saying that the judicial investigation must cover the whole event and not merely the bus episode.[5] He went on to accuse Israel of creating the tense climate on 13 April which had led to the bus massacre. All this was a ploy to divert attention from the real issues, since the LKP was being assisted by Israel in preparing for a large-scale confrontation. In addition, previous clashes between the LKP and the Resistance, and the LKP's general position on the Palestinian presence in Lebanon, made it difficult for the LKP to convince others that it was innocent. The party's history and its conduct during the conflict, as we shall see later on, indicate the fundamental reasons that brought about the bus massacre.

As early as 1974, the LKP had engaged the Resistance in armed clashes to create conditions in which the state could conspire with the LKP and other right-wing militia in an all-out war with the Palestinian Resistance. In April 1975 the right-wing engaged the Resistance, on the understanding that if the latter were successfully dealt with, it would be easier to prevail over the LNM. Another reason for these clashes was the right wing's (correct) assumption that the Resistance was divided over the issue of a Palestinian mini-state. While the mini-state figured prominently in the designs of Fateh and other smaller commando groupings, it was anathema to the Rejection Front (which was part of the PLO).[6] The right-wing calculation was that the PLO, and especially its leadership, would moderate the conflict in a way that would ultimately weaken the Rejectionists' position. In this way, the pro-imperialist forces that were in favour of a regional settlement could become supreme and the right wing would be able to re-establish its control over the Lebanese polity.

It also appeared that the right wing recognized that the PLO was aligned with Syria against this US imperialist-sponsored settlement, and that, although Syria was against this particular settlement, it was nevertheless in favour of some kind of a settlement that would include its concerns.

Three distinct stands on the settlement of the regional issue (the Palestinian question) became evident. The right wing identified with the US-sponsored plan. The PLO and the Syrians were open to negotiations if this would include them.[7] But the Rejection Front within the PLO was against all plans that came up with partial, compromising solutions to the Palestinian issue, since it considered this to be the crux of the dilemma in the Arab East.

The proponents of the first stand hoped that, with the elimination of the Rejectionists and the taming of the PLO through financial and military pressure, they could convince the PLO to join the Middle East settlement plan, especially if the result were perceived later by the PLO to be some kind of a Palestinian state. These well-thought-out calculations did not take account of one extremely important consideration, which was basic to the success of any strategy: the conflict was to be fought out on Lebanese soil. What this meant in practice was that, despite the PLO leadership's position in favour of the mini-state, that position remained officially undeclared because of its unpopularity among the Palestinians, especially those in Lebanon and the occupied territories.[8]

The LNM and its mass base were solidly behind the Resistance. They also rejected, on the Lebanese level, any division within the Palestinian Resistance. The popular slogan regarding Palestine among the Lebanese masses that comprised the LNM's spontaneous base was 'Total liberation, a democratic state'.

Consequently, any in-fighting among the Resistance groups under conditions of a right-wing offensive would have been condemned by the Lebanese spontaneous mass movement. Certainly it would have been condemned by the fully-mobilized Palestinian masses in the refugee camps.[9]

While certain elements in the Palestinian leadership were willing to come out against the Rejectionists, the leadership as a whole was unwilling to do so openly. Instead, the PLO leadership opted for a 'neutral' position: 'What occurs in Lebanon is an internal affair; we do not want to be party to the conflict.'[10] A complement to this ideological expression was that 'the enemy wants to divert our attention from the main goal (the liberation of Palestine). It wants to drive us into a side-battle.'[11]

While Fateh's (and the PLO's) 'neutral' stance was dominant, there were different trends within the ranks that forced the leadership to enter battle at various times on the side of the LNM. The thirteenth of April was a case in point. Palestinian units spontaneously went on the offensive against the Maronite right wing without waiting for orders from the high command. Arafat, the PLO chairman, was caught by surprise at the reaction of his own commando units.[12] He called upon the Arab states to intervene in the matter to stop the fighting.

The cease-fire of 16 April did not last long. The right wing engaged the

Palestinian Resistance once more the next day. And once more the Resistance's retaliation was spontaneous, and again its military supremacy was unquestionable. The situation began to get out of hand on the political level too. In a major significant sense, the state as a power centre for the bourgeoisie began to experience certain contortions that for a while changed its character as a power centre. The LNM was in a strong political position, heavily represented in the cabinet, with major anti-regime elements within the parliament aligned with the anti-system LNM against the extreme right wing. The LNM proceeded to exploit this position by creating a political and constitutional crisis within the system, in the hope that the LKP and its allies would, in the words of ex-President Helou, 'respect the rules of the game'. The ideological underpinnings of such a tactic will be considered later on. But first consider the tactic.

## Putting Pressure on the Phalangists

The roots of the tactic were the decisions of the LNM to isolate the LKP (the Phalangists) from Arab politics and the Lebanese state. This was a realization on the part of the LNM that if the LKP were pressured by the Arabs it would reconsider its options in dealing with its opponents. Once the first cease-fire crumbled, it was also necessary to isolate the LKP, the major right-wing factor, from Lebanese politics. Prime Minister Rashid al-Solh's address to parliament on 15 May was the form which the tactic took. The significance of this address was not that it accused the LKP and the Army Command of complicity and conspiracy, which it did, but that the Prime Minister enunciated a plan of action to resolve the problem through effecting reforms in the political system. In effect, the address articulated the same points that the LNM was raising in its 'Minimum Programme'.

Solh called for measures to (1) reform the election laws; (2) guarantee an even distribution of authority among the various offices (the Presidency, the Premiership, the Parliament Speaker); (3) support the Palestinian cause and defend Lebanon from Israeli attacks; (4) amend the Army Law, make the army answerable to the political authorities and keep it separate from internal politics; (5) reform the naturalization law to alleviate the misery of those that this law segregated against; (6) reform the income-tax structure to raise money to finance social services and social and economic projects needed to carry out essential social and economic reforms.[13]

In this address the Prime Minister also announced his resignation in disgust. Lebanon was now faced with a crisis on two levels: the first, the armed conflict; the second, the incapacity of the system to deal with this, especially after the constitutional crisis that followed the resignation of the Premier.

The reform plan was extremely popular. Not even the conventional Muslim establishment was against it (at least openly). In point of fact, the plan proposed many areas of reform that were in concurrence with those advocated by the Muslim establishment. Consequently, none of the Muslim politicians were willing or able to form a new cabinet should the President ask them to do so. Their first condition for the formation of a cabinet was that the President agree to institute the reforms put forward by Solh.

It soon appeared that the President had no alternative but to settle with the LNM and the conventional Muslim establishment. At that time, this was the only rational way to resolve the constitutional crisis precipitated by Solh's resignation.

Given the military power of the LKP and the other right-wing parties, the state was in no position to maintain the cohesion of the Lebanese social formation when these right-wing political actors no longer had hegemony in the cabinet or parliament. More important perhaps, the President, who occupied the most authoritative state position, shared many of the views of the other right-wing parties. These major views had to do with the Palestinian issue and social and political reforms, especially those pertaining to the offices of the Presidency and the Premiership. Further, the right wing had opted for a military solution and had been pressuring the state since 20 April to have the army intervene in the conflict. All these factors militated against any 'traditional' solution to the crisis. Accordingly, the President acquiesced to right-wing pressure and resorted to a non-conventional and potentially dangerous solution when he appointed a military cabinet headed by Brigadier Rifai.[14]

The formation of the military cabinet came against a background of opposition events. These included an LNM rally whose slogan was 'no cabinet except that of the patriotic demands'.[15] It also came three days after the second round of fighting between the Resistance and the LKP, which had started in Dikwani (north of Beirut). When the cabinet was formed on 23 May, the LNM declared a general strike, hoping to bring down the military cabinet. On 24 May an Islamic conference was convened to demand that Rifai resign.[16]

A Syrian initiative to mediate in the conflict took place on 24 May when Khaddam, the Syrian Foreign Minister, and the Syrian Defence Vice-Minister, General Jamil, arrived in Beirut. Apparently, they convinced the military cabinet that it should resign, which it did on 26 May. The Syrians also persuaded Franjieh to ask Karami, the Tahaluf (alliance) candidate for the premiership, to form a cabinet. Karami accepted the offer on 28 May. However, both he and the LNM were adamant in their refusal to include the LKP in the new cabinet.[17] Given this predicament, Syria was instrumental in convincing the LKP to accept the formation of the cabinet without the LKP being represented in it.

The LNM then called for a new National Pact that reflected the various changes and developments that had occurred in Lebanon in the last 30 years.[18] The LNM also wanted to prevent any military officer from assuming the posts of Defence Minister and Interior Minister, since the army was clearly biased in favour of the Maronite right wing. Furthermore, it intended to bar the LKP and its allies from any future cabinet, so as to isolate the party from Lebanese politics. This last position did not sit well with the

Muslim establishment, which wanted to leave its options open as regards the LKP. On 1 June 1975, Jumblatt stated that the Muslim establishment had agreed with him on this last point. However, Salam, Musa Sadr and others were quick to deny it.[19]

This internal political crisis went on unabated, taking on new dimensions as it festered. The LKP drew upon President Sadat of Egypt as a counter-weight to Karami and his Syrian backers. Arafat also entered the picture when he met with Chamoun on 13 June in an attempt to facilitate the form-ation of the cabinet and thus end the crisis.[20]

Meanwhile, on 15 June Israel attacked the south (Arkoub and Nabatiyeh). These attacks coincided with isolated LKP attacks in Beirut which attempted to resume the fighting on a large scale. The fighting was intended to abort the formation of a cabinet that precluded LKP participation. The problem was compounded when the Syrian mediation efforts failed to reach a solution by 17 June. This situation prompted Jumblatt to meet with Hafiz al-Asad, the Syrian president, in Damascus in an attempt to revitalize efforts to isolate the LKP from mainstream Lebanese and Arab politics.

The failure of Syrian efforts to convince the LKP not to be included in the cabinet allowed the LKP to make further threats to 'Cypriotize' Lebanon (partition the country and internationalize the crisis through United Nations intervention) if it were not included in the cabinet. In an attempt to bring about a peaceful solution to the constitutional and political crisis, Arafat met with President Franjieh on 24 June, four days after this LKP threat. The LKP, however, with the Israeli card in its favour, banked on a military solution to guarantee its participation in the cabinet and to sabotage the Palestinian attempt to defuse the crisis. To this end, the LKP initiated hostilities on 24 June, attacking the Chiyyah area of Beirut from its strong-hold of Ayn al-Rummaneh. This attack signified the beginning of the third round of fighting.[21] The armed forced entered the battle on the LKP side, by helping to shell the LNM area of Chiyyah. The LKP followed these attacks by a visit to the President, in an attempt to influence him over the formation of the cabinet.

This LKP offensive forced Imam Musa Sadr to take action in opposition to the LKP. By openly undermining the LKP, the Imam attempted to convince the predominantly Shiite area of Chiyyah that not only the LNM but also the traditional Muslim establishment (he himself being in that category, in this instance) was on the side of the people. To further exemplify his point, the Imam went into seclusion in the Amliyyah mosque and vowed not to come out until the LKP stopped its attacks on the Chiyyah area.[22] Undaunted, the LKP continued its offensive and carried out another attack in another largely Shiite area, Karantina, where Marxist LNM and PFLP forces were powerful. This 29 June attack, however, was completely defeated by these forces.[23]

On 20 June, Jumblatt left for Egypt to consult with Sadat on the Lebanese situation. This visit was a part of a series of meetings that Jumblatt con-ducted with Franjieh, Asad, Khaddam, Kazem al-Khalil (the Vice-President of the Party of Free Nationalists, the PFN) and the Muslim establishment. The visit was also part of a tour by Jumblatt that included Rumania. Despite the fact that some LNM fighters had entered battle in support of the Resistance and to defend LNM areas, Jumblatt's visit indicated that the LNM was still committed to a diplomatic solution to the crisis. In point of fact, the Jumblatt forces (the Druze followers and the SPP) held back, as did most of the LNM organizations.[24]

## July 1975: A Karami Cabinet

On 1 July 1975, Karami formed his cabinet and also assumed the post of Defence Minister. Chamoun, the PFN chief, took the post of Interior Minister. The other members were: Osseiran, Taqla, Arslan and Tueini. One of the cabinet's first acts was to register 55 complaints against Israel with the United Nations.

On the day the cabinet was formed, the LKP decided to extend the conflagration to the Bekaa region. On the same day the Imam ended his seclusion to seek an end to the fighting in the Shiite town of Qa in the Bekaa. On 7 July, hostilities spread to the north of Lebanon, when the city of Tripoli (an LNM stronghold) and Zgharta (where the Franjieh family comes from) became the scene of fierce fighting.

The entire month of July was also witness to intense Israeli raids. Several air strikes occurred on Palestinian refugee camps all over Lebanon between 7-13 July. Other raids took place on 19 and 23 July. These raids were accompanied by intermittent explosions, kidnappings and killings, mainly in Beirut.[25]

The LKP offensive against Karantina, which was defeated by the LNM and the PFLP, signalled a shift in the LKP's portrayal of the Lebanese problem. Because of its insistence on entering the cabinet, its propaganda and fighting arms attacked those forces that were behind the decision to isolate it. These attacks were facilitated by Israeli raids which preoccupied most of the Resistance forces, especially when these raids were targeted against all Palestinian refugee camps in Lebanon.

Although hostilities in the Bekaa and in the north were contained, the Israeli raids and the ceasefire violations, mostly by the right wing, were serious enough to threaten the peace. In fact, as early as 6 July Jumblatt predicted a new round of fighting.[26]

With regard to the formation of the Karami cabinet, it must be said at the outset that the isolation and non-participation of the LKP was at least a propaganda victory for Jumblatt and the LNM. Matters, however, were deeper than that. The LNM was not represented in this new cabinet, and the LNM slogan regarding 'the cabinet of patriotic demands' was not being fulfilled. Furthermore, the right wing, despite the lack of the LKP participation in the cabinet, still emerged with a supreme position in the state. It had the Presidency, the Army Command, the Ministry of the Interior and at least one other cabinet post (Arslan's). The rest of the cabinet members were not very sympathetic to the LNM. The Muslim establishment was very well represented by Karami.[27] As it turned out, LNM's diplomatic efforts (domestic, Arab and international) to defuse the crisis worked against the movement. The LNM entered into all these deals at a time when it was apparent that the right wing was unwilling to compromise, and was adamant in its efforts to strengthen its position, in order to prevail in the polity at the expense of its enemies, mainly represented by the LNM.

The right wing was so powerful in the state that on 15 July the army ordered a curfew in the south without the knowledge of the Prime Minister. The right wing, through its state machinery, further exercised power by conducting mass arrests of LNM members in LNM areas. The following day, 18 July, the LNM warned the state of the serious consequences that these arrests might have. The LNM threatened to call for a general strike if its members were not released.[28]

These tactics made it abundantly clear that the right wing was not interested in a peaceful resolution of the crisis. Nor was it willing to tolerate constitutional reform that was inimical to its interests. The struggle to secure the best deal in the cabinet was merely a political move to enhance the LKP's position and its ability to 'legally' utilize the armed forces and other state institutions to its benefit. This enhanced legal position allowed the right wing to utilize methods otherwise inaccessible in its dealings with international efforts to stabilize Lebanon in the interest of the LKP.

With the LKP and its allies firmly in control of the state, the only rational course open to the LNM was to seek a political resolution of the crisis. The LNM was militarily weak and its ally, the Palestinian Resistance, though militarily strong, had opted for a diplomatic solution which was in concurrence with Syrian policy aims for Lebanon. Furthermore, the LNM realized that there was considerable conflict between major groupings of the Muslim establishment, the LKP and the PFN. This made the LNM believe that it could win the Muslim establishment to its side, and that in the long run the LNM could prevail upon the Muslim establishment through mass action to agree to the LNM-sponsored reforms. This line of thinking was plausible, at least in theory, since the Muslim establishment relied on a mass base that was increasingly shifting to the LNM. In addition, other pro-system Maronites and other Christians were anti-LKP. It was auspicious for the LNM to ally with these forces to isolate and weaken this formidable right-wing encroachment.

The LNM also realized that Arab policies were in favour of a solution whereby Karami would become Prime Minister and as an old Chehabist, would institute certain reforms.[29] In point of fact, the result of Jumblatt's Arab politicking may be summed up in one sentence: 'Lebanon needs a president who carries on the thought of Chehab.'[30] The fundamental reason for the LNM position, however, revolved around the specific make-up of the LNM coalition. Diverse ideological commitments and rivalries made it extremely difficult for all LNM member groups to agree on the same policies.

This explains, in large part, the passive resistance of the LNM during the first several months on the military front.

## Syria's Special Relationship

In carrying out its first political initiative in Lebanon, Syria's concern was to maintain stability and prevent (or at least restrict) other Arab rivals (Iraq and Egypt, primarily) from intervening diplomatically in Lebanon. To this end, Syria convinced the Saudi government that, with its special relationship with Lebanon, Syria could bring about a solution that would be congruent with Arab policies. Arab policies were then seeking stability in the region and the status quo through a comprehensive settlement of the Arab-Israeli problem and its core, the Palestinian question.[31]

That Syria had a special relation with Lebanon was beyond question. In more recent times and before the 13 April bus massacre, a summit meeting had been held between Asad and Franjieh on 7 January 1975 at Shtura in the Bekaa. A joint communiqué was issued at that time that assured Lebanon of Syria's readiness to support it militarily against external enemies (in reference to Israel). The two countries also agreed to political and military co-ordination between them. Syria followed this by a call on 24 March to all the Arab countries to join in a unified military command. Meanwhile, talks were under way between the PLO, the Syrians and the Lebanese concerning the Syrian proposal of a joint Syrian-Palestinian leadership.[32]

Syria's position in Lebanon was extremely strong. It also reflected the mandate that Saudi Arabia and other Arab states had given Syria to pursue a policy in Lebanon that was congruent with the Saudi position (primarily) on the regional settlement. Indeed, Karami's appointment as Prime Minister was a triumph for these policies and a defeat for Israeli attempts, in Lebanon and in the region, to counter the Syrian and Arab position on the settlement issue. Israel's means of derailing this Arab plan in Lebanon were its air raids and its co-ordination with the right wing, especially the LKP, to escalate the situation as early as the late 1960s. Even as early as 1973, Syria attempted to counter these Israeli moves and the Kissinger step-by-step diplomacy in the area by forming a unified political-military committee with Jordan on 6 June 1973.[33] While all elements in the region were in favour of containing the revolutionary process, whose storm centre was the PLO/LNM alliance, their co-operation (direct and indirect) ended there. This was even clear in the case of the LKP and Israel's co-operation in Lebanon.

## The Phalangists Shift Their Ground

Seeing that Arab policies were not in its favour at that time, the LKP reverted to tactics of rapprochement. The month of July and most of August 1975 saw diplomatic efforts by all the parties to the conflict to enhance their respective positions vis-à-vis each other. Israeli raids continued, which had the potential of sabotaging the Arab drive for a comprehensive settlement and enhancing the right-wing position, if only for the simple reason that such raids diverted Palestinian forces away from engaging right-wing troops.

These right-wing tactics were not new. The LKP had earlier resorted to them when the need arose. As early as 1 January 1975 the LKP chief had attacked the political and military work of the Palestinian Resistance as a whole in Lebanon. This was contrary to his earlier divide-and-rule tactic of the 'honourable' versus the 'dishonourable' Palestinian guerrilla activities. A second verbal attack on the Resistance followed shortly afterwards, while a third came on 20 February. These attacks, it seems, were a part of the LKP strategy that eventually led to the April bus massacre.

On 23 April 1975 the LKP was supported by the Permanent Conference of the Maronite Order of Monks, which warned of 'the loss of the Lebanese character'[34] due to subversive ideologies. These ideologies, of course, meant Arab nationalism and communism. When the LNM decided to isolate the LKP as a response to the bus massacre, the Maronite League attacked the decision on 28 April and the LKP accused the 'extreme' left of working to subvert the political system. However, the LNM was still working to arrive at a peaceful solution to the crisis, and the Palestinian Resistance had repeatedly declared its concern for Lebanese sovereignty and the unity of the Lebanese, and in reciprocation Premier Solh emphasized Lebanon's concern for the Resistance on 29 April 1975. Franjieh also expressed his feelings about the Resistance's position on Lebanon and declared that there was no problem between the Lebanese authorities and the Resistance.[35]

Having realized that it was isolated, the LKP softened its stance and began to talk of national unity. This was also a reaction to the LNM's call on 13 July 1975 to abolish confessionalism and reform the electoral law. The following day Asaad called for a new National Pact. These developments prompted Gemayel, the accomplished anti-leftist, to declare that he distinguished between a 'positive Lebanese left' and a 'subversive international left'.[36] On 17 July, however, Gemayel attacked the Resistance and those who dragged it into the fight to impose socialism in Lebanon.[37]

The talk about national unity was crucial to the LKP and the right wing in general. They intended to counter the LNM's proposals and split the Muslim establishment and other pro-system forces that supported certain reforms proposed by the LNM. When the Assembly of Catholic Bishops called for national unity on 22 July Jumblatt, who had recently returned from a trip to North Africa, renewed the LNM's call to abolish confessionalism and develop the system. The Mufti (the Muslim religious leader), however, welcomed the bishop's statement. To counter the LNM's call for reform, the Maronite Monks called for a 'comprehensive and conscious cultural revolution'.[38] This incomprehensible statement was followed by the commencement of Muslim-Christian dialogue on 31 July, at the suggestion of the President of the Maronite League.[39]

## August 1975: Israel Keeps up the Pressure

The month of August witnessed increased Israeli attacks. Tyre was hit from land, sea and air on 5 August. Two southern villages were hit on 7 August, and still another, Yarine, was hit on 11 August. These attacks came hard on the heels of Karami's visit to Damascus, where Syria re-affirmed its commitment to the defence of Lebanon.[40]

On 13 August the LNM discussed the final draft proposal it intended to present to the state dealing with the reform of the political system. The LNM's position was reinforced when, on the 15th, the Greek Orthodox Patriarch, Elias the Fourth, attacked the LKP, confessional privileges and the National Pact. On the same day the Nasserist member of the parliament, Wakim, called for the direct election of the President by the people and for reform of the political system.[41]

Assessing that the situation was not favourable to it, the LKP called for 'dialogue', the support of the Resistance and the respect of Lebanon's sovereignty and the Lebanese-Palestinian accords. The LKP 'rejects the attempt to lure the party towards any conspiracy and calls upon the state to realize equality and be just to the deprived and supports the struggle of the Palestinian people . . .'.[42]

On 18 August Jumblatt announced the LNM's programme for political reform. It called for a new Arab, patriotic and democratic Lebanon where confessionalism would be abolished and basic human rights would be protected. It also called for a new electoral law whereby Lebanon would become one electoral district and every 10,000 citizen voters would be represented by one member of parliament. Other points in the programme dealt with the rights of the President and other executive offices. They also specified a Supreme Defence Council and a Council of the Armed Forces to limit the authority of the Army Commander. The programme also dealt with the separation of powers between the three branches of government, and with administrative reforms.[43]

While these events were taking place, Israel attacked Tyre on 16 August, and the Arkoub region, Maroun al-Raass, Sidon, and other areas of the south on 19 August. Other attacks followed the next day in the Bekaa and the town of Sirghaya on the Lebanese-Syrian border.[44] Meanwhile, Sadat of Egypt attacked the Resistance on 21 August. As he put it, he feared for 'the Resistance's future in Lebanon, if its positions remained contrary to the general Arab position.'[45] He further suggested the transfer of the PLO headquarters from Beirut to Cairo. On that day Kissinger arrived in the region. Talks between Israel and Egypt were held on the following day. On 24 August rallies were held in Beirut and other areas of Lebanon to protest at the partial Sinai agreements. On 27 August, Israel called for an end to the Resistance's activities in Lebanon.[46]

On 23 August, the LKP had sent a memorandum to Franjieh and to the Maronite Patriarch calling for the secularization of the state as a basis for the abolition of confessionalism. The LKP sought to accomplish two major goals by sending the memorandum: the first was to make it clear to the Lebanese that it too was for secularization; the second was to counter the LNM reform programme, which specified that the first step towards complete secularization was reform of the electoral law to do away with confessional representation in parliament. The first step would also abolish confessionalism from the army, the civil service and the local government, while leaving the offices of President and Premier to be reformed in a second stage. It appeared that the LKP was more radical than the LNM because it was for total secularization of the state in a single step. The choice, as far as the LKP was concerned, was either that its suggestion would be followed or that no secularization could occur in Lebanon.[47]

Meanwhile, Israeli land and air attacks and shelling occurred on 25 August, followed by other attacks on 28 August on the town of Bourgholiyyah. Tyre was also shelled on 29 August, and Kfarshouba was attacked on 31 August.[48]

The fourth round of fighting began on 28 August because of the deteriorating situation in the Bekaa. Suddenly the right wing began to talk about the partition of Lebanon.[49] In opposition to partition, Eddé, the prominent Maronite leader, declared: 'A Christian Lebanon will be a second Israel.'[50] Eddé had opted for a unified Lebanon, with certain reforms that would not drastically change the political system. He and the Maronite Patriarch were considered to be 'doves', whereas the Maronite 'hawks' were Gemayel, Akl, Chamoun and Father Kassiss (of the Maronite Order of Monks).

The events that followed the formation of the Karami cabinet and which culminated in the outbreak of violence on a large scale on 28 August proved that a political solution was neither desirable nor practical for the Maronite right wing. This right wing was not prepared to share Lebanon with other reform-oriented groups. It seemed that the LNM was cognizant of this fact, yet it kept pursuing a political solution. Aside from the reasons that were given earlier as an explanation of the LNM position, the fundamental reasons need to be discussed in some detail.

## Three Trends within the LNM

It must be stated at once that the LNM was formed as a coalition in reaction to the right-wing attacks on the revolutionary movement in 1969. The LNM comprised diverse ideological groups with allegiances to various countries and/or classes. The major categories within the LNM were: (1) the pro-Syrian groups, (2) the independent Lebanese group and (3) the pro-Iraq groups. The Baath Party Organization (BPO), the Union of Working Peoples' Forces (UWPF – one of four Nasserist organizations) and Imam Musa Sadr's Movement of the Deprived (MD) belonged to the first category. The SPP (led by Jumblatt), the major SNP group (led by Imam Ra'd), the Communist Party (CP), the Organization of Communist Action (OCA), the Arab Socialist Action Party (ASAP), the Independent Nasserist Movement (INM) and two other Nasserist movements belonged to the second category. In the third category was the Arab Baath Socialist Party (ABSP).

Each of the categories displays ideological variations within it. This kind of categorization is valid, however, for the following reasons.

(1) Groups in the first category remained allies throughout the war. They consistently supported Syria and at one point split from the LNM to form their own front.

(2) The second set of groups was not under the direct or indirect influence of any country. They took positions on issues guided by their own analyses which at times coincided with Syria's strategy and at times did not. More important, however, unlike the groups of the first category, they were the authors of the LNM 'minimum programme'.[51]

(3) The ABSP is not included in the second category only to reflect the fact that it was heavily supported by Iraq, where the all-Arab National Command of the party has its headquarters. Major strategies and directives emanated from the Command. The ABSP, however, had policy positions close to the SPP and the CP. Some of its leaders were also special envoys of the LNM to Europe and other places. The party was also among the authors of the 'minimum programme'.

(4) Finally, a categorization by ideology which is abstracted from the concrete conditions of Lebanon would: (a) lump all the Nasserist organizations together, regardless of their different positions vis-à-vis Syria, to the detriment of the analysis of events; (b) include the ABSP and BPO together, regardless of the glaring animosities between the two wings of the Baath; (c) face problems in categorizing the SPP and the SSNP — the first being strictly Lebanese but pro-Arab, while the second is Syrian Nationalist with Marxist undertones; and (d) have to include the CP, OCA and ASAP together as Marxist-Leninists, rather than as independent Lebanese parties in the sense that the term was used above. The difficulty with this categorization is that these Marxist-Leninist parties have different positions on Arab nationalism and Arab policies in general.[52]

The presence of pro-Syrian components within the LNM certainly influenced the course of action that the LNM took, especially in relation to participation (or lack of it) in the Karami cabinet. Since the various LNM components did not fully prepare themselves militarily for the conflict, the LNM had to rely upon Syria for supplies. This weakness precluded any serious thinking about an all-out offensive against the right wing.

The CP and the OCA, although they were for reform in Lebanon along the lines spelled out in the 'minimum programme', shared the same views as the Syrians and the Resistance on a Middle East settlement. An offensive against the right wing at that time would have upset Syria's calculations for a settlement opposed to Kissinger's step-by-step negotiations. A quick and peaceful solution, they reasoned, must be sought for Lebanon while efforts were to be made to effect peaceful change in Lebanon. Diplomacy and Arab pressure, they felt, were enough to convince the right wing to reconsider its methods. The capacity of the right wing and Israel to sabotage any attempt to reach a peaceful solution that did not favour the right wing was apparently overlooked in this analysis.[53]

The SPP also sought a peaceful solution, on the grounds that the majority of the political forces and people in Lebanon were in favour of reform and in support of a pro-Palestinian policy. The main strategy to reach such a solution was to apply maximum pressure on the right wing to give up its military options. As with the CP and the OCA, the SPP did not realize that the right wing had reached the point of no return and that any pressure against the Maronite right wing would be eased by Israeli military action and by the inconsistencies of Arab politics, which the right wing was skilled in exploiting.

The fourth round of fighting proved beyond a shadow of a doubt that the LNM, if it were to implement its reforms, must smash the right wing militarily. The 'fear' of Israeli raids of intervention if a military solution were pursued was for the most part unjustified. Lebanon was already experiencing almost daily attacks on its southern borders and heavy Israeli incursions deep into its territory. Because of these attacks, Jumblatt had in fact called for the shelling of Israeli settlements in retaliation for the destruction of Lebanese villages by Israel.[54]

The few parties within the LNM that called for a tougher military stance against the right wing were in practice overruled. All the parties, save the pro-Syrian groups, were in agreement on the nature of the Lebanese system and its conservative establishment. What separated them, however, was how to effect change.[55] Indeed, these months revealed the actual ideologies (labels aside) of the parties and organizations that comprised the LNM.

## September 1975: Beirut's Destruction

The fourth round of fighting continued in September. On the first of the month, major clashes occurred in Zahle. In addition to continued fighting in Zahle on 2 September, fighting erupted in Tripoli and Zgharta in the north, and intensified on 4 September. On 9 September, Beirut exploded and by then the fighting was raging throughout Lebanon. Concurrently, Israel conducted air strikes against Hasbaya on 2 September and against Tyre the following day. Israel also attempted a naval landing at Sidon the following day.[56]

Meanwhile, the right wing pressured Karami to use the army in the conflict, and in fact he called upon the army to intervene on 3 September. Jumblatt, who had already called, the day before, for the resignation of the cabinet because it was unable to keep the peace, intensified his attacks against the state for its use of the army. To appease the LNM, the President dismissed Army Commander Ghanem on 10 September, and appointed Hanna Said in his place.[57]

On 15 September, Jumblatt announced that without reform it was impossible to bring an end to the fighting. This announcement was countered by the Maronite League, which declared that the source of the problem was an Israeli creation.[58] The League was implying that if it were not for the Palestinians in Lebanon, there would have been no fighting, and thus reforms were unnecessary.

The September fighting resulted in the complete destruction of Beirut's commercial district and its city centre. In an attempt to prevent any further damage, the cabinet formed a reconciliation committee. The PLO, which since 9 September had announced that it did not wish to be involved in the fighting, was instrumental in the reconciliation efforts. Arafat met on 19 September with the traditional leaders Yafi, Salam, Karami and Mufti, to discuss reconciliation.[59] The next day Gemayel threatened to internationalize the crisis. To further complicate matters, the LKP set up a clandestine radio station (the Voice of Lebanon) to propagandize its cause.

## October 1975: National Dialogue

The LNM's pressure against the state, and Arafat's efforts with the traditional leaders, bore fruit. On 24 September the combatants agreed to discuss their differences in a newly-formed National Dialogue Committee (NDC).[60] The following day the NDC met in the presidential palace, where Khaddam, the Syrian Foreign Minister, attended the conclusion of its meeting. The NDC met nine times altogether; its last meeting was held on 14 November. On 13 October, the NDC decided to form three subcommittees to consider political, economic and social reforms. The most important of these was the political reform committee, which altogether had six meetings; the first was held on 16 October and the last on 14 November.[61]

The NDC consisted of 20 members, most of whom represented the various factions of the dominant class in Lebanon: Yafi, Salam, Eddé, Taqla, Jumblatt, Gemayel, Chamoun, Tueini, Asaad, Arslan, Osseiran, Rabbat, Khalaf and Qansu.[62] The last two plus Jumblatt were the LNM representatives. The representation was along confessional lines, which was opposed by the LNM. However, the LNM agreed to enter the committee after registering its reservation over the committee's make-up. The LNM's main concern at that time was to begin dialogue to effect change.[63]

The first meeting was typical of the rest of the meetings in all the committees and subcommittees, and set the tone for those that followed. Two major trends were evident in the NDC. Jumblatt and the traditional leaders (Muslim and Christian), save for the LKP and PFN representatives (Gemayel and Chamoun, respectively), were for constitutional changes and other reforms. The LKP and PFN wanted no reform whatsoever. In the first meeting Jumblatt presented the 'minimum programme' of the LNM, while Salam and Yafi advanced the need for constitutional change to reflect the demographic changes that had occurred in Lebanon over the past three decades (i.e. the fact that the Muslims were now the majority in the country).[64] Gemayel would not hear of any change and proclaimed:

The present Lebanese framework is one that safeguards our national unity and it is the successful framework.

Further,

With regard to amending the constitution we in the LKP are against this discussion, and if there is insistence upon it I will allow myself not to attend the meetings . . .

My basic observation is that the Lebanese Muslim holds on to the present Lebanese framework [confessionalism?], as for other thoughts [on changing the political system] they are imported either from some Arab system or inspired by Israeli conspiracies.

As for social justice, it cannot be through slogans. And we created in Lebanon, which has no petroleum, a national economy that guarantees for the citizen the highest levels. And it might require development, but not change.[65]

A study of Lebanon's politics and economics clearly shows these statements to be pure rhetoric. More important, perhaps, is that these statements reflect what could generally be termed the political thought of the Maronite right wing.[66] And certainly it would be rational to assume that the LKP was not interested in dialogue to bring about reform. In point of fact, each time the NDC or its political-reform subcommittee raised the question of reform, the LKP took exception to it and instead raised the issue of law and order as a requirement that must be met before any dialogue could take place.[67] In essence, this meant that the LKP was against any peaceful solution and did not want any compromise. From the outset the right wing, which was cornered into accepting participation in the NDC, was probing for ways in which to undermine it. On 30 September a massacre was committed in an LKP stronghold against Palestinian Christians living in Ayn al-Rummaneh. The crime sabotaged the NDC's third meeting.[68]

On 8 October, fighting erupted throughout Lebanon and Karami threatened to resign if the fighting did not stop. The following day the Permanent Conference of the Order of Monks issued a statement rejecting the efforts of the NDC. Franjieh was also against the NDC, especially when it was dealing with constitutional amendments to limit his powers as President, and when some of its members (Salam and Eddé) were calling for his resignation.[69]

The LKP began to agitate for the Arabization of the crisis.[70] The party was aware that the NDC was heavily influenced by the Syrian position, which concurred to varying degrees with those of the LNM and the pro-system forces in opposition to the Maronite right wing. The LKP hoped that the direct involvement of other Arab countries would counterbalance Syria's influence in such a way that the LKP would be able to legitimize its efforts against the LNM. Furthermore, the LKP, in dealing a heavy blow to the LNM and the Resistance, would have weakened the anti-settlement forces in the region. This line of thinking, of which the LKP's opponents were aware, prompted the LNM to reject and work against Arabization. Qansu of the BPO announced that 'no Arab country has the right to intervene in Lebanon except Syria.'[71]

The right wing continued its efforts to sabotage the NDC. On 14 October, the Maronite League and the Maronite Order of Monks issued a joint memorandum which they delivered to Franjieh, rejecting any dialogue before Lebanon regained its sovereignty (this referred to the Resistance's presence in Lebanon).[72] This statement was in support of Gemayel's position in the NDC. The communiqué included another important feature: it called for the internationalization of the crisis. On 16 October, Gemayel came out in full support of the communiqué. This was significant in that it showed that the Maronite right-wing components were in agreement on the NDC and on internationalization. It appeared that Gemayel agreed to internationalization after his version of Arabization came to nothing when the Conference of Arab Foreign Ministers failed to reach any decision on Lebanon at its meeting on 15 October.[73]

A fifth round of fighting began on 19 October which paved the way for the LKP to withdraw from the NDC. In an attempt to block internationalization, Jumblatt met with Asad and they both stated that Syria and the LNM had been successful in preventing the partition of Lebanon, and that both were against the internationalization of the crisis. Two days later, on 23 October, Karami attacked the President and Chamoun, and insisted that the army must not get involved in the fighting. Karami was supported by the Lebanese Islamic summit meeting in Aramoun. The presence of Arafat and Jumblatt at this meeting, which took place on 25 October, showed that the Maronite right wing was alone in its demand to involve the army in the fighting.[74]

In Beirut, a new front was opened when the 'battle of the hotels' started on the day of the Aramoun summit. During the next two days, fierce fighting raged throughout the country, with reports that the army, acting on orders from Chamoun, was assisting the right-wing forces. The LKP and the other right-wing forces, however, were defeated on all fronts, especially in Beirut.[75]

Karami went into seclusion in the Sarail (the Cabinet's headquarters), where he formed a security committee in an attempt to stop the fighting. The next day, 29 October, he arranged a cease-fire, which held in Beirut and other areas except in Zahle. Apparently, the right wing agreed to the cease-fire because, among other things, it meant that the LNM would pull out from positions it had captured in the fighting.[76]

## November 1975: Collapse of the NDC

By 4 November, reports from the Lebanese security forces indicated that the LKP had violated the cease-fire on various occasions.[77] On the same day the complicity of the Army Command with the right wing became clear when a huge ship loaded with arms docked at the Acqua-Marina in Junieh, the right-wing makeshift capital. The ship was unloading arms in plain view of the army. Furthermore, the ship could not have entered port without the army having been aware of it.[78]

On 12 November, the political-reform subcommittee of the NDC agreed to abolish confessionalism in the civil service, the judiciary and the armed forces. In addition, confessionalism was to be abolished in the electoral laws. It was further agreed that reference should not be made to the higher offices (the Presidency, the Premiership, the House Speaker) since the constitution did not include statements that indicated the confessions of the people who could fill these offices.[79] In fact, only the National Pact specified that the President must be Maronite and the Premier Sunni Muslim.

Edmond Rizk, who was substituting for Gemayel, was in agreement with these points, which were proposed at an extended meeting that included representatives of all the parties to the conflict. The sixth meeting of this subcommittee, which took place on 14 November, confirmed the agreements reached in the previous meeting. The meeting, however, was not attended by the LKP representative, while two other members, Rabbat and Salam, sent word that they were unable to attend. The meeting was attended by other NDC members.[80]

The following day, the extended meeting to discuss the agreements reached at the fifth meeting of the political-reform sub-committee on 12 November was held. Gemayel and Chamoun, who were present, opposed the recommendations of the sub-committee.[81]

The ninth meeting of the NDC, held on 24 November, was dominated by Gemayel and Karami: Salam used it to accuse the Interior Minister, Chamoun, and the President of being responsible for the continued crisis. Both of these people, he argued, had private armies at their disposal which were fighting with the Maronite right wing. The meeting ended with a major squabble as to the responsibility of the President for the continued crisis. This degeneration in dialogue marked the end of the NDC period.[82]

The demise of the NDC was also related to concentrated international efforts to end the crisis. As was mentioned earlier, the right wing had opted for internationalization, while the LNM and Syria were trying to combat these actions.[83] On 12 November, the Greek Orthodox representatives clarified to the Papal envoy, who had arrived in Beirut three days earlier, the need for change in the political system, for dialogue and the need to support the PLO.[84] This was followed by a US announcement opposing partition. Couve de Murville, the French envoy, also came out against partition while Eddé, on 20 November, attacked right-wing schemes that were designed to partition the country.[85] Eddé was followed by Jumblatt, on 25 November, who attacked the President and Chamoun and asked for their resignation.[86] The following day UN Secretary-General Waldheim arrived in Beirut, where he declared that the solution was in the hands of the Lebanese, who must avoid any foreign intervention.[87] The right-wing plan began to crumble when Couve de Murville supported Syria's efforts in Lebanon and suggested that some reforms were needed in the political system. The following day, 28

November, Chamoun presented Couve de Murville with a partition plan, while Karami began to prepare a plan for reform to bring about stability.[88] The LNM agreed to Karami's proposals, but warned that the plan should not be at the price of diluting the essence of the crisis.[89]

A part of the plan called for expanding the Cabinet. On 30 November, the President did expand it. The LNM regarded this move as an effort to dilute the essence of the crisis by making it seem as if it were a squabble over the number of Cabinet seats. For this reason, the LNM demanded that reform should precede the Cabinet expansion. The Sunni Muslim summit meeting on 5 November at Karami's residence advised him to work for reform before enlarging the Cabinet.[90]

## December 1975: Differences within the LNM

An important development began to take shape within the LNM during this period. Differences arose between the pro-Syrian component and the other components of the LNM regarding the method of dealing with the attempts at internationalizaiton. Jumblatt was of the opinion that the rest of the Arabs must help in pressuring the Lebanese right wing and other countries to relinquish attempts to internationalise the conflict. Furthermore, Jumblatt attacked Karami, when the former returned from an Arab tour on 4 December. When the LNM rejected expanding the Cabinet, Qansu of the pro-Syrian BPO lauded Karami's cabinet decision.[91] It appeared that the Syrians wanted to assure the LKP that a solution to its liking could be achieved without resorting to international efforts. It also seemed that this was a clever move by Syria, which could convince the LKP to co-operate with Damascus especially when the foreign envoys were against partition and foreign intervention.[92]

The LKP was quick to realize Syria's intentions, which became clear when Asad extended an invitation to Gemayel to visit Damascus on 6 December. There Gemayel announced that co-operation between Syria and Lebanon was a 'safety valve' to the two countries.[93] Meanwhile, Asad informed Yafi (who was visiting Damascus) that Gemayel had given guarantees to Syria that the LKP was in favour of the expansion of the cabinet. The expansion of the Cabinet signalled the beginning of co-operation between Franjieh and Karami, who were at odds with each other up until late November. The LKP gave Asad assurances that it would work in support of the Karami-Franjieh co-operation.[94]

The Syrian decision to invite the LKP was an affront to the LNM, which had been working to isolate the party from Arab politics. The LNM took exception to this move, especially when the LKP was involved on 6 December in what came to be known as Black Saturday. That day LKP party members killed 70 innocent civilians and kidnapped 300 others at various LKP checkpoints in Beirut. On 7 December the LNM demanded that the state put the LKP on trial for these atrocities.[95]

The period of 8-13 December witnessed heavy fighting throughout

Lebanon and the LKP was forced to retreat in the face of LNM attacks on all major fronts, especially in the hotel areas. On 10 December Franjieh accused 'the left and Zionism' of instigating what had been happening in Lebanon. This accusation drew heavy fire from the LNM and other pro-system leaders, who accused Franjieh of demagogy.[96] The LKP shelled residential quarters in LNM-held areas on 11 December to ease pressure on its fighters in Beirut.[97] The LNM, however, kept up its offensive until a cease-fire was negotiated and took hold on 14 December.

To further counter LKP efforts to sabotage the LNM's efforts to reach a settlement through peaceful means, Jumblatt visited Damascus on two occasions in an attempt to convince Asad not to co-operate with the LKP. Jumblatt also tried to convince Asad of the need to reform the political system along the lines specified by the LNM.[98]

Back in Lebanon, Jumblatt accused the President of violating the Constitution by siding with the right-wing forces. Jumblatt also demanded the President's resignation. On 19 December General Hikmat al-Chehabi, the Syrian envoy, met with Franjieh, Chamoun, Gemayel, Karami, Salam, Yafi, Sadr and Arafat in an attempt to reconcile the conventional zuama with each other. The PLO's position was reflected by Arafat's meeting with these conventional zuama, and it was echoed the following day in Kuwait by another top PLO official, Abu Iyad, who announced: 'The Resistance needs neither victory nor defeat in Lebanon. We respect our commitment towards the government . . . We will prevent partition.'[99] This position was in congruence with Syria's position on Lebanon.

On 20 December, the Governor of Northern Lebanon, an SPP member, was assassinated. The incident touched off a fight between Karami and Franjieh in which the former accused the latter's militia of engineering the assassination. The next day Karami left for Damascus to consult with Asad. The Maronite Order of Monks came out in support of the President against Karami and declared that there was a 'Sunni' threat to Lebanon, and further accused the Palestinians of fomenting trouble. Furthermore, the Order announced that the best solution was to go back to the old Lebanon (Mount Lebanon). The Order also expressed these desires to de Murville, telling him that independence was a joke and that the only solution was the state of Mount Lebanon.[100]

Gemayel followed the Order by rejecting Arabism and threatening to work for partition if a 'no victor/no vanquished' solution was not found. He further accused 'international communism' of creating trouble.[101] These right-wing moves came hard on the heels of a statement by Eddé from Washington, DC, on 20 December, in which he accused Zionism of having a plan to create confessional states in the region. Eddé followed these statements by accusing the US on 27 December of being behind plans to partition Lebanon.[102] In Jumblatt's opinion, however, the right wing wanted to dilute the patriotic demands for reform by threatening to bring about partition if a 'no victor/no vanquished' solution was not adopted.[103]

Having failed to achieve its goals so far, the right wing resorted to the old tactics of Arabizing the crisis. It hoped once more that the Arab states would be able to help it defeat the LNM and the Resistance, which Syria wanted only to contain. The Order of Monks called for a federated state. Saudi Arabia took a position against partition and Arabization of the conflict and declared that any Arabization would have to be through Syria's efforts.[104] Meanwhile, Eddé warned of another round of fighting in the making which would enhance the right-wing position in any future negotiations. He was referring to the right-wing plan to attack and occupy LNM areas, a move that would encourage partition.

## January 1976: The Threat of Partition

Indeed, the right-wing offensive began on 4 January 1976, with sniper fire and kidnappings in Beirut and a concentrated attack by the LKP and PFN troops on Tal al-Zatar.[105] Fearful of a serious attempt at partition by the right wing, Syria's Foreign Minister Khaddam announced that 'Lebanon was a part of Syria and we will get it back in any partition attempt; either it will remain unified or it goes back to Syria.'[106] This statement prompted Gemayel and Chamoun to attack Khaddam.

Meanwhile, on 7 January, Jumblatt left for Saudi Arabia and upon his return declared that the Saudis were against partition. On that day the fighting spread throughout Beirut, the north, the Bekaa and to parts of the Mountain. On 9 January, Chamoun ordered the army to fight the LNM, especially in the Bekaa. All the Lebanese, except the Maronite right wing, protested at the measures that called upon the army to openly take sides in the conflict. The LKP, however, demanded more involvement by the army against the LNM.[107]

Israel issued several statements in January in which it warned that it could not remain on the sidelines and watch 'Muslim power' grow or any outsider intervene in Lebanon. On 10 January, Prime Minister Rabin issued a similar warning which was designed to counter Khaddam's announcement on the annexation of Lebanon to Syria.[108] On the same day President Sadat of Egypt supported Chamoun against Syria on the issue of annexation.

Khaddam accused Chamoun of co-operating with Israel to bring about partition. He further claimed that Chamoun had presented Syria with a partition plan which Syria had rejected.[109] On 11 January, the LKP surrounded the Palestinian camp of Dubayye. This move was part of the escalation that the right wing was seeking. The camp was the smallest one in Lebanon and was in the midst of LKP territory 15 miles north of Beirut. Any partition plan would have had to call for its surrender.

In an effort to ease the pressure on the camp, which was militarily indefensible, the Combined Forces (the LNM and the Palestinian Resistance now under one command) attacked on many fronts principally in Beirut and the south, and were able to advance against LKP and other right-wing positions. The Resistance clearly saw that the right wing was working to partition the country. Since partition was against the Resistance's policies, it used all its force to try to prevent it. The Combined Forces reoccupied the hotel areas from which the LNM had withdrawn under the stipulations of the last cease-fire, and occupied the strategic Beirut bridge linking Beirut with Mount Lebanon. The Combined Forces also occupied those Beirut suburbs under LKP control where pockets of Palestinian and pro-LNM population existed, such as Tal al-Zatar and Nabah.[110]

The Combined Forces also surrounded Damour in the south and occupied Mishrif, Nameh and other areas along the coast south of Beirut. The offensive appeared to blunt the right-wing offensive.[111] However, the lonely Dubayye camp fell on 14 January to LKP and PFN fighters, who were aided by the army.[112] This right-wing victory came one day after its summit, which had issued a statement that the struggle was with the Palestinians. On 15 January the LKP and PFN attacked Karantina, another LNM area in the midst of right-wing territory in Beirut, which was a threat to the LKP-held port of Beirut and other strategic LKP facilities. As with Dubayye, Karantina had to be occupied to effect partition.

Jumblatt warned that the LKP would commit atrocities against the population if it were allowed to capture Karantina. Arafat met with Arab ambassadors in Beirut, while the Lebanese Islamic summit meeting in Aramoun warned that the army might split if the Army Command aided the LKP in Karantina.[113]

The LKP shrouded its offensive in a diplomatic smokescreen when it called, on 16 January, for an Arab 'initiative' to solve the crisis. The following day the Arab ambassadors met with Karami and Franjieh and informed them that the Arabs supported the Syrian initiative.[114] The LKP's efforts to Arabize the crisis had failed. This failure prompted the LKP to take the issue to the UN. On 18 January the LKP and PFN troops entered Karantina after fierce fighting. The Karantina residents were evicted in buses and were sent to the west side of Beirut. The result of the Karantina takeover had given the right wing the geography of partition.[115]

On 19 January the fighting intensified throughout Lebanon, and a division of the Palestine Liberation Army (PLA) stationed in Syria crossed the border into Lebanon from the Bekaa and the north with heavy equipment.[116] Without any prior consultation with Jumblatt or the LNM, the Resistance leadership gave orders to the Combined Forces to overrun all right-wing areas south of Beirut.[117] The offensive was led by Abu Musa, the Fateh commander in the south. On 20 January all the right-wing positions fell, including Damour and Sadiyyaat, where Chamoun fled from his palace by army helicopter.

On the same day Chamoun called for the internationalization of the crisis. Jumblatt replied that internationalization would not work, because the international community would support the LNM.[118] On that day too, the right wing held talks that sought the unification of its military forces, which included the LKP, PFN, Cedar Guards and Al-Tanzeem, among others.[119]

Around the middle of January, many army units that despised the complicity of the Army Command with the right wing began to withdraw from the army to form the Lebanese Arab Army (LAA) under the command of Lieutenant Ahmad Khatib.[120] This development, plus the victories of the Combined Forces, convinced the right wing to lie low and negotiate with its opponents. The Syrians, who had given their blessing to the Combined Forces' offensive in the south, renewed their initiative of 16 January that had been halted by the right-wing offensive. The right wing (now that it had tried almost everything to block the Syrian initiative) tried to win what it could diplomatically, hoping that having the geography of partition in its hands would enhance its bargaining position.

On 22 January, the LKP, the PFN and the LNM agreed to the Syrian solution: the President would remain a Maronite; the Prime Minister would be elected by Parliament instead of being chosen by the President, subject to parliamentary vote of confidence in the Cabinet; and the parliamentary seats would be distributed equally between Christians and Muslims. A cease-fire was agreed upon, supervised by a military committee made up of Lebanese, Syrian and Palestinian military officers.[121]

On 24 January, despite some cease-fire violations, Jumblatt announced that the war was over.[122] Two days later he called for Franjieh's resignation. The Syrian role, however, was not appreciated by Israel, which was concerned about Lebanon becoming a confrontation state. The US had a different view of Syria's role. It acknowledged the 'positive role that the Syrian government play[ed] in Lebanon'.[123] On 31 January, the Maronite summit welcomed the Syrian initiative and announced that the Maronites had formed what they termed the Front of Freedom and Man.[124] The Resistance also expressed its belief that the war was over.

It appeared that Syria's efforts had been successful in defeating partition and in keeping the political system virtually unchanged. The pro-Syrian forces within the Resistance and the LNM launched a campaign of terror against voices which opposed this solution. On 31 January these forces attacked the left-wing *Al-Muharrer* newspaper in Beirut and killed many of the workers and writers.[125]

On that day Salam rejected the Syrian proposal that the Maronites should retain the Presidency and instead advanced what he had proposed a few days earlier: a Presidential Council of six which would represent the confessions.[126] Meanwhile Jumblatt accused the LKP and PFN of preparing for another round of fighting in the spring. All these events were indications that many problems remained in the way of the solution envisioned by Syria. Nevertheless, the Syrians were adamant in their efforts to stabilize the country.

## Conclusion

Despite the great strides the LNM had achieved on the level of the 'political', the Maronite right wing was in firm control of the state machinery, especially the presidency and the army. The right wing opened up the conflagration with the intention of smashing the LNM and the Resistance through the use of the state's most formidable organ — the army. They had already used the army against the Resistance and unarmed demonstrations of students and workers, even before the Sidon February 1975 incident which, along with the events of 13 April 1975 (bus massacres), ignited the Lebanese Civil War. The Sidon incident, in which Maruf Sa'd, the city deputy who had headed the demonstration of fishermen, was killed, and the subsequent bus incident when members of the LKP ambushed and murdered everyone on board, indicated that the right wing was intent on recouping the other organs of the state from LNM influence. The co-existence of the LNM, the LKP, the PFN and other pro-system forces in the same cabinet, was certainly a temporary arrangement and — given the irreconcilable contradictions between the two forces (LNM and right wing) — unworkable.

The resignation of the military government on 26 May 1975 was a defeat for the right wing and testimony to the fact that the LNM and its allies were powerful enough to challenge the president's prerogative. A regrettable mistake, however, was that the LNM did not pursue its demand for a cabinet in which it would have been heavily represented. This was for various reasons, primarily because it did not want to undermine the Syrian initiative, which was instrumental in the formation of this new cabinet. Furthermore, the LNM preferred a peaceful resolution to the conflict and was banking on resolving this antagonistic contradiction through reformism and the parliamentary process.

The resultant formation of the Karami cabinet on 1 July 1975, and the National Dialogue Committee on 24 September 1975, was an obvious indication that the right wing was unyielding and determined to secure power through all means available. In fact, at that time, the right wing was already preparing for an offensive that would secure the geography of the partition of Lebanon. The LNM responded to this breach of faith by appealing with diplomatic and political pressures. These efforts were, however, incapable of preventing this right-wing option from continuing. Although the LNM had anticipated such an offensive, at that time they were incapable of mounting a pre-emptive offensive to link West Beirut with Karantina, Nab'ah and Tal al-Zatar, since they were still relying on the political process.

Contradictions within the Lebanese polity, however, soon propelled the LNM forward and forced it to assume more 'radical' methods in its fight against the right wing. External contradictions in relation to Syria further forced an LNM with a radical, petty bourgeois ideology to differentiate itself from the pro-Syrian forces. This was an important milestone for its own revolutionary development. Another step followed when the LNM decided to go it alone on the Mountain offensive in March 1976.

# Notes

1. K.S. Salibi, *Crossroads to Civil War: Lebanon 1958–1976* (Delmar, NY, Caravan Books, 1976), 97.
2. *An-Nahar*, 14 April 1975.
3. Salibi, op. cit., p. 99.
4. Ibid., p. 101.
5. *An-Nahar*, op. cit.
6. The name Rejection Front denotes the 'rejection' of anything short of the total liberation of Palestine.
7. Salibi, op. cit., pp. 88, 122.
8. Officially, the PLO calls for a secular democratic state to be established in all of Palestine.
9. The Saiqa, for instance, was quickly condemned by the masses for its clashes with other Resistance groups.
10. *Message from Fateh to the Lebanese People* (A Fateh publication, 26 October 1969), 8.
11. Ibid.
12. Salibi, op. cit., pp. 98–99.
13. *An-Nahar*, 16 May 1975.
14. *An-Nahar*, 24 May 1975.
15. *At-Tariq* (January–August 1976), p. 325.
16. Ibid.
17. Ibid., p. 326.
18. Ibid.
19. *Lebanon's War* (Beirut, Dar al-Masseerah, 1977), 219.
20. *At-Tariq*, op. cit.
21. Ibid.
22. *An-Nahar*, 29 June 1975.
23. *At-Tariq*, op. cit., p. 327.
24. Up until June 1975, the fighting was between the Resistance and the right wing. See, for example, M. Deeb, *The Lebanese Civil War* (New York, Praeger, 1980), 1.
25. *At-Tariq*, op. cit., pp. 327–328.
26. *Lebanon's War*, op. cit., p. 220.
27. Karami was a member of the Tahaluf which included Salam. He is also a traditional zaim.
28. *The Two Year War* (Beirut, Dar an-Hanar), p. x.
29. The Syrian diplomatic initiative, for instance, convinced Franjieh to ask Karami to form a Cabinet.
30. *Lebanon's War*, op. cit., p. 220.
31. M. Bannerman, 'Saudi Arabia', in P. Haley and L. Snider, eds., *Lebanon in Crisis* (New York, Syracuse University Press, 1979), 122–126.
32. *The Two Year War*, op. cit., p. IX.
33. *Lebanon's War*, op. cit.
34. Ibid., p. 217.
35. Ibid., p. 218.
36. Ibid., p. 220.
37. Ibid.
38. *The Two Year War*, op. cit., p. X.

39. *Lebanon's War*, p. 221.
40. Ibid.
41. Ibid.
42. Ibid.; *At-Tariq*, op. cit., p. 328.
43. *At-Tariq*, op. cit.
44. Ibid.
45. Ibid.
46. Ibid.
47. *Lebanon's War*, op. cit.
48. Ibid., p. 222.
49. *At-Tariq*, op. cit., p. 329.
50. *Lebanon's War*, op. cit.
51. The pro-Syrian groups were in support of 'reform' that would have consecrated confessionalism.
52. Samih Farsoun and W. Carroll, 'The Civil War in Lebanon: Sect, Class and Imperialism', *Monthly Review* (June 1976), 24.
53. The entire history of the conflict is proof of this observation.
54. *Lebanon's War*, op. cit., p. 221.
55. The ASAP called for the need to defeat the right wing militarily.
56. *Lebanon's War*, op. cit., p. 222.
57. *At-Tariq*, op. cit., p. 329.
58. *Lebanon's War*, op. cit.
59. Ibid.
60. *At-Tariq*, op. cit.
61. Minutes of the NDC meetings, in *At-Tariq*, op. cit.
62. Ibid.
63, LNM statement on the political situation, 24 September 1975.
64. Minutes of NDC first meeting in *At-Tariq*, op. cit.
65. Ibid., pp. 101–102.
66. For an excellent treatment of right-wing ideology, see, for example, F. Abdallah and K. Hani, 'Fascist Features in the Economic Thought of the Lebanese Bourgeoisie', in *At-Tariq*, op. cit., pp. 45–67.
67. Minutes of NDC first meeting in *At-Tariq*, op. cit.
68. *At-Tariq*, op. cit., p. 330.
69. *Lebanon's War*, op. cit., p. 222.
70. Ibid., p. 223.
71. Ibid.
72. *The Two Year War*, op. cit., p. XI.
73. *At-Tariq*, op. cit., p. 330.
74. *Lebanon's War*, op. cit., p. 224.
75. *At-Tariq*, op. cit., p. 331.
76. *Lebanon's War*, op. cit., p. 224.
77. *At-Tariq*, op. cit.
78. *The Two Year War*, op. cit.
79. Minutes of NDC meeting in *At-Tariq*, op. cit.
80. Ibid.
81. Ibid.
82. Ibid.
83. *Lebanon's War*, op. cit., pp. 224–225.
84. *At-Tariq*, op. cit., p. 332.

85. *Lebanon's War*, op. cit., p. 224.
86. Ibid., p. 225.
87. *At-Tariq*, op. cit.
88. *Lebanon's War*, op. cit.
89. Ibid.
90. *At-Tariq*, op. cit., p. 333.
91. *Lebanon's War*, op. cit.
92. *At-Tariq*, op. cit., p. 332.
93. *An-Nahar*, 12 July 1975.
94. *Lebanon's War*, op. cit., p. 226.
95. *At-Tariq*, op. cit., p. 333.
96. Ibid.
97. Ibid.
98. Ibid.
99. *The Two Year War*, op. cit., p. XII.
100. *At.-Tariq*, op. cit., p. 334.
101. Ibid.
102. Ibid.
103. Ibid.
104. *Lebanon's War*, op. cit., p. 227.
105. *At-Tariq*, op. cit., p. 335.
106. *Lebanon's War*, op. cit., p. 176.
107. Ibid., p. 228.
108. Ibid.
109. Ibid.
110. Ibid.
111. Ibid.
112. *An-Nahar*, 15 January 1976; interview with Dubayye camp residents.
113. *At-Tariq*, op. cit., p. 336.
114. *Lebanon's War*, op. cit.
115. After the fall of Maslakh, the right-wing forces were able to connect their Beirut areas with the Mountain by way of the coastal road.
116. *Lebanon's War*, op. cit.
117. Jumblatt, *This is My Will* (Al-Watan al-Arabi, June 1978).
118. *Lebanon's War*, op. cit.
119. Ibid.
120. *At-Tariq*, op. cit., p. 337.
121. *Lebanon's War*, op. cit., p. 229.
122. Ibid.
123. Ibid., p. 230.
124. *At-Tariq*, op. cit., p. 337.
125. Ibid.
126. *Lebanon's War*, op. cit., pp. 229–230.

# 7. The Left-Wing Offensive: 1976

By mid-January 1976 it was clear that the army, bureaucracy, parliament, judiciary and Cabinet were unable to function. This was especially the case when the President and some Cabinet ministers, such as Chamoun (Minister of the Interior), were parties to the conflict and even had their own private militias. The Syrian-backed southern offensive of 20 January had convinced the right wing to accept the latest Syrian peace initiative. The pro-system forces allied to the Lebanese National Movement (LNM) were convinced that, this time, the Syrian initiative would bear fruit. And there was reason to believe it. The right wing, it seemed, had exhausted all its efforts to break away from Syrian peace initiatives. These pro-system forces had hoped that the Syrian initiative would enhance their position in the political system within the context of an 'improved' confessional arrangement.

The LNM, however, had reason to believe that the right wing was preparing for a new round of fighting to isolate these forces within the LNM which would not opt for a confessional solution and to strengthen the Maronite position in future negotiations with other rival pro-system forces. The LNM had no choice but to accept the Syrian initiative, because of the pressure that the leadership of the Palestinian Resistance had applied on it and because some groups within the LNM wanted to resolve the crisis through Syria's intervention.[1] The condition for LNM acceptance of the Syrian initiative was that negotiations must proceed along the lines of the 'minimum programme'.

The Syrian initiative, however, intentionally bypassed the LNM and its programme. Syria was not interested in instituting reforms that would do away with the confessional system in Lebanon. It was only interested in stabilizing the situation in Lebanon so as not to allow a progressive democratic system to be established on its borders, and to bring the country to accept Arab initiatives on a regional settlement with Israel. The Syrian initiative dealt with the confessional Muslim establishment and the Maronite right wing. This tactic left the LNM no choice but to stage an offensive, which was soon joined by the Resistance, against the right wing. The LNM recognized, although belatedly, that the only way to succeed in implementing its programme was to defeat the right wing militarily. This decision was in itself a development in the LNM's perception of methods of effecting political change. This new outlook came, however, after bitter lessons grasped while dealing with its adversaries and enemies in 1975.

This chapter focuses on two significant events. The first is the Constitutional Document that attempted to consecrate confessionalism. The second is the offensive itself, which generated a major split between the LNM and the Resistance on the one hand, and the Syrians on the other.

On 1 February 1976 the Maronite right-wing elements which comprised the Front of Freedom and Man (FFM) lauded the Syrian effort, while the LKP's Pierre Gemayel, one of its members, attacked Jumblatt and the left. The LKP (Phalangist) chief also expressed the need for a new round of fighting against the left.[2] The Syrian initiative gained momentum on 7 February when President Franjieh went on a visit to Syria. The immediate result of the visit was a joint communiqué that guaranteed the implementation of the Cairo Agreement (between the Lebanese state and the Palestinian Resistance) in letter and spirit. It also laid the basis for the unity of Lebanon and agreed to the need for political reform in the Lebanese system. The next day the communiqué was welcomed in most Arab capitals and by all sides in the country.[3]

During this period kidnapping occurred in the right-wing areas and Israel attacked the south on 2 February. These incidents threatened the cease-fire which was being supervised by Lebanese army and Palestinian units. Meanwhile, Raymond Eddé of the National Bloc attacked Israel and accused it of fomenting trouble in the country. He also accused Franjieh of being responsible for what had taken place in the country thus far. He further announced his belief that Lebanon was Arab and must remain democratic, and that his party stood against the fighting and partition and was for social democracy, justice and the secularization of the state.[4]

The FFM announced that it was for keeping the presidency with the Maronites and, if that failed, it would demand complete secularization of the entire system.[5] In this fashion the FFM hoped to sidestep the LNM's gradual plan to implement secularization and at the same time drive a wedge between the LNM and the pro-system forces allied to it.

## The Constitutional Document

The Franjieh visit to Syria made possible what came to be known as the Constitutional Document (CD). This was the result of hard negotiations and comprised 17 points, the most significant and disturbing feature of which was the consecration of confessionalism. On that score, the CD stated that the President would be Maronite, the Prime Minister Sunni and the House Speaker Shiite. While this was enshrined in the National Pact, it was not part of the Constitution.[6] The CD also stated that parliamentary seats would be divided equally between Christians and Muslims. Furthermore, electoral law would be amended taking these changes into consideration. Other points in the document called for the realization of 'social justice'; the decentralization of the civil service; the strengthening of the army; the creation of a planning and development council; the amending of the naturalization law; the specifying of the President's responsibilities; the election of the Premier by parliament; deconfessionalizing the civil service, except for top posts which would be equally divided between Christians and Muslims; the creation of a special court whose function would be to look into the constitutionality of the laws and decrees emanating from the executive. These were the major points of the CD.[7]

The Constitutional Document was proclaimed by Syria as the most important event in Lebanon since the National Pact.[8] However, it came under attack from many quarters. Curiously enough, the LKP attacked it, saying that it would consecrate confessionalism.[9] In fact, the LKP attacked the CD because it gave more clout to the Muslim establishment at the expense of the Maronite sector of the bourgeoisie. Salam and Yafi (representing the Sunni Muslim élite) also attacked the CD, as they too regarded it as a measure that would consecrate confessionalism.[10] The Independent Nasserist Movement (INM), a component of the LNM, also attacked the CD. The LNM accepted eight of the 17 points. The points it rejected were those that consecrated confessionalism or those that it regarded as mere patchwork. The LNM, however, did not reject the CD as a basis upon which reform could begin to be implemented.[11]

Seeing that the LNM had a more positive stance on the CD, the LKP held an emergency meeting (on 23 February 1976) and decided to confirm its belief in what it termed 'the Lebanese framework' and the secularization of the state and announced its support of the CD and the Syrian initiative.[12]

On the same day Jumblatt held a press conference in which he reiterated the LNM's position on the CD. He further elaborated that the discussion of the CD should make it clear that the 'minimum programme' must be implemented in full. He also declared that the LNM had already convinced the masses that there was no alternative but to implement the programme. At a press conference on 8 March Jumblatt stated:

> This is the reality that Franjieh and Karami must face, and it must be faced by the Arab governments including our Syrian friends; the battle of the barracks and their capture [by the Lebanese Arab Army — that part of the army which had broken away and allied itself with the LNM] indicates that a new wind of revolution is blowing in Lebanon.[13]

Jumblatt further announced his condition that the LNM be heavily represented in the new Cabinet in recognition of the mass support the LNM enjoyed. This, he said, was the only way for a peaceful solution to Lebanon's problems.

Meanwhile, the Lebanese army was disintegrating, and this of course interfered with Syrian efforts to reach a solution. The Lebanese Arab Army (LAA) had enhanced the position of the LNM during the 'battle of the barracks' and the LNM was gaining ground in the military arena. The appointment of a new Lebanese Army Commander on 2 March could not do anything to stop 'the battle of the barracks'. By the end of March, the LAA had total control of the barracks in the south, the Bekaa, the Mountain, most of the north and Beirut. About 75% of the army joined or affiliated to the LAA.[14] These events were a crushing defeat for the Lebanese state, whose last vestige as a state had crumbled. The right wing, which had depended upon the army in its attempt to stop the development of the revolutionary process, grew more dependent upon the Syrian initiative to reach a solution to the crisis. A few army units, which were already assisting the right wing, openly declared their political affiliation. The few barracks that did not join either side were confined to Beirut and its environs. The officers who belonged to these barracks were trying to reunite the army. They favoured a general amnesty for all those who had defected and a change in the army law to address the needs of the defectors. Hanna Said, the Army Commander, was amenable to such a move. Franjieh and Chamoun, however, would not hear of such a thing. In fact, Franjieh asked Karami to take action against the Army Command.[15]

The right wing unanimously supported Franjieh and Chamoun on the army question. However, the general feeling in Lebanon was that Franjieh was becoming an obstacle to any peaceful solution of any question. Calls for his resignation were heard from every quarter. The Syrians sent a delegation to try to moderate between Franjieh and his opponents, but Franjieh refused to compromise on any issue.

## The 'Television Coup'

Subsequently, on 11 March Brigadier Aziz al-Ahdab of the Beirut garrison staged a 'coup' which had the support of the Lebanese Army Command. Ahdab made a public announcement that the President must resign since the army was now in charge. The coup was dubbed the 'television coup' since, in fact, the Beirut garrison really had no power to implement its demands. When Ahdab went to the television station to announce this 'coup' he was accompanied by bodyguards from the Palestinian Resistance.[16]

There is reason to believe that the 'coup' was supported by the Syrians, who were interested in reuniting the army in an effort to weaken the LNM by containing this revolutionary development. At any rate, Saudi Arabia expressed its support of Ahdab by sending him congratulations on the occasion of the Islamic feast.[17]

In a clever move to counter any possible right-wing tactics, Lieutenant Ahmad al-Khatib, the LAA Commander, agreed to co-ordinate with Ahdab to begin negotiations to reunite the army. This showed that the LAA was attempting to find a peaceful solution to the army question. The LKP did not take a position on the Ahdab move until two days after its initiation. Smaller right-wing groups, however, came to Ahdab's support from the beginning because they saw the 'coup' for what it was: an attempt to co-opt the LAA and thus weaken the LNM.[18]

On 14 March 66 members of parliament signed a petition asking Franjieh to resign, but the President rejected it on the grounds that it was not constitutional. Al-Asaad, the Parliament Speaker, came out in support of Ahdab and indirectly called upon the President to make a 'sacrifice' and resign so that the army could be reunited.[19]

On 15 March a contingent of the LAA was advancing toward Beirut from the south to bolster its defences there. The pro-Syrian Palestinian Saiqa guerrilla group blocked the contingent's way and prevented it from advancing beyond Khalde, a few miles south of Beirut.[20] The incident was significant because it confirmed Syria's fear that Franjieh's opponents wanted to oust him by force. This became clear when Issam Qansu, leader of the pro-Syrian Baath Party Organization (BPO) in Lebanon, declared that the difference between his pro-Syrian organization and the others was on the method to be used to oust Franjieh. Qansu further stated that military force would lead to the partition of the country.[21]

At the same time the situation in Beirut began to deteriorate, and by 18 March Beirut and the Mountain areas witnessed heavy fighting. Due to these developments the 'coup' lost its significance. The LKP opened up a new front in the Mountain, which indicated that it was not interested in reuniting the army or in resolving any questions other than on LKP terms.

Initially the LKP was capable of surrounding isolated LNM areas in the Mountain.[22] In response, the LNM opened up the fighting in Beirut on a full scale, and by 23 March the LNM had established full control of the hotel area and Starco.[23] In the Mountain, the following areas witnessed some of the fiercest fighting: Aley, Kahala, Dhour Shwere and Beit Merry. The LNM announced that no cease-fire would be accepted unless the LKP lifted its siege of the LNM Mountain areas and the right wing accepted the 'minimum programme'.[24]

These LNM victories were contrary to Syria's designs for Lebanon. They strengthened the democratic forces in a neighbouring state and had the potential of propelling forward the revolutionary process in the entire region. Consequently, Syria unleashed the Saiqa forces on the Palestinian Rejectionists who were actively supporting the LNM's operations in Beirut and other areas. Syria also began to attack the LNM verbally from Damascus and Beirut, accusing it of contributing to the partition of Lebanon.[25] Unheeded, the LNM kept pushing on with its offensive. Ironically, the Syrian position was now in support of the right wing at a time when LNM Mountain areas were under siege.

Initially the Resistance (except for the Rejection Front) was not involved in the fighting. However, many considerations were pressuring it into fighting. The Palestinian masses expected the Resistance to fight alongside their ally, the LNM. Equally important was the fact that since late January 1976 the Syrians had been working hard to secure dominance over the Resistance. This Syrian encroachment did not sit well with the Fateh leadership, which dominated the PLO, much less with the Rejectionists.

On 25 March the LAA in support of the Combined Forces (LNM forces and Resistance units) advanced towards the presidential palace, which was being shelled by LAA and LNM artillery. The heavy shelling forced the President to flee to the port of Junieh, a right-wing stronghold. His flight was facilitated by (pro-Syrian) Saiqa forces which stood in the way of the advancing LAA and Combined Forces.[26] The President's flight was looked upon by Chamoun with disdain, since he regarded it as giving in to the LNM. LAA guns were now trained on Junieh ready to shell it and the town's residents panicked because of the threat of attack.

This incident led Syria to assert a stronger stance against the LNM and the Resistance. In so doing, Syria continued its verbal attacks against Jumblatt: 'We want to end political and economic feudalism in Lebanon, but we look for Lebanon's interest . . . and not that of one person [Jumblatt].'[27]

Meanwhile, the LNM turned the tide of the fighting in the Mountain against the right wing. Ayntoura, Mtein and other Mountain areas were liberated on 26–27 March. Unsure of the next move, Syria halted its attacks against Jumblatt and the LNM. Undaunted by Syria's view of him, Jumblatt went to Damascus to convince Hafiz al-Asad, the Syrian President, not to interfere with the LNM offensive. He also asked Asad to look the other way for two weeks, by which time Jumblatt was confident that the Combined Forces would bring total defeat to the right wing and force it to sit down and negotiate.[28] On the very same day Gemayel threatened to internationalize the crisis and Franjieh contacted Asad by phone in an attempt to counter Jumblatt's visit.

The following day fighting in Beirut and the Mountain raged. Out of frustration against the advancing Combined Forces, the right wing shelled the residential quarters in the LNM areas.[29] For the third time since the beginning of the war, Beirut's port was on fire.

Back in Beirut, Jumblatt announced 'Asad's understanding of the LNM's position'.[30] However, Syria was unwilling to compromise with the LNM on its strategic view of Lebanon, which ran counter to the LNM's. Consequently, the BPO (pro-Syrian Baathists) attacked Jumblatt verbally and accused him of being a US agent and traitor. Syria also threatened Jumblatt by stating that it would stop allowing arms shipments to reach the LNM through its territory. Ironically, the Resistance was also putting pressure on the LNM to stop the offensive, since the PLO leadership was wedded to a regional settlement, along the lines favoured by the Saudis, which Syria was trying to implement through her manoeuvrings in Lebanon.[31] The Resistance leadership saw clearly that a victorious LNM could derail this Saudi strategy in pursuit of a regional settlement.

## A New Cease-fire, and the Dean Brown Mission

Due to these pressures, Lebanon's thirty-fourth cease-fire was granted by the LNM, which at this time, with the Resistance and the LAA, enjoyed a superior military position against the right wing. Therefore, the cease-fire was granted on the grounds of certain LNM stipulations. The cease-fire was to last for 10 days so that a new President could be elected to replace Franjieh, who was called upon to resign unconditionally and immediately. Furthermore, the LNM demanded that political reform proceed along the lines of its programme, and that in implementing the cease-fire the LNM troops were not going to pull out from their advanced positions.[32]

During the cease-fire, concentrated diplomatic contacts were being conducted by the US envoy, Dean Brown, who had arrived in Beirut on 31 March. On 1 April Brown met Franjieh, Chamoun and Gemayel, then the Maronite Patriarch, Al-Asaad and Karami. Al-Asaad, who supported the Syrian position, contacted Waldheim, the United Nations Secretary-General, and informed him of his rejection of the internationalization of the crisis. King Hussein of Jordan announced that day (1 April) his support for Syria's intervention in Lebanon, since it prevented 'the attempt of the extremist Muslims to change the Lebanese system.'[33] All these moves were designed to show Brown the extent of support Syria's role in Lebanon enjoyed.

Despite the cease-fire of 2 April, the Combined Forces liberated Ayntoura for the second time, while fierce fighting raged in Aley, Mtein-Bolonia, Beirut and its environs, and in the north of Lebanon.[34] On the same day, Brown continued his talks with the Lebanese leaders. He met separately with Imam Musa Sadr, Salam and Jumblatt.

The Brown mission was looked upon with suspicion by Syria, especially when the LKP and the Cedar Guards were agitating for the internationalization of the crisis.[35] The Syrians did not want to take any chances and risk being shunted aside in Lebanon. They resisted any effort which they perceived would weaken their position regarding a general settlement in the Middle East. What the Syrians wanted to prove was that they were the only force in the area capable of restoring peace to Lebanon, and that they were an indispensable force which must be included in regional negotiations.

The BPO and other pro-Syrian forces in Lebanon came out against the Brown mission. A tug-of-war ensued between the Syrians and the United States with respect to diplomatic and military initiatives in Lebanon. To moderate the situation somewhat, Kissinger reiterated the US position on Lebanon: the United States opposed any foreign military intervention in Lebanon. Kissinger described Syria's role as one that was keeping extremists at bay.[36]

The pro-Syrian Saiqa and Kamal Shatilla's Nasserist organization launched scathing attacks on Jumblatt because of his talks with Brown and his call to 'Arabize' the crisis. The pro-Syrian groups correctly perceived these moves as an attempt by Jumblatt to limit the Syrian role in Lebanon. Meanwhile, Qansu and Amin of the BPO left for Syria to consult with their bosses.[37]

As a rebuttal to these Syrian-inspired attacks against him, Jumblatt announced that the LNM would maintain Syria's friendship. He followed this announcement by another on the following day (2 April) stating that his party, the SPP, was not working to defeat the Syrian initiative. These announcements blunted Syrian-inspired attacks against Jumblatt and the LNM.

The LKP, meanwhile, welcomed the Syrian initiative and called for a deterrent military force composed of Arab and foreign troops. Such a force, the LKP reasoned, would contain the LNM and force it to withdraw from its advanced positions. The BPO and the Saiqa, however, redirected attention to the fact that the cease-fire was supposed to precede the election of a new president.[38] They further warned that any breach of the 2 April cease-fire would not be tolerated by them.

The following day was witness to further talks between Brown, Eddé, the Mufti (the Sunni religious leader), Elias Sarkis and the French ambassador to Lebanon. The Mufti informed Brown that no solution was possible unless confessionalism was abolished.[39] On 4 April, Jumblatt attacked Syria's military presence in Lebanon in the form of the Saiqa and other Lebanese organizations. The PLO came out in support of the LNM on this issue, warning that its alliance with the LNM was strategic and that it was ready to strike without mercy against any attempts (by the pro-Syrian groups) to dissolve this organic linkage.[40] These statements were also designed to influence Brown's efforts and to relay to him, indirectly, that the Resistance was a major force which he must meet if his mission were to be fruitful (earlier Brown had refused to meet with the Resistance because the United States did not recognize the PLO).[41]

Brown continued to meet Lebanese leaders. This time he had talks with Gemayel, Franjieh, Chamoun and Malek, all of whom were in the Front of Freedom and Man (FFM). The pro-Syrian organizations intensified their attacks on the Brown mission. They also attacked Jumblatt for his lack of co-operation with the Syrian initiative and for his 'ingratitude' for Syria's aid to him and the LNM since 1975. They also blamed Jumblatt for not restraining the LNM in the face of cease-fire violations by the right wing.[42]

On 6 April the Resistance attacked the Brown mission and at the same time interceded to end the propaganda war between Syria and Jumblatt. The LNM welcomed the Resistance's initiative for a number of reasons, primarily because it did not want a final break with Syria, at least not before a new President was elected.[43]

## France Opposes the US

On 8 April France expressed its support of the Syrian initiative in Lebanon and declared its opposition to the US efforts there.[44] Meanwhile, Jumblatt had another meeting with Brown to impress upon him the need to reform the political system. At the same time another LNM leader, Ibrahim Qulailat (of the Independent Nasserist Movement), called for the adoption of the LNM programme as a basis for a solution. The LNM followed these moves by its call to amend Article 73 of the Constitution to allow parliament to elect a new President before August. The LNM also expressed its commitment to seek a political solution within the 10-day cease-fire period it had already granted on 2 April.[45]

However, matters started heating up between the Saiqa and the Rejection Front and resulted in the two groups clashing militarily near Beirut's international airport. The Combined Forces were also advancing in the north toward Franjieh's town of Zghorta. To avert any break between Syria and the LNM as a result of these military moves in the north, the Resistance called for a meeting between Syria and Jumblatt. On the same day (9 April) the Resistance attacked the Brown mission once more, while Jumblatt issued a statement announcing the existence of an international conspiracy against both the Resistance and the LNM. He then called for an Arab League meeting to discuss ways by which this conspiracy could be averted.[46]

To check LNM advances and to apply maximum pressure on it, Syrian units entered Lebanese territory from the east. With this move, popular displeasure in the Bekaa against the Syrian troops was extreme and was followed by warnings from the LNM and the Resistance to Syria against the use of its troops in Lebanon.

Meanwhile, the French envoy, de Murville, met Chamoun, Gemayel and the Maronite Patriarch to talk about possible presidential candidates. He then met Al-Asaad, Karami and Arafat.

French and US policies on Lebanon and the region diverged. The French were for the Syrian initiative in Lebanon and against the US mission. After meeting with the French envoy, Arafat, the PLO chief, accused the United States of conspiring against the Resistance, the LNM and Syria.[47] On 10 April, President Ford announced that the United States was trying to prevent Syria from controlling Lebanon. Brown followed his boss's announcement by suggesting the creation of a local deterrent force which would include US advisers.[48]

The LNM, whose leaders had also met the French envoy, took a different stance from that taken by Arafat. It condemned all forms of intervention (Syrian, United States...) and reiterated its adherence to Lebanon's sovereignty and unity. Jumblatt, who was as usual speaking for the LNM, expressed the need to Arabize the crisis. He further claimed that some Arab states did not want confessionalism to be abolished, as that would detonate the situation in the entire region and threaten their regimes.[49]

The timing of Syria's small-scale military intervention was one day before parliament met to amend Article 73 of the Constitution. Once the Constitution was amended, the Syrians wanted to be sure they had enough military power in Lebanon to influence the election. On 11 April the LNM again warned Syria of the dangers of its military adventure in Lebanon. To press for the speedy election of a President before Syria's pressure became insurmountable, the LNM announced that it had ceased to co-operate with foreign envoys until the election of a new President.[50] The LNM also called upon the Arab countries and foreign powers to intervene to stop the Syrian military intervention.

The situation was further complicated by a series of Israeli attacks on

Lebanese towns and Palestinian refugee camps during the month of April. Israel followed these attacks by a threat of military intervention in Lebanon.[51] In doing so, Israel wanted to strengthen the right-wing position in Lebanon against the LNM and the Resistance. It also wanted to remind the United States, France and the other states in the region that Israel's interests had to be taken into consideration in arriving at a solution to the Lebanese problem.

Despite the fact that the LKP had been violating the cease-fire by shelling residential quarters in the LNM areas and by committing massacres in its own areas, Syria was opposed to the LNM retaliating on the military fronts. The LKP took advantage of this Syrian policy and attacked Beit Shabab in the Mountain and occupied it. The PFN (Chamoun's party) also besieged the village of Byaqout. These and similar attacks were accompanied by statements from Gemayel praising Asad and Syrian socialism.[52] The LKP continued to improve its military situation in the Mountain and by 14 April occupied another LNM area, Dhour Shwere.[53]

The general situation in April prompted Eddé to renew his warning of the existence of an Israeli plan, in co-operation with the right wing, to partition the country.[54] The French envoy called for French military intervention to guarantee the election of a new President and to help stabilize the country.[55] To counter these French moves and to provide legitimacy for Syria's limited military intervention, Karami (Prime Minister of Lebanon) announced that there was a need for the Syrian military presence as a force interested in maintaining order.[56] In an indirect way Israel approved of the Syrian move, announcing that there was a 'red line' beyond which it would not tolerate Syrian activities.[57] It was anybody's guess where this line was, or whether it was simply a physical boundary. It is plausible, however, that Israel had indirectly agreed to the Syrian role in Lebanon, since Syria was capable of containing the LNM and was operating in favour of its right-wing allies.

On his arrival in Beirut from Damascus on 15 April, the French envoy announced his approval of Syria's role in Lebanon. On the next day he ended his mission to the region. This was in fact a triumph for Syria. The Resistance was quick to appreciate that fact: it decided to further mend fences with Syria. On the same day the French envoy left the area, Arafat left for Syria, where he reached an agreement with the Syrians. The agreement included the following points: (1) an end to the fighting; (2) re-establishment of the military committee to supervise the cease-fire; (3) opposition to the partition of Lebanon; (4) opposition to Arabization; (5) opposition to US efforts; (6) opposition to the internationalization of the crisis; and (7) support of the Syrian initiative in Lebanon.

The next day the LNM welcomed the Damascus agreement as an interim one until a new President was elected. The only force that was obviously against the agreement was the Rejection Front.[58] It regarded it as a sell-out by the Palestinian leadership of the LNM and the Palestinian revolution and as a means of pursuing the mini-state solution.

On 19 April the right wing severely attacked the agreement and the Resistance. In response to this verbal attack, the National Front, which had been established by the pro-Syrian Lebanese organizations, warned the right wing against escalating the fighting. The LKP's efforts to internationalize the crisis finally crumbled when Dean Brown declared that the solution must be a Lebanese one.[59] On 23 April Brown left for London to meet with Kissinger.

At that point the LNM's military position, despite some losses in the Mountain, was still strong. Up until that period in the war the LNM had not set up local administration in its areas. There were only popular committees in many of the LNM areas to take care of security, food distribution, housing and medical supplies. But these committees were not co-ordinated and operated haphazardly.[60] To establish a firmer control on what was happening in its areas, and to mobilize the masses and take care of their needs in an efficient manner, the LNM announced that it was establishing a local authority. This was also a move to try to deny the local traditional zuama the support of any mass base they might still have enjoyed. The traditional leaders were quick to oppose such measures and were aided by the National Front, which attacked these measures as contributing to the partition of Lebanon.[61]

## Syria Secures its Presidential Candidate

On 26 April two main contenders for the presidency emerged: Raymond Eddé, the LNM's choice, and Elias Sarkis, who was supported by Syria, Karami and the right wing. To the Syrians Eddé was unacceptable because of his close ties with the LNM and because of his consistent opposition to any foreign intervention, including Syria's. Sarkis was more to Syria's liking because he lacked a mass base and an army. Consequently, he would have to rely upon Syria for support.

The LNM announced that its participation in the election of the President depended upon the candidates' acceptance of its programme. It argued that this was a realistic demand since the LNM represented 75% of the Lebanese and controlled 80% of the country.[62] However, this condition was preempted by the Syrian role in the Lebanese presidential elections.

On 6 May the LNM refused to recognize the convening of parliament to elect the new President, accusing Syria of using political and military pressure on members of parliament to vote for Sarkis. Predictably, on 9 May Sarkis was elected through Syrian intimidations and threats. Eddé was unable to reach the area where the meeting was held because his security was not guaranteed by the authorities.[63]

Syrian troops shelled Palestinian refugee camps where demonstrations were taking place to protest at Syria's intervention in the presidential elections. Similar demonstrations were also held in the south.[64] The LNM rejected the election results, but was incapable of doing anything about it. On the other hand, this was a welcome outcome for the United States. Dean Brown, who had been back in Lebanon since 1 May, held a press conference on 11 May praising parliamentarism and declaring it was impossible for any group to win militarily. He urged reconciliation among the warring parties so that reform could take place.[65] As a signal to Israel, he also declared that Lebanon would not become a confrontation state (meaning that Lebanon would not be belligerent to Israel).

While these developments were taking place on the diplomatic level, military battles for hegemony were still being fought. During an LKP visit to Syria, the party, on 5 May, was simultaneously intensifying its attacks against the LNM in the Mountain. Apparently the Syrians, who claimed neutrality, did little to discourage the LKP from violating the cease-fire. Between 9 and 10 May the LKP met with crushing defeats in Ayntoura, which it was trying to recapture. To ease the LKP pressure on Ayntoura, the LNM opened another Mountain front in Oyoun al-Seimaan. Unable to defend itself against LNM attacks, which it had provoked, the LKP called upon Syria to intervene militarily in Lebanon.[66]

In conjunction with these requests, Syria announced that it was against any group which sought to continue the fighting. The LNM understood this announcement to mean: do nothing against the LKP attacks. On 14 May Jumblatt, Khatib (of the LAA) and Habash (of the PFLP) denounced Syria's intervention and declared their belief that Syria had intervened militarily to prevent the LNM from winning a clear-cut victory against the right wing as the only possible way to bring an end to the war.[67]

During May, the deteriorating military position of the LKP spurred it on to shell residential quarters in LNM areas. In an attempt to play for time, Bashir Gemayel (the son of the LKP chief) made some conciliatory remarks to the LNM by calling for a Lebanese agreement on the 'common denominator'.[68] This nebulous statement was not taken seriously by the LNM, which announced that it was for a coalition which would include itself, the Resistance and Syria, but that it was against Syria's heavy-handed behaviour in Lebanon. Furthermore, despite its initial rejection of Sarkis's election, it demonstrated its willingness to co-operate with the President-elect by holding a meeting with him on 19 May, with Arafat and Abu Iyad of the Resistance attending.[69]

The LNM and the Resistance also rejected a renewed French proposal to send French army troops to Lebanon. On the same day (23 May), Imam Musa Sadr, who had visited Syria the week before, attacked the LNM and its programme. He also attacked secularization specifically. Since he was a member of the National Front, it was safe to assume that he was reflecting Syria's position on reforms in Lebanon.[70]

The right wing resorted to assassination attempts and cold-blooded killings in an effort to create the conditions for an open confrontation between the Syrians and the LNM. On 25 May, an LKP–PFN assassination plot against Eddé failed. The day before, the LKP attacked Jubail, the coastal town north of Beirut and Eddé's stronghold, and killed 30 of Eddé's supporters.[71] Perhaps one of the most cold-blooded murders was committed against Jumblatt's sister, who was killed in her home in Furn al-Shubback, in the right-wing held part of Beirut. The following day, Bashir Gemayel announced that the LKP had captured three of her assassins.[72]

The last few days of May witnessed an escalation of fighting throughout Lebanon. The result was more crushing defeats for the right wing in the face of the advancing Combined Forces. The right wing responded by renewing its shelling of residential quarters in LNM-held parts of Beirut.[73]

In the north Colonel Mimary, who was affiliated with the LAA, was accused by Abu Iyad, the Resistance chief, of shelling Christian villages in an effort to create sectarian conflict as a prelude to a possible Syrian military intervention. In essence, Abu Iyad was accusing the pro-Syrian organization in Lebanon of creating the conditions for Syria to be looked upon as the saviour.[74]

These right-wing and Syrian tactics were to bear fruit in the last phase of the conflict. But there were still many duels between unequal forces to be fought. Politically, however, the Mountain offensive was all but over.

## Conclusion

The LNM Mountain offensive came as a result of specific events that left the LNM no choice but to fight. The Syrians attempted to consecrate confessionalism through the agreement they reached with Franjieh that culminated in the Constitutional Document. The LKP also besieged LNM Mountain areas, a move which indicated that the Maronite right wing was not in favour of reaching an accord with the LNM. Furthermore, LKP attacks eroded the extremely weak 'coup' by Brigadier Ahdab which attempted to reunite the armed forces and pressure Franjieh to resign.

The Mountain offensive brought about rapid victories for the LNM. Because of pressure from Syria and the Resistance, however, the LNM had to settle for a cease-fire. Fearful that the increasing Syrian role could severely limit its options, the LNM called for Arab and foreign diplomatic intervention to counter it. As it turned out, however, French diplomatic efforts supported Syria's role in Lebanon and were a major factor in countering the initial US diplomatic effort.

Sarkis's election to the presidency indicated Syria's dominant role in Lebanon. The right wing was quick to adjust itself to this, as it tended to support Syria's diplomatic and military initiatives against the LNM. Both Syria and the right wing intended to blunt the Mountain offensive and defeat the LNM militarily.

The limited military Syrian intervention on the eve of Sarkis's election was an indication that the Mountain offensive was politically all but over. The LNM was still strong militarily, but the stage was already set to deal with it on this level also.

# Notes

1. These were the pro-Syrian groups. See, for example, M. Deeb, *The Lebanese Civil War* (New York: Praeger, 1980), 106.
2. *At-Tariq* (January–August, 1976), 337.
3. *Lebanon's War* (Beirut: Dar al-Masseerah, 1977), 231.
4. Ibid.
5. Ibid.
6. See chapter 2, p. 33–4.
7. Franjieh's message to the Lebanese people and the text of the CD, 24 February 1976.
8. *Lebanon's War*, op. cit.
9. Ibid.
10. Ibid.
11. Ibid., p. 232.
12. Ibid.
13. Jumblatt at a press conference on 8 March 1976.
14. The only barracks that did not join were certain ones around Beirut.
15. M. Deeb, op. cit., p. 89.
16. John Cooley, 'The Palestinians', in P. Haley and L. Snider, eds., *Lebanon in Crisis* (New York: Syracuse University Press, 1979), 40.
17. *Lebanon's War*, op. cit., p. 234.
18. Ibid.
19. Ibid.
20. Ibid.
21. Ibid.
22. Ibid., p. 235.
23. *At-Tariq*, op. cit., p. 339.
24. Ibid.
25. *Lebanon's War*, op. cit.
26. *At-Tariq*, op. cit.
27. Ibid.
28. Jumblatt, *This Is My Will* (Al-Watan Al-Arabi, June 1978).
29. *At-Tariq*, op. cit.
30. Ibid.
31. M. Deeb, op. cit., p. 110.
32. *Lebanon's War*, op. cit., p. 236.
33. *At-Tariq*, op. cit.
33. Ibid., p. 237.
36. Ibid., p. 236.
37. Ibid.
38. Ibid.
39. *At-Tariq*, op. cit., p. 340.
40. Ibid.
41. Ibid.
42. *Lebanon's War*, op. cit., p. 237.
43. M. Deeb, op. cit.
44. *Lebanon's War*, op. cit.
45. *At-Tariq*, op. cit.
46. Ibid.

47. *Lebanon's War*, op. cit.
48. Ibid.
49. Ibid.
50. Ibid.
51. Ibid., p. 238.
52. Ibid.
53. *At-tariq*, op. cit.
54. Ibid.
55. Ibid., p. 239.
56. Ibid., p. 238.
57. Ibid.
58. Interviews with Rejection Front members, 15 August 1978.
59. *Lebanon's War*, op. cit., p. 239.
60. The popular committees also took care of defence. The Resistance used to arm them. The situation was so chaotic, however, that it prevented coordination with other popular committees or with the LNM top leadership.
61. *At-Tariq*, op. cit., p. 341.
62. Ibid.
63. *Lebanon's War*, op. cit.
64. *At- Tariq*, op. cit., p. 342.
65. *Lebanon's War*, op. cit.
66. Ibid.
67. *At-Tariq*, op. cit., p. 343.
68. *Lebanon's War*, op. cit., p. 240.
69. Ibid.
70. Ibid.
71. *At-Tariq*, op. cit., p. 344.
72. *Lebanon's War*, op. cit.
73. *At-Tariq*, op. cit.
74. Ibid.

# 8. The Syrian Invasion: June 1976

Up until this point in the conflict, the Combined Forces (the LNM and the Resistance) had been fighting Israel, the right wing and, occasionally, the pro-Syrian forces. Despite these formidable enemies the revolutionary movement had been able to frustrate the grand design for its annihilation and/or the de jure partition of Lebanon. Furthermore, the revolutionary movement had proved capable of mounting an offensive that almost succeeded in bringing about a new form of state in which the LNM could have been hegemonic in the power bloc. All this was frustrated, however, because of the Syrian role in Lebanon. The revolutionary movement had yet to contend with another military machine with which it was not equipped to deal either militarily or psychologically. On previous occasions the LNM and the Resistance had been reluctant to enter battle with proxy Syrian troops who entered Lebanon in the form of the PLA and Saiqa. Given a choice between fighting the Syrians or yielding to their demands, the LNM tried to steer a middle course, hoping to bring diplomatic pressure (Arab and international) to bear upon the Syrians and so loosen their grip.

The 1 June 1976 full-scale Syrian invasion, however, changed the situation dramatically. It became a matter of survival for the revolutionary movement, which had no choice but to fight the invading forces. This was a clear-cut choice, especially when the Combined Forces were fighting the right wing and Israel concurrently at the time of the invasion. Syria's invasion rolled back the gains of the Mountain offensive. This was regarded as a service rendered to the enemy. No component of the LNM or the Resistance could have collaborated with the Syrians and still hoped to retain its legitimacy within the mass movement.

This chapter deals with the way in which the invasion was able to contain the revolutionary movement by preventing it from achieving a clear-cut victory. It also deals with the roles which the external forces played in attempting to restore confessionalism.

The right wing supported the invasion since Syrian troops entered into fierce fighting with the Combined Forces. Internationally, the US and France were, to varying degrees and for different reasons, in support of the Syrian invasion. The US saw that Syria was attempting to contain the Resistance and the LNM. An Israeli invasion of the same magnitude would have brought about a confrontation between Syria and Israel, derailing the step-by-step Middle East peace negotiations. Furthermore, such an invasion would have isolated the right wing from the Arabs and contributed to revolutionary development in Lebanon and perhaps in Syria. It appeared that Syria's and the US's objectives of containing revolutionary development coincided. This containment was a prerequisite to the imposition of a Middle East settlement. France too was not in favour of radical change in Lebanon.

Certainly, the National Front and the Saiqa were in full support of the invasion, as was Colonel Mimary in the north. Al-Asaad was also affiliated with the National Front, as were some lesser traditional zuama.

The invasion was devastating for the LNM, which was already weakened when major forces had split from it to form the pro-Syrian front. It was apparent that, if the LNM were to have a fighting chance against Syria, the Resistance had to ally with it all the way. The Resistance, however, was not a monolith. Fateh, the Rejection Front and Saiqa each had varying views and goals. Although Fateh and the Rejectionists supported the LNM militarily against the Syrians, there were military and other reasons, having to do with their views on a Middle East settlement, which precluded Fateh from pursuing this option on a long-term basis.

The precarious situation of the LNM prompted it to intensify its diplomatic and political activities. Jumblatt called upon the Arab masses to support the steadfastness of the Resistance and the LNM; he also called for a general strike in Lebanon to protest at the invasion. On the same day (1 June) the LNM handed to the Soviet ambassador to Lebanon a memorandum explaining its position on the Syrian action.[1]

On 2 June, Jumblatt met Sarkis in the presence of the Fateh chief, Abu Iyad, The meeting was followed by a statement from Jumblatt that he and Sarkis had agreed to end the fighting and begin negotiating with the right wing. To make good his statement, Jumblatt followed it by a meeting with Bashir Gemayel of the LKP (Phalangists) in the presence of Abu Hassan, the PLO security chief who had arranged the meeting.[2] By holding these meetings Jumblatt sought to show that there was no need for Syrian military intervention in Lebanon.[3]

Meanwhile, Saiqa forces clashed with the Resistance in Beirut, and Syrian forces were reinforced in Akkar, the Bekaa and the north. On 6 June the Combined Forces, in retaliation against the NF and Saiqa forces, occupied the offices of all the pro-Syrian Lebanese and Palestinian parties and organizations and arrested many of their leaders.[4] The next several days witnessed major clashes between the Syrians and the Combined Forces in the Mountain and Sidon. In Sidon the Syrian attack was repelled; in the Mountain the Syrian forces were able to advance towards Sofar.[5]

## The Arab League Initiative

The LNM's and the Resistance's diplomatic initiatives were fruitful in bringing about a meeting of Arab Foreign Ministers on 9 June. The meeting decided to: (1) send a symbolic Arab force to replace the Syrians; (2) call for a cease-fire; (3) form a committee to represent the Arab League in Beirut; (4) call for national reconciliation under Sarkis; and (5) support the Palestinian revolution.[6]

These decisions did not sit well with Franjieh or any other right-wing component. On 11 June, the right-wing Lebanese Front called for the withdrawal of Lebanon from 'the League of the Muslim Arabs'.[7] On that same day the military committee formed by the Arab League arrived in Beirut and was followed by Sudanese, Libyan and Algerian troops to begin implementing the League's decisions.

These efforts led to the withdrawal of some Syrian units from Beirut on 12 June. In the Mountain, however, the Syrians besieged the Combined Forces in the north of Al-Matn and shelled the Arkoub in the south, and Ayntoura and Sinneen in the Mountain. The next day the Mountain battles raged in Farayya-Oyoun al-Seeman, Aynsiha-Falougha and Aynzhalta-Ayndara. In addition, the shelling of the LNM and Resistance areas in Beirut and Sidon ensued, and the Syrians entered Arkoub and defeated the Resistance there.[8] The Syrians quickly declared they were ready to withdraw from these areas, provided the Lebanese authorities agreed to have Arab troops take their positions. Since Franjieh was against the Arab League's decisions, he was not about to agree to this.[9] The move also showed that the Syrians were not serious about withdrawing.

On 14 June, Jumblatt informed the Arab ambassadors to Lebanon that the immediate goal of the LNM was to make Lebanon democratic without changing the economic or social character of the country.[10] The intensified diplomatic initiatives led to meetings between Arab envoys, especially the Libyan ambassador, with the LKP and the Syrians to explain to them the need for the implementation of the League's decisions. Seeing the ascendancy of the League's position, the right wing quickly reversed its position toward the League's policies. Gemayel talked of the need to comply with the Cairo Agreement, while the Lebanese Front welcomed the League's decisions.[11]

The military fronts were just as busy as the diplomatic. The Syrian invasion prompted defections of many units of the PLA, which was under Syrian control, to the Combined Forces.[12] These developments, however, did not stop the deterioration of the Combined Forces' military situation. They were being shelled in the Mountain and Sidon by the Syrians and at the same time they were repelling right-wing attacks in Beirut and its suburbs and also in Akkar in the north.[13]

On 21 June battles raged in the commercial areas of Beirut and in the Mountain. More significantly, however, a right-wing/Syrian offensive began on Tal al-Zatar and Jisr al-Basha. The north and north-east of Beirut, Nabah, Dikwani, Sin al-Feel and Mansouriyyeh also came under attack.[14]

The Syrian position was reinforced by Asad's visit to France, which started on 17 June and culminated in a communiqué on 19 June. Syria and France were agreed on Lebanon and on a Middle East settlement. A visit by Asad to Rumania further strengthened his position on the Middle East in general.[15]

The Resistance exerted every effort — diplomatic and military — to try to stop the takeover of Tal al-Zatar, but to no avail. The siege could have been lifted by the right wing had the Syrians wished it. All they needed to do was move their troops, which were preventing Resistance troops from reaching the camp. The Syrians and the right wing, however, were intent on decimating the Resistance in Tal al-Zatar, especially since the camp was an important mass base for the PFLP, which was the major component of the Rejection Front.[16]

Militarily, the Combined Forces fared no better in July than in June. Tal al-Zatar remained under siege, and fierce fighting raged around it. At first, however, the Combined Forces were capable of inflicting heavy losses upon the attackers despite Syrian buffer troops.[17] This was a clear indication that the will of the Combined Forces to fight was capable of surmounting almost any barrier. In addition, despite Syrian and Israeli blockades on LNM areas, food and military supplies were reaching the fighters.[18]

Saudi and Sudanese units that arrived on 1 July took up positions in Beirut and Sidon. They were equipped with tanks and troop carriers. They were helpless, however, in supervising the cease-fire.[19] Fighting in Beirut and the Mountain continued and the Combined Forces were capable of advancing against right-wing positions there. The cease-fire, Lebanon's fifty-first, which was announced on 2 July, crumbled the same day. Fighting again erupted around Tal al-Zatar.[20]

On 4 July, Bakradoni of the LKP was in Syria for talks with Asad. Jalloud, the Libyan envoy, was also in Damascus trying to reconcile Asad with the LNM and the Resistance. On the same day, the Arab League committee held a meeting with the Resistance and the Syrian Foreign Minister.[21] All these efforts failed, however, and fighting raged on all fronts. By 5 July Tal al-Zatar had repelled the forty-seventh major right-wing offensive. The eighth of July marked the nineteenth day of the siege of the camp, and by that time it had repelled 50 attempts to penetrate its defences.[22]

In the north, the coastal town of Shekka was recaptured by the right wing. The northern right-wing offensive was generally successful, because Syrian troops blocked roads to prevent men and supplies from reaching the Combined Forces.[23] The shelling that the Syrian army directed against Tripoli in the north and Zahrani in the south compelled Jumblatt to threaten Syria with a people's war. He also renewed the call for the establishment of local administration in LNM areas.[24]

Syrian troops met with stiff resistance in the north, the south and the Bekaa. After a devastating defeat of Syrian tanks near Sidon, Syria withdrew from the area on 13 July. In the Bekaa Syria was able to enter Baalbek, while in the Mountain its troops cut off Aley from Al-Matn.[25]

Anticipating Syrian predominance in Lebanon, some members of parliament joined in a National United Front that was based on three principles of unity: the rejection of partition, an end to intervention and the implementation of the 1969 Cairo Agreement. These efforts were made by the LNM in a futile attempt to counter Syria's actions diplomatically.[26] Meanwhile, co-ordination between Syria and the right ensued when, on 11 July, a high-level delegation went to Syria for talks. The delegation comprised Bashir Gemayel, Bakradoni, Danny Chamoun, Lucien Dahdah and Joseph Mughabghab.[27]

On 13 July a second Arab Foreign Ministers' meeting was held. It called for a cease-fire and dialogue between the Resistance and Syria. The Ministers also agreed to beef up the Arab Security Forces.[28]

Concurrently, Tal al-Zatar continued to repel attacks, amidst talks of a Palestinian delegation to be sent to Damascus to patch up Syrian–Palestinian differences. On 18 July an LKP (Phalangist) delegation went to Damascus for talks, while the LNM intensified diplomatic contacts with some Arab governments that could pressure Syria to moderate its position toward the LNM.[29]

On 19 July, a tripartite conference of Saudi Arabia, Egypt and Sudan was held in Jeddah, Saudi Arabia. Among other things, the conference discussed Lebanon and decided to recommend a cease-fire, the implementation of Arab League decisions and roundtable reconciliation talks.[30] On the same day Arafat confirmed that the Resistance had decided to send a delegation to Damascus.

## A Syrian–Palestinian Agreement

On 21 July the Palestinian delegation went to Damascus. The talks resulted in a Syrian–Palestinian agreement on 26 July 1976.[31] Both sides agreed upon the following: (1) that the Constitutional Document of 14 February 1976 would serve as a basis for national dialogue; (2) that the Resistance would not intervene in Lebanon's affairs, and that relations between the two parties must be governed by the 1969 Cairo Agreement; (3) that the Resistance had the right to operate from all Arab fronts including Lebanon; (4) that a cease-fire in all of Lebanon should be accepted by all the parties to the conflict; and (5) that a tripartite committee, headed by the Arab League, should supervise the cease-fire.[32]

In addition, the Damascus Agreement included many secret points, chief among them: (1) the separation of Lebanese demands from those of the Resistance; (2) the Resistance's agreement not to demand withdrawal of Syrian troops from Lebanon; (3) the cessation of the propaganda war between the two sides; (4) continual consultation with Syria, which must approve all steps to be taken by the Resistance; (5) the determination of where to have Palestinian concentration centres before sending them to the future Palestinian state; (6) the returning of Saiqa offices to that organization in Beirut; and (7) a new Cabinet to be formed in Syria with Khlaifawi as Prime Minister.[33]

The agreement was rejected by Chamoun and Gemayel.[34] The Rejection

Front also attacked it as interference in Palestinian affairs and claimed it bypassed the LNM completely.[35] In point of fact, the agreement was a triumph for the Syrian side. It appeared that the Palestinians agreed to it because it allowed them to operate (at least theoretically) from all Arab fronts. Also, the main concern of the Palestinians at that moment was to lift the siege from Tal al-Zatar and bring stability to Lebanon. As long as they were allowed to operate from Lebanon, they were willing to abide by the Cairo Agreement of 1969.

Despite the Damascus Agreement, however, the Tal al-Zatar and Nabah battles did not stop. Furthermore, Syria kept on shelling the south and the Mountain and did not lift its blockade of Tripoli.[36]

Meanwhile, the LNM began to organize the areas under its control so as to enable it to administer health care, food, water, electricity and security. Previously, each component of the LNM had performed these tasks separately. The LNM wanted to centralize these activities.[37] A Central Political Council was formed to take care of these matters and also to co-ordinate in a more efficient way the activities of the various LNM components. Jumblatt was the Council President and Rafii was elected First Vice-President and Ra'd, Qulailat and Hawi, Vice-Presidents. Ibrahim was elected Executive Secretary. Bureau chiefs for all districts and functions were also elected.[38] Under pressure, the LNM was forced to seek a more efficient and effective organization. This, however, was at least a year too late. Such a move had been needed from the beginning of the conflict to channel the efforts of the mobilized masses according to a general plan. But such a move was still welcome, as it signified that the LNM was insisting upon the implementation of its programme, and was gearing its efforts in that direction.

## The Fall of Tal al-Zatar

The first several days of August witnessed intensified right-wing military activities, in which the main objective was to clear all areas north of Beirut of the LNM and the Resistance. For this reason the battle raged in Tal al-Zatar, and other LNM areas were shelled. The Mountain fronts were especially important to the right wing, which sought to isolate West Beirut from its sources of supply in the Chouf mountains. On 4 August the right wing announced it had conquered Nabah.[39] This LNM defeat made it more difficult for Tal al-Zatar to resist. The attackers were amassing more troops for a major assault on the camp. Meanwhile, the LNM announced that it had no other option but to fight. Habash, of the Rejection Front, confirmed the LNM position by announcing there would be no concessions, only resistance, and that the liberated areas were to remain as such.[40]

The Resistance intensified its diplomatic efforts on the Arab and Lebanese levels in an attempt to prevent the camp from falling. It expressed its willingness to abide by the Cairo Agreement and called upon Syria to begin the implementation of the Damascus Agreement.[41] The Syrians, however, were unwilling to do so. They first wanted to weaken the Combined Forces and pressure them to withdraw from the Mountain. The Syrians and the right wing were adamant in wanting to bring about the fall of the camp, which threatened the security of the right-wing areas in Beirut and the lines of communications of East Beirut with the Mountain. In addition, the fall of the camp would relieve 10,000 troops for Mountain operations.

On 12 August 1976, Tal al-Zatar fell after 52 days of daily shellings and repeated assaults. Its 2,500 defenders were almost annihilated in house-to-house fighting after the camp's defences were penetrated. The remaining 12,000 camp residents were evicted and it was subsequently bulldozed.[42]

Soon after the fall of the camp the right wing began preparing for the Mountain battles. Tank battles also raged in Beirut. The victorious right wing renewed its call for partition. Gemayel, for instance, called for 'decentralization' and for what he termed 'unity in multiplicity'.[43] The LNM reacted by calling upon the Arab League to protect Lebanon's unity. Jumblatt followed this by declaring that the LNM was not ready to negotiate with its adversaries who wanted partition.

## Moves Towards an Arab Summit

To arrest this deteriorating situation, Saudi Arabia and Kuwait were calling for an Arab summit meeting to take action against partition. Sudan supported the efforts to hold such a meeting.[44]

On 16 August the right wing began to fight in Ayntoura. The Resistance announced it would continue to fight and not compromise by relinquishing its positions in the Mountain. This announcement was in defiance of the Syrians, who were pressing the Resistance to pull out from the Mountain. Three days later the right wing announced its intention of fighting until it 'liberated' all of Lebanon.[45] Meanwhile, Gemayel announced he was for dialogue between Christians and Muslims.[46] These announcements were in fact designed to counter the diplomatic efforts of the LKP's adversaries, who were pressing for an Arab summit. Another attempt to derail the movement towards an Arab summit came when Franjieh instructed the Lebanese ambassador to the UN to enter a complaint against 'the tampering of the PLO with Lebanese sovereignty'.[47] This request was interpreted as an attempt to internationalize the conflict.

The (Saudi) Commander of the Arab Security Forces in Lebanon met Jumblatt and Salam in an attempt to reach a cease-fire agreement. One of its provisions was to secure an LNM withdrawal from the Mountain.[48] Jumblatt rejected the proposal since no cease-fire had ever held during the conflict. The LNM regarded the proposal as a way to surrender ground to the Syrians and the right wing.

On 21 August, Jumblatt pressed for the convening of an Arab summit. Saudi Arabia suggested the meeting be held in Riyadh, the Saudi capital.[49] Meanwhile, the LKP announced that diplomatic solutions had failed in

Lebanon, and that there was no alternative but to fight.[50] In effect, the LKP was repeating what the right wing had said earlier in its attempt to put hurdles in the way of the Arab summit. This right-wing position was congruent with Dean Brown's statement in Washington, DC, on 22 August. He was of the opinion that the armed conflict was going to be a long one and that 'cantonization' — partition — was the solution which would prevent Lebanon from turning left.[51] Partition was 'creeping' in on Lebanon. In his capacity as Education Minister, Chamoun signed an order that allowed the opening of branches for all colleges of the Lebanese University in East Beirut.[52] This move further solidified partition.

By 24 August, it was apparent that the right-wing Mountain operations were unsuccessful. The right wing redirected the fighting to Beirut and shelled West Beirut. These moves were accompanied by renewed attempts toward rapprochement with the Muslim traditional zuama in an attempt to isolate the LNM from any further negotiations on the Lebanese or Arab level. This was crucial to the right wing since the Saudis were criticizing Jumblatt's position and had called for a Palestinian–LKP reconciliation.[53] This meant that the Saudis regarded the conflict as one between the Palestinians and the Lebanese. This portrayal of the conflict was in the interest of the LKP, which wanted to leave nebulous the internal contradictions brought about by the Lebanese system.

The Arab Security Forces Commander was still attempting to effect a cease-fire that stipulated the withdrawal of the LNM from the Mountain and the implementation of the 1969 Cairo Agreement. The LNM again rejected the cease-fire proposal. The Resistance argued that one of the parties to the 1969 Cairo Agreement (the Lebanese state) was non-existent. The Resistance, however, expressed its willingness to abide by the Cairo Agreement and pull out from the Mountain as soon as a Lebanese state became a viable entity.[54]

Meanwhile the fighting was raging on all fronts. To deal with this situation the Arab League asked for an emergency meeting of the Arab Foreign Ministers. The meeting was set for 4 September.[55]

On 31 August, President-elect Sarkis met with Asad in Damascus, where Syria reaffirmed its support for his presidency. During the last several days of August, Israel was claiming that a military and political vacuum existed in the south of Lebanon. On the last day of the month Israel intervened militarily in the southern town of Aynebel and announced that it was not allowing a reconciliation in Lebanon to occur behind its back. On 1 September, Israel 'offered' to 'protect' the southern Christian villages and began to amass troops in Aynebel. Israel also declared it was not going to allow the Resistance to return to the south.[56]

Meanwhile, Gemayel demanded the cancellation of the Cairo Agreement and called upon the Arab League to resolve the conflict. On 5 September, however, he accepted an invitation to visit Damascus and then attacked the Arab League's initiative to resolve the crisis.[57] The Arab initiative began the previous day when the Arab Foreign Ministers met to determine the time and place of the Arab summit meeting. On the same day as the ministers' meeting, fighting escalated in Lebanon. The Saudi commander accused the right wing of escalating the fighting.

On 5 September the Arab League announced the time and place of the summit meeting: it was to be held in Cairo some time during the third week of October. Furthermore, the League established a committee composed of some of the Arab Foreign Ministers to try to calm the situation in Lebanon before the convening of the Arab summit.[58]

On 8 September, Chamoun visited Damascus following a visit by the LKP delegation three days earlier. He met Asad and Khaddam, the Foreign Minister, and declared that Syrian troops were to remain in Lebanon as long as the Lebanese authorities were willing to accept them.[59]

Jumblatt countered these right-wing moves by declaring that the LNM was not so pressed as to negotiate with anyone. He also said that Sarkis could help resolve the conflict if he were able to transcend narrow interests.[60] What this meant was that Sarkis must not side with the Maronites, be amenable to Syria's position on Lebanon or agree to measures that consecrated confessionalism.

On 11 September the Resistance and the Syrians met in Shtoura in an effort to iron out their differences. Arafat reiterated the Resistance's position regarding its withdrawal from the Mountain. Jumblatt also called for the abolition of confessionalism and the adoption of the LNM reform programme. He also attacked the traditional zuama for their reluctance to move toward the LNM position.[61]

In point of fact, these zuama had been intensifying diplomatic contacts to bring about a solution to the conflict since Sarkis had assumed the presidency. On 15 September Salam met with Asad in Damascus. Egypt was also instrumental in that regard. President Sadat of Egypt had separate meetings on 14 September with Karami, Imam Musa Sadr and an LKP delegation. Taking advantage of their visit, Karami and Bashir Gemayel met in the Cairo Hilton on 15 September, where they discussed matters relating to Sarkis and stability. The Mufti also met with Asad in Damascus before leaving for Egypt.[62]

These meetings indicated that these traditional zuama were trying to find a solution that would preclude the LNM and its programme. At a meeting in Shtoura between Sarkis and Arafat on 17 September, Sarkis demanded the Resistance withdraw from the Mountain. Sarkis's position was congruent with Franjieh's and Chamoun's, who had earlier announced that no negotiations were possible before the Combined Forces withdrew from the Mountain. The Resistance and the LNM in turn announced their unwillingness to withdraw from the Mountain before a solution to the conflict had been found.[63]

A second tripartite meeting was held in Shtoura on 19 September. The meeting reached deadlock on the question of a pull-out from the Mountain. The stalemate remained even after Sarkis assumed the presidency on 23 September.[64] The LNM was hoping that the Arab summit would curtail

Syria's influence somewhat. The Resistance, meanwhile, confirmed that diplomatic contacts were under way to convene a mini-Arab summit prior to the 18 October full summit.[65]

## A Syrian Fait Accompli

Unwilling to take chances with these summits, Syria decided to present the Arabs with a fait accompli in Lebanon. In an offensive that lasted four days against LNM Mountain positions, Syria entered most of the LNM-held areas.[66] The LKP also fought the LNM in the Mountain and announced that it was going to continue the fight even if the Syrians were to stop. Sarkis and other traditional zuama (including Salam) had prior knowledge of the offensive.[67]

On 29 September, the second day of the Syrian offensive, Egypt called for a mini-summit to be held within 48 hours. On the first day of the offensive Jumblatt was already in Cairo to press for Arabization of the conflict. He later left for Saudi Arabia and Baghdad and returned to Cairo, where he consulted with Sadat on the mini-summit.[68]

On 1 October the Lebanese army, under Army Commander Said, was deployed in Aley against the LNM. The right wing also shelled West Beirut and the Palestinian refugee camps. Meanwhile, an LKP delegation went to Damascus for talks with Asad.[69]

In Cairo, Jumblatt called, on 3 October, for a mini-summit. He then left for Paris, where he called upon France to intervene diplomatically to end the fighting.[70] On 4 October, Qansu (of the BPO) announced that Syria was continuing its military solution and that it stood against any initiative that did not support its plans.[71]

Despite the end of the four-day Syrian offensive, fighting raged in Beirut and the right wing kept shelling West Beirut. The Mountain fronts were occasionally busy. The LNM kept pressing for a French initiative. These moves led Qansu to attack the LNM, the Resistance and the LAA.[72]

After Paris, Jumblatt visited Algeria and Libya on 7 October, where he asked both countries for material help. This prompted a Libyan delegation to leave immediately for Syria. But other events pre-empted these efforts. On 8 October, the LNM criticized the Resistance for having met with representatives of Sarkis. The LNM was of the opinion that such meetings were counter-productive and detracted from the Arab and French initiatives. On the same day, Israel aided the right wing in shelling an LNM area in the south. The following day, Israel and the right wing escalated the fighting in the south, and by 10 October the Combined Forces were under attack in the south, the Mountain and Beirut.[73]

The LKP renewed its threats to 'liberate' all Lebanese territory. Syria also helped by its attempt to discredit Jumblatt among the Druze. Syria propped up certain Druze leaders to fight Jumblatt in co-ordination with the LKP. While battles were raging throughout Lebanon, an LKP delegation visited

Syria on 13 October accompanied by Danny Chamoun (Camille's son) and the Druze Faisal Arslan. Later that day they were followed by Bashir Gemayel.[74] On the previous day the right wing had opened a new front east of Sidon at Room-Jizzine. Street fighting raged there for five days.

These tactics were intended to derail the Arabization effort. On 15 October, however, Saudi Arabia called for a mini-summit to be attended by Sadat, Asad, Sarkis, Arafat, King Khaled of Saudi Arabia and Prince Sabbah of Kuwait. The date was set for 17 October in Riyadh.[75]

The mini-summit was held on schedule. It decided upon a cease-fire, the creation of an Arab Deterrent Force (ADF) under Sarkis's command and a committee of four to guarantee the implementation of the Cairo Agreement within 90 days. The Riyadh mini-summit also called for dialogue among all the Lebanese warring parties. The full Arab summit was postponed until 25 October.[76]

The right wing, however, with Israel's help, kept fighting in the south. The object was to defeat the Riyadh agreement — and Israel was intent on not allowing the Resistance to return to the south. The right wing also wanted to crush the Resistance and the LNM.[77]

Gemayel suggested that the ADF should have international supervision. Chamoun, however, refused to allow the ADF to enter right-wing areas once it started its mission in Lebanon.[78]

On 25 October the Cairo Arab summit meeting rubber-stamped the Riyadh agreement. Six countries agreed to participate in the ADF: Saudi Arabia, Sudan, Yemen, Libya, the United Arab Emirates and Syria. The ADF was to have 30,000 troops, over two-thirds of which were to be Syrian.[79] In effect, the ADF became a cover for the Syrian invasion.

On 27 October, Palestinian reinforcements from Syria moved to the south, while others left the Mountain and Jizzine to bolster forces in the south.[80] At this time the Syrians needed to strengthen the Resistance to help bring about a Middle East settlement in which Syria would be included.

Despite its initial refusal to allow the ADF to enter its areas, the right wing finally accepted, lest the tide of war turn against it. After much delay the ADF entered (1) many areas (on 8 November) including Junieh, the right-wing capital north of Beirut, and Khaldeh, south of Beirut; (2) (on 9 November) the right-wing Mountain areas of Kahala, Bekfayya and Aynsaadeh; (3) (on 15 November) Beirut [eastern and western areas]; and (4) (20 November) Sidon and Tripoli. The ADF had control of all major areas in Lebanon except the south.[81]

On 8 December Sarkis asked Dr Hoss, an economist, to form a Cabinet of technocrats so that reconstruction could begin. The Cabinet included the following ministers: Bizri, Raphael, Doumit, Salam, Sheito, Boutross and Rizk.[82]

After the Cairo summit, Lebanon re-emerged with a confessional system and state as before. It re-emerged, however, maimed and divided. No longer did one hear the name Beirut without the adjectives 'East' or 'West'. There were right-wing areas and LNM areas. A 'Christian' Lebanon existed in the south along the Israeli border. Confessionalism, thanks to Arab reactionaries and imperialism, had been maintained. This confessional state, however, had lost its major feature: cohesion. Without cohesion such a state ruled only with the direct support of external forces.

Most significant perhaps was the fact that the LNM had been contained. It still, however, enjoyed the allegiance of the majority of the Lebanese. It had also matured under fire and most important of all, it never relinquished its guns.

## Conclusion

The Syrian invasion was instrumental in the containment of revolutionary development in Lebanon. All gains the LNM had achieved during the Mountain offensive were pushed back with the 1 June 1976 Syrian invasion of Lebanon. Internally, the invasion was supported by the National Front and other zuama affiliated to it, and also by the Maronite right wing. Once the Syrians were in Lebanon, the majority of the Muslim sector of the bourgeoisie chose to co-operate with Syria rather than with the LNM. Additionally, many groups within the LNM opted for co-operation with Syria to bring stability to Lebanon. These options were compelling at this time since Israel and the right wing had opened a new military front in the south of Lebanon. This co-operation, however, was not an alliance between peers but one between a victorious occupation army and a contained LNM.

The Syrian invasion allowed the right wing to attack Palestinian and LNM areas. Tal al-Zatar and mountain positions came under heavy attack both by the Syrians and the right wing. The Syrians also tried to drive a wedge between the Resistance and the LNM through the Palestinian–Syrian agreement of 26 July 1976. But the agreement was not implemented since the Syrians refused to pressure the right wing to lift the siege of Tal al-Zatar or to move their buffer troops out of the way of the Combined Forces' relief columns.

A major problem with the LNM was that it still was unwilling to break with Syria, even though Syria had frequently betrayed its interests. The traditional nationalist and anti-imperialist role Syria had played in the past, and especially Syria's role in the 1973 October war, obfuscated the nature of the Asad regime from most of the political parties that comprised the LNM. Only the Arab Baath Socialist Party (ABSP) consistently warned the LNM of the Machiavellian trickery that Syria was enacting. The LNM was, however, reluctant to heed these warnings, since it was cognizant of the animosity that the two wings of the Baath (ABSP and the pro-Syrian Baath Party Organization – BPO) harboured for each other.

It was also very difficult for the LNM to sever ties with Syria, since most of its arms were Syrian supplied. Syria utilized this dependence to maximize and realize its own interests within Lebanon and to control the extent to which the LNM could achieve success. As Kamal Jumblatt pointed out in his book, *This is My Will*, on various occasions the pro-Syrian BPO was selective in delivering arms to the various LNM components that bought the merchandise.

Because the LNM was militarily weak and dependent upon Syrian arms, its success could be realized only within the parameters of Syrian designs. This ultimately worked to the detriment of LNM objectives. Prior to the Battle of Lebanon, a frontal attack on the state would have been premature and perhaps counter-productive. In the initial confrontation with the state the LNM seemed to be improving its position through 'peaceful' means. The state was obliged to grant some reforms in order to preserve its institutions. The LNM should have realized, however, that in the final analysis, the state will ultimately protect the interests of its own ruling class. The LNM should have become cognizant of this fact when it discovered that in many situations the organs of state power were frequently used against it. It would have been wise for the LNM to prepare for other eventualities. This failure to perceive the true nature of the state and to prepare adequately for armed conflict were perhaps the major errors the LNM committed prior to the Battle of Lebanon.[83] Other important factors in its failure was its lack of clarity in regard to the Syrian role, and its benevolent estimations of the right-wing intentions. This last matter could have been avoided if the LNM had been clearer about the power relations in the state and the right-wing necessity of maintaining hegemony at all costs.

The Syrian invasion was not in the least inimical to the immediate interests of the US and Israel. Both countries were interested in the defeat of the LNM and the Resistance, which Syria was more than willing to accomplish. The fall of Tal al-Zatar and Israeli intervention in the south of Lebanon, indicated the immediate common interests among Israel, Syria and the Maronite right wing.

The LNM also suffered because of errors in the area of organization. These errors were serious setbacks that prevented the LNM from consolidating its gains.

One reason why the LNM was reluctant to engage in battle was because it did not want its adversaries to accuse it of working for partition (a charge was later levelled at the LNM by Asad in any case). Because the LNM did not opt for a military solution until a late stage in the Battle of Lebanon (1976), it failed to centralize and take charge of administering the areas under its military control. As with the NDC, the reluctance to set up a central political council allowed many traditional leaders, who lost legitimacy among the population, to stay on the loose and pretend to exercise more power than they in fact had. As with the NDC, the non-existence of a political council allowed these zuama to pretend to represent the masses while they contacted other Arab and foreign states to work out a solution that could keep confessionalism intact.

Jumblatt himself regretted that this central political council was not established earlier. He did, however, advance policies, such as implementing land reform in the LNM-liberated areas, that other groups within the LNM rejected.[84] Local administrations that did exist in LNM areas were set up spontaneously and haphazardly, and were also unco-ordinated with each other; this left the populations in many of these areas subject to the whims of profiteers. Instead of individual efforts being directed in a more efficient manner to support the LNM, they were misdirected or unfulfilled. The spontaneous mass movement that wholeheartedly supported the LNM was not given proper direction in organizing itself, consolidating its gains and protecting its interests through an organized and independent political body. For these reasons the spontaneous mass movement lost a great opportunity to mature and in this process, propel the LNM further along the road of revolutionary development.

When the Central Political Council of the LNM was finally established it was compelled by the imminent Syrian invasion. At this late stage, however, the Central Political Council was not equipped or prepared to handle the monumental task of a comprehensive and co-ordinated defence against Syria, which at that time was in collusion with the right wing, Israel, the US and the reactionary Arab regimes. These major actors all had a vested interest in maintaining the status quo and procuring the defeat of the LNM.

Evidence of complicity among these forces was overwhelming, and this complicity allowed the LNM no choice but to develop organizationally to meet the reactionary onslaught, and to this end the Central Political Council (CPC) was formed. The formation of the CPC was, however, as already mentioned, too late to be effective. Arab diplomatic moves were already under way to bring about an end to the conflict. The Riyadh mini-summit and the Arab summit in Cairo resulted in the containment of the LNM and the Resistance, and provided confessionalism with a new lease of life.

The LNM was in control of 80% of Lebanon's territory before the Syrian invasion. An organized, armed and disciplined political apparatus with clear strategic aims could have assumed state power at that point. As it turned out, the LNM opted for a political solution to the conflict that co-opted its gains and left intact the mechanisms for its later defeats. It was this petty bourgeois radicalism and reformism that resulted in the serious setback to revolutionary development in that area and the ascendancy to power of the right wing in Lebanon, whose dominance was finally secured with the Israeli invasion of Lebanon after 6 June 1982.

## Notes

1. *Lebanon's War* (Beirut, Dar al-Masseerah, 1977), 241.
2. Ibid.
3. *At-Tariq* (January–August 1976), 347.
4. Ibid., *Lebanon's War*, op. cit., p. 242.
5. *At-Tariq*, op. cit., p. 345.
6. *Lebanon's War*, op. cit.
7. Ibid.

8. Ibid.
9. Ibid.
10. Ibid.
11. Ibid.
12. Interview with Fateh, The Revolutionary Council, 9 September 1978.
13. *At-Tariq*, op. cit.
14. *Lebanon's War*, op. cit., p. 244.
15. Ibid., p. 243–244.
16. Interview with Rejection Front members, 15 August 1978.
17. *At-Tariq*, op. cit., p. 348.
18. Interview with Rejection Front Members, op. cit.
19. *At-Tariq*, op. cit., p. 245.
20. *Lebanon's War*, op. cit., p. 245.
21. Ibid.
22. Ibid., p. 246.
23. Ibid.
24. Ibid., p. 247.
25. Ibid., p. 246.
26. Ibid.
27. Ibid.
28. Ibid.
29. Ibid., p. 247.
30. Ibid.
31. H. Hassan, *Lebanon from Ayn-El-Rummaneh till Riadh* (Baghdad, Thawra Publication), 81.
32. Ibid.
33. Ibid., pp. 81–82.
34. *Lebanon's War*, op. cit., p. 249.
35. Ibid.
36. *At-Tariq*, op. cit., p. 351.
37. *Lebanon's War*, op. cit., p. 247.
38. Ibid., p. 249.
39. Ibid.
40. Ibid.
41. Ibid., p. 250.
42. Ibid.
43. Ibid.
44. Ibid.
45. Ibid.
46. Ibid.
47. Ibid.
48. Ibid.
49. Ibid., p. 251.
50. *The Two-Year War* (Beirut, Dar An-Hanar), XV.
51. *Lebanon's War*, op. cit.
52. Ibid.
53. Ibid.
54. Ibid.
55. *The Two-Year War*, op. cit., p. XVI.
56. *Lebanon's War*, op. cit., p. 252.

57. Ibid.
58. Ibid.
59. *The Two-Year War*, op. cit.
60. Ibid.
61. *Lebanon's War*, op. cit., p. 254.
62. Ibid.
63. Ibid.
64. Ibid.
65. Ibid.
66. Ibid., p. 255.
67. Ibid.
68. *The Two-Year War*, op. cit.
69. *Lebanon's War*, op. cit., p. 256.
70. Ibid.
71. Ibid.
72. Ibid.
73. Ibid., p. 257.
74. Ibid., p. 258.
75. Ibid.
76. *The Two-Year War*, op. cit.
77. This is evident from many statements by right-wing leaders.
78. *Lebanon's War*, op. cit., p. 258.
79. There were already 20,000 Syrian troops in Lebanon.
80. *Lebanon's War*, op. cit.
81. The south was below the 'red line' which Israel had warned the Syrians not to cross.
82. *Lebanon's War*, op. cit., p. 263.
83. According to Jumblatt, the Palestinian Resistance did not really want to see the LNM militarily independent. This LNM weakness limited its options during the Battle. (Kamal Jumblatt, *This is My Will*, Al-Watan Al Arabi, June 1978; translated into English as *I Speak for Lebanon*, London, Zed Press, 1982.)
84. Ibid., pp. 124, 145–6.

# 9. Israel's Invasion of Lebanon: 6 June 1982

Despite Syria's preponderance in Lebanon and her containment of the LNM, the LNM retained great prestige among the masses, especially because Kamal Jumblatt was at its head. Jumblatt emerged from the war as an international figure widely known in European and United States political circles. No solution for Lebanon could have been envisaged by these circles without considering Jumblatt's position, although from time to time he proved to be a great impediment to counter-revolutionary designs. On 16 March 1977 he was assassinated — by whom remains a mystery. It is evident, however, that his death simplified the task of imperialism in the region.

Walid Jumblatt succeeded his father, Kamal, to the leadership of the LNM and the SPP. Walid also steered the LNM to a pro-Syrian position. The events that followed reflected the conflict among the various actors in the area. Without a consensus among the warring factions Lebanon's stabilization was impossible, but the various interests involved prevented such a consensus forthcoming. These irreconcilable interests left Lebanon divided — de facto — and this de facto partition intensified instability. The LNM was calling for its programme to become the basis for a new, stable political solution. On the other hand, Arab reactionaries, Israel and the US all had an interest in preventing a new political arrangement that would give the LNM a role or strengthen the LNM-PRM alliance. These contradictions contributed to precipitating the Israeli invasion of Lebanon on 6 June 1982. Before discussing this invasion it is necessary to provide some background to developments that followed the Riyadh mini-summit and the 1976 Arab summit in Cairo which wrapped up the 1975–76 Lebanese civil war.

The Lebanon events of 1975–76 were part and parcel of an imperialist push to bring about a regional settlement. The Arab East is one area that seems to offer some sections of US capitalism the opportunity for a partial recovery from its own crisis of overproduction. US imperialism has, therefore, sought a way to maintain control of the area, its production and consumption. With US hegemony there, about 150 million consumers would be in the market for more goods and services, and petro-dollars could be spent on development projects by US industries and multinationals. Also, without the Arab East 'distraction', imperialism would be able to concentrate more attention and resources towards directing a deadly blow against the Latin

American revolutionary movement. It is thus understandable why the US has a vital interest in stabilizing the Arab East.

Revolutionary developments in parts of the Arab world were presenting problems for imperialist interests. In Egypt, the proletariat were moving dramatically in presenting a threat to Sadat's regime. During 18–19 January 1977 massive demonstrations in all the major cities and towns of Egypt were held to protest Egyptian rapprochement with Israel and the United States.[1] Rapprochement with Israel had begun immediately after the October War. Egypt was moving steadily towards a 'peaceful' solution to her problems (the return of the Sinai) with Israel. Although the opening to the West (Al-Infitaah) had started before the October War, it was given impetus and further justification after 1973. The object of the Infitaah was to tie Egypt more directly and strongly to the international capitalist market. Al-Infitaah soon led to more inflation, more unemployment and general misery for the proletariat in Egypt.[2]

The rebellion, mercilessly suppressed by Sadat, spurred him to move quickly in negotiations for the return of the Sinai. Sadat knew that while he was able to strike a severe blow to the proletariat, if he did not move fast with negotiations, the situation would become more problematical. These major domestic considerations prompted Sadat to fly to Jerusalem on 19 November 1977.

The defeat of the Egyptian proletariat in its first major challenge to Sadat's regime and the subsequent trip to Jerusalem had wakened the revolutionary forces comprising the Arab Revolutionary Movement (ARM). This also had an effect on the LNM and the PRM, but they were already in a weak position since their containment during the Battle of Lebanon. To recapitulate, the general situation in Lebanon then was characterized by the predominance of Syria, the ascendancy, as never before, of the fascist forces (LKP, etc.), the resurrection of confessionalism, with all its implications, and a subdued LNM and PRM.

With this situation in Lebanon, Israel soon mounted a major offensive against the LNM–PRM alliance in the South of Lebanon. Israel's March 1978 offensive had the following objectives:

1. Deal a heavy blow to the LNM–PRM alliance.
2. Extend Israel's influence into Lebanon by establishing a six mile wide area inside Lebanon along her border.
3. Counter Syria's influence.
4. Strengthen the Lebanese central government's bargaining position with the LNM therefore improving the fascist forces position within this government.
5. Improve her position in any imperialist imposed regional solution.

With this offensive, Israel was able to accomplish some of her objectives. Most notably, she was able to maintain her forces within the six mile zone she had established. This zone was patrolled and scouted by the puppet Lebanese army major Saed Haddad.

Immediately after this invasion, a major showdown began to develop between the LKP and the Syrian troops of the Arab Deterrent Forces (ADF). Syria, who during the last phase of the Lebanese civil war came to the rescue of her makeshift LKP allies, now found herself the object of attack. The LKP entered this confrontation aided by units of the Lebanese army. The LKP felt it could handle the sufficiently weakened LNM, and press to improve its position within Lebanese politics, once Syria was forced to agree to LKP ascendancy. The LKP attack resulted in the removal of Syrian forces from key positions in LKP-held areas of Beirut (especially from the bridges at the northern entrances to Beirut). Syrian forces were replaced by Saudi forces working within the ADF, which were later removed.

The Israeli and LKP attacks improved both the central government's and LKP's positions vis-à-vis the LNM, Syria and the PRM. Right-wing manoeuvring was being facilitated primarily due to the strategic thrust of Syrian policy in Lebanon. Syria was against any fundamental change that might in any way threaten the Syrian regime. In fact, this was the main reason for Syrian intervention in Lebanon. This policy worked to the advantage of the right-wing at that time since it checked the ascendancy of LNM–PRM advances.

Another reason for this relative ease of right-wing manoeuvring was that the LNM was mostly a coalition of various organizations forced to come together under fire. They did not have the co-ordination, the discipline or the consensus to carry it further. Another complication arose with Jumblatt's assassination, which brought the LNM closer to Syrian policy.

LNM gravitation toward the Syrian position left the masses perplexed as to the movement's real objectives. Since the LNM was not communicating a clear political line vis-à-vis Syria they were losing an important opportunity to harness the spontaneous efforts of the masses in implementing a programme perceived to be in their interest. Thus the revolutionary movement was unable to achieve political independence that would have allowed it to seek alliances for the realization of its strategic goals without being compromised.

In part, failure of the LNM (and the PRM) was due to the class structure obtaining in Lebanese (and Palestinian) society which reflected the class make-up of the LNM political parties and organizations. Dominated by petty bourgeois radical nationalists, the LNM was guided by bourgeois ideology and a form of idealism that was of little help to the Movement in its fight against fascism.

While these reactionary moves were taking place in the region, the Arab Revolutionary Movement (ARM) was incapable of generating any consequential counter-move or strategy. The only significant eventuality was the creation of the Steadfastness and Confrontation Front (SCF) in 1978. The Front comprised Syria, Libya, South Yemen, Algeria and the PLO.[3] It primarily came into being to combat the Camp David 'peace' process. A plan to confront these imperialist designs was needed but the Front failed to develop any real plan. No state within the Front was capable of fully supporting a war of attrition against Israel, and except for Syria, no Front states shared borders with Israel. Syria was unwilling to precipitate such a bold move lest it provoke Israel to a war which could prove detrimental to Syria. In addition, Syria was still banking on diplomatic efforts to solve the Lebanese situation and return the Golan Heights.

Syrian strategy was to work for a comprehensive regional 'peace' settlement. This position agreed with the USSR's policy objectives in the region. Syria felt that Soviet support was contingent upon the diplomatic option. The USSR was pursuing a strategy of detente. Consequently, it would not want to unnecessarily endanger (as the USSR saw it) this global detente with imperialism. For all these reasons, the Front was little more than a political effort without much effect. Even the Arab masses had little hope in its efficacy; they had already lost faith in most of its participants and Syria's role in support of fascism was still fresh in their memories.

A seeming peculiarity about the Front was the absence of Iraq. Iraq had consistently opposed all 'peaceful' solutions. Iraq was, however, at odds with Syria owing to the rivalry between the two Baath factions of Iraq and Syria. These antagonisms were responsible for setbacks in Arab policy towards Israel. When Arab public and official pressure attempted to force Iraq into joining the Front, Iraq quickly responded with a counter-proposal to that suggested by the Front. Knowing the strategic thrust and the weaknesses of the various Front states, Iraq proposed a complete plan, with a place for a military budget and troops with a unified command.[4] Iraq also pushed for a war of attrition against Israel. Furthermore, Iraq demanded that the Front must come against all 'peaceful' solutions and not only against Camp David. What she meant by that was obvious: against 'all' such solutions, including the Geneva-type conference supported by Syria and the USSR. This was a situation that would bring differences among the members of the Front since they did not hold the same position on the Geneva Conference; it was a clever move on Iraq's part; she justified her position to the Arab masses by claiming that the Front was not serious in confronting Israel.[5]

Instead of joining the Front and struggling from within for more militant positions, Iraq chose the opportunist tactic that ultimately contributed to the Front's ineffectiveness. Iraq could have polarized the situation in favour of the Arab progressives and exposed those states that did not want to actively oppose imperialism. But Iraq herself was not seriously interested in countering Camp David from within the Front, so she clothed her rhetoric with ultra revolutionary exhortations. The battle against counter-revolutionary solutions could have been initiated with Camp David. Once Camp David was defeated (through united Front action), there would have been a possibility to develop the Front for further action against other such 'peaceful' solutions.

The joint Arab opposition to the Camp David Accords came in the form of the Baghdad Ninth Arab Summit of November 1978. The meeting was unable to stop the motion towards the signing of the Egyptian–Israeli peace treaty of 26 March 1979. Politicking after the 1978 Summit, however, resulted in the consecration of Egypt's isolation from the rest of the Arab world. Because of their interest in a comprehensive settlement of the Palestinian issue, the reactionary Arab states were unwilling to accept the Camp David Accords as a framework for 'peace'. These Accords neither constituted nor led to any viable solution. As it turned out, Israel and the US were capable of achieving their objective of politically isolating Egypt from the rest of the Arab world; Israel no longer had to worry about Egypt in any Israeli–Arab confrontation. Egypt, too, opted to go it alone. The price, however, was steep, for Egypt and the rest of the Arabs.

A by-product of the Arab Summit of 1978 was increasing Iraqi regional prestige. That was significant, especially after the rapprochement between the Iraqi and Syrian regimes at the end of 1978. Talks of union between Syria and Iraq were initiated. Iraq seemed to be preparing herself to become a viable Gulf power. Iraq's sudden tilt towards Syria while continuing with her rapprochement with Saudi Arabia – which had started before the Baghdad Summit – reflected two major trends within the Iraqi Baath regime. While Iraqi policies towards Syria and Saudi Arabia were not necessarily incompatible in principle, they were headed by two different groupings within the regime. Sadam Hussein's grouping was against rapprochement with Syria. This grouping had dealt a severe blow to the Communist Party when, in 1977–78, it imprisoned and later executed many leading Communists. Factions within the Iraqi Baath were against the attack on the Communists. They felt this purge was a prelude to rapprochement with Saudi Arabia. By the time of the Baghdad Summit of 1978 there were clear indications that Iraq was moving to the right. The policy of anti-imperialism the regime had followed was coming to an end. This policy enabled Iraq to complete the nationalization of her oil and use the oil revenues to build infrastructures and increase her industrialization. The state capitalist regime felt it had consolidated itself to the point where it could begin to seek an important role within the international capitalist market. To do so, however, the Hussein grouping had physically to eliminate, not only the Communists, but also its opponents within the Baath Party, which it did in early 1979. As a result, Syria and Iraq remained enemies.

The Iranian revolution of February 1979 was another perceived threat to the Iraqi regime, already worried about its own future as early as 1978. Therefore, it carefully watched the development of the revolutionary situation on its borders. Sadam Hussein, however, put Iraq on a collision course with the new Iranian regime as soon as he chose to ally himself with Saudi Arabia – Iran's worst enemy in the Gulf.

Meanwhile, the signing of the Israeli–Egyptian peace treaty in April 1979 prompted the Arab states to convene their tenth Summit meeting in Tunisia. This Summit did not amount to much. The reactionary Arabs, led by Saudi Arabia, were in favour of a comprehensive settlement to the Arab–Israeli problem. The US, however, was wedded to the Camp David process. This Arab summit failed to influence US policy in favour of the Arab position.

1979 represents a year of transition for the entire region. Soon after the Camp David Accords were signed in 1978 and the Iraqi regime had shifted to the right, US interests were being threatened by the Iranian revolution.

The occupation of the US Embassy in Iran in late 1979, prompted the United States to rethink her tactics and strategy regarding the region. Having secured Camp David, she drew her attention to the Gulf. This did not escape the Arab reactionaries, especially Saudi Arabia and Iraq; both countries saw a chance for genuine co-operation with imperialism. They felt that they could guarantee the Gulf for the international capitalist market in exchange for a comprehensive settlement that, in turn, would guarantee both Saudi Arabia's and Iraq's regional interests, including the resolution of the Palestinian Question.

Iraq's invasion of Iran in September 1980 represented the new, close co-operation between the US and the Arab reactionaries. The war is financed by the Arab Gulf states, primarily Saudi Arabia, while military and logistical support has been coming from Jordan and Egypt. The reactionary Arabs and imperialism were unable to accomplish their goals (the defeat of the revolutionary process in the Gulf region) through the Iraq–Iran war. Despite their failure, however, both the Arab Revolutionary Movement (ARM) and the Iranian revolution suffered heavily.

The 1980 Amman Summit — which neither the SCF Arab states, nor the PLO attended — was primarily orchestrated by Saudi Arabia to give support to Iraq in the imperialist war against Iran. Syria and Libya did not want to be railroaded into supporting such a war in the name of Arab solidarity; South Yemen, the PLO and Algeria wanted no part of the Summit either, and this boycott underscored Arab disarray. Furthermore, this imperialist war was a major diversion of Arab resources from the main battle, the liberation of Palestine. Reactionary attempts to link this war, on the basis of its results, to the achievement of a comprehensive 'peace', all but failed; consequently, other means were sought. It was at this time (August 1981) that Crown Prince Fahd (now king) of Saudi Arabia presented a comprehensive 'peace' plan to serve as the basis for negotiations with the US and Israel. Fahd's plan called for the withdrawal of Israel from the territories she occupied in the 1967 war, the establishment of a Palestinian mini-state in the West Bank and Gaza and recognition of the state of Israel by the Arab States. The plan, however, did not mention the PLO as the sole, legitimate representative of the Palestinian people.[6]

To varying degrees, many Arab countries favoured the plan. Arafat was also in favour of it but objected to the fact that it did not mention the PLO as the sole, legitimate representative of the Palestinian people. Nevertheless, a situation seemed to exist that favoured the convening of an Arab summit meeting to adopt Fahd's plan as the unified Arab position in negotiations with the US and Israel. Arab reactionary thinking regarded such a plan as countering the Camp David Accords and pressuring the US to deal with the Arabs along the lines of the creation of a Palestinian state. These Saudi-led moves, however, were being conducted against a background of increased Arab weakness in fighting capabilities. The Gulf war was consuming tens of thousands of lives on both sides. In addition, Iraq's material and moral position was further weakened in terms of her effect on the Palestinian

Question when, in June 1981, Israel successfully bombed the nuclear reactor near Baghdad.

## The AWACS Deal — US–Israeli Contradiction

In bombing the nuclear reactor, Israel tried to score a point with the US. Israel's military arm could reach the Gulf to protect imperialist interests. Israel had an eye on the AWACS deal that the United States had negotiated with Saudi Arabia. The bombing was one of the tactics used to influence the voting in the United States Congress on this subject.

It had become increasingly clear since 1973–74 that the US could not rely on Israel as the main defender of US interests in the region. The US recognized that to secure the Gulf for imperialism she would have to depend upon the Arabs. Israel alone could not successfully deal with a growing Arab revolutionary movement. Internal rebellions in the Gulf had to be effectively countered through local gendarmes. Furthermore, to achieve Pax Americana requires co-operation between Israel and her Arab reactionary adversaries; consequently, glaring antagonisms that prevented this needed to be resolved. The Achilles' heel in US policy has, however, been in the nature of the country's relationship with Israel. Therefore, a contradiction existed in the method of securing United States interests in the region and, until this could be resolved, these interests could not be fully secure. The contradiction is: the United States is unwilling to forsake Israel in favour of the Arab reactionaries — a fact Israel fully understands. She has, however, been unwilling to acquiesce to any US move towards the Arabs that might endanger Israel's premier position in the region. Israel has consistently opposed such moves, at the risk of creating temporary but real differences with US policy in the region. Israel was confident that the US would not severely penalize her for any 'misconduct'; consequently Israel had opposed the AWACS deal and the Palestinian mini-state and, in June 1982, even dared to invade Lebanon.

Arab reactionaries have been aware of Israel's territorial ambitions, but they have had no way of effectively stopping her pursuing these ambitions. Arab reactionary support for the PLO and Syria has been minimal in relation to the tasks needed to apply pressure on the US to balance her support between Arab reactionaries and Israel. Full support for the PLO and Syria has been minimal because the inherent revolutionary character of the PLO, despite its leaders, is fundamentally antagonistic to reactionary designs and the survival of Arab reactionary regimes.

## Fez I Fails

A few weeks after the bombing of the nuclear reactor, Israel took further advantage of Arab squabbles and, in July 1981, bombed Palestinian civilian targets in Beirut. These bombings were also an Israeli attempt to upset the delicate balance that was tipping in favour of the Saudi AWACS deal. Saudi Arabia remained on target however, and secured the deal.

Meanwhile, Sadat's assassination on 6 October 1981 created a new problem for imperialist policy in the region. Camp David was no longer a viable process. Recognizing this, Fahd quickly filled the void by presenting his plan (August 1981). Saudi Arabia called for the convening of the twelfth Arab summit meeting to adopt the plan; Arab heads of state assembled in Fez, Morocco in November 1981 for the Summit. As mentioned earlier, Arafat was in agreement with the Fahd plan, objecting only to the absence of any mention of the PLO. This was a clear indication that the right in the PLO was in the saddle, ready to recognize Israel provided she would be amenable to the mini-state solution. What seemed to be a foregone conclusion was, however, defeated by Syria. The Fez Summit failed to convene beyond its initial sessions. Since the Fahd plan failed in Fez, there was no viable plan left for negotiations. A situation now existed conducive neither to Israel, the US nor the Arab reactionaries. It was clear that the anti 'peace' forces had to be defeated prior to any real move towards Pax Americana.

## Pax-Americana: An 'Even-Handed' US Policy in the Middle East

To pave the way for such stability, it was imperative to wipe out the Palestinian Revolutionary Movement (PRM), and the Lebanese National Movement (LNM) which latter was an effective, developing force against a Pax Americana in the region. The timing of the Lebanese civil war (1975-76), which had an internal (to Lebanon) dynamic of its own, had much to do with regional and international forces that really fed the civil war to serve their own particular interests.

The Camp David Accords were an attempt to ensure these goals. Recognizing that the revolutionary movement in the Arab world was threatening to disrupt their plans, the US imperialists searched out ways to contain this process. As mentioned earlier, this meant that the US would have to increasingly rely on the reactionary Arab regimes to destroy the Palestinian and Lebanese revolutionary movements, as well as those within their own countries.

Since 1980-81 the US began to realize that no Arab country, other than Egypt, was willing to join the Camp David Accords. Thus, the US began to take steps to realign its policy in the area; the clearest indication of this was the AWACS deal with Saudi Arabia. Much to the dismay, and despite the protests of Israel and a section of the US capitalists, the AWACS deal indicated that US policy had tilted irreversibly towards the reactionary Arab regimes.

The achievement of an 'even-handed' reliance both on the Arab regimes and Israel was long a goal of 'trilateralist' foreign policy, although the conditions for realizing it were slow to materialize. Israel, however, was loathe to accept this increasing US reliance on its Arab 'enemies'.

The US bourgeoisie itself was split on how to proceed. Brzezinski, sharply critical of Reagan's State Department's heavy-handed shift to reliance on the Arab reactionary regimes at the time of the AWACS deal, warned that these tactics would push Israel to invade Lebanon.

## Israel's Invasion of Lebanon (6 June 1982)

The 'Black Jews' (Black Israelites) around Begin, advocates and practitioners of terror and extermination against the Palestinians, recognized that they could not have peace with the Arab regimes as equal partners. These forces took advantage of this split in US policy, and seized the initiative with the invasion of Lebanon in June 1982 in an effort to try to force the US back into a straight alignment with Israel against the Arabs. In addition, the Iran–Iraq war in which Iraq was fulfilling strategic US imperialist policies, provided Israel with a free hand to conduct military operations against the PLO-LNM alliance and a reluctant Syria. In taking advantage of Arab disarray, Israel attempted to prove to the US that it was the only country in the area that could guarantee US interests. Israel tried to do that earlier by bombing Iraq's nuclear reactor, and by showing that Israel can deal with revolutionary forces in the area better than Syria could (Lebanon invasion and the strategic blow to the PLO-LNM alliance). With the invasion of Lebanon, Israel also wanted to prove to the US that it could discipline and, if necessary, wipe out Syria as a military power, and be a regional power broker (in Lebanon, for instance), and most of all, that Israel was the US's only really dependable ally in the area.

In doing so, however, Israel was exhibiting a desperation unparalleled in Israeli policy. The Israeli invasion of Lebanon was a major attempt, the last of a series, to disrupt the US–Arab rapprochement. Israel had bet on the likelihood that the Arab states would take to war against her thus bringing the US to Israel's side, which, in turn, so Israel thought, would arouse Arab outrage against the US.

The Arab reactionary states, however, with much invested in their relations with the US, did not take the bait; even Syria fought a face-saving limited engagement with Israel during the invasion. Feeling secure enough to withstand any domestic, popular backlash, the Arab reactionary states, led by Saudi Arabia, did not feel obliged to give even token help to the PRM/LNM. Instead, they opted to counter the invasion through diplomacy. In this way, they hoped to check Israeli political advances through international pressure. They also wanted to share in weakening the PRM and installing a viable right-wing government in Beirut that would remain within the reactionary Arab (as opposed to Israeli) sphere. Both the Arabs and Israelis were competing for influence in Lebanon; both were out to get the PRM/LNM. But each party tried to do it in its own way: Israel, by attempting to eliminate them physically; the Arabs by arranging to pull Palestinian fighters out of Beirut, neutralizing and dispersing them in the Arab world.

When Saud El-Faisal and Abd El-Halim Khaddam, the Saudi and Syrian Foreign Ministers respectively, visited the US during Lebanon's invasion, they were primarily discussing modalities and conditions of PLO withdrawal from Beirut. This withdrawal was being discussed even before a US promise was secured to pressure Israel into withdrawing completely from Lebanon concurrently with the PLO pull-out. Arab reactionary states were also depending upon the bourgeois control of the Palestinian Revolutionary Movement (PRM) to keep the PLO a viable entity, despite military defeat, and which could be utilized to bring about a resolution to their liking of the Palestinian problem.

The flurry of Arab diplomacy showed that the Arab regimes by and large opted for the US solution. Immediately after his visit to the US in the summer of 1982, Saudi Arabia's Prince Saud El-Faisal began to hint at the 'autonomy' as opposed to a 'mini-state' solution for the Palestinians. This entailed trying to identify and bring forth local Palestinian leaders who were willing to negotiate Palestinian national rights away for the privilege of administering their own garbage pick-up and sewer disposal and the other inconsequential jurisdictions that a phony autonomy would allow. Faisal's 'autonomy' dropped the binding of control of land to political autonomy, thus making it a meaningless abstraction.

With Israel having the upper hand and Beirut under seige PLO leaders then stopped talking of both the mini-state and autonomy, and concentrated on withdrawal from Beirut. The moderate leaders of the LNM were clearly moving towards reconciling the various warring factions in Lebanon. A clear precondition for this was withdrawal of the PLO, even though it must have been recognized that this would heighten the possibility of Israeli and Phalangist attacks against the LNM and Palestinians. The results of these imposed decisions have already been written in blood. In pulling out of Beirut and surrendering their arms the PLO violated two cardinal rules of revolutionary struggle: 1. Never give up your arms; and 2. Never tail behind the reactionary leadership of the national bourgeoisie — whom Arafat represents as the so called 'moderate' component of the PLO. A similar mistake was committed by the Communist Party of Iraq (CPI) in 1959 when the CPI, at that time the largest and best organized party in the Arab East, relinquished their arms and allied with the nationalists. As a consequence hundreds of Iraqi Communists were tortured and murdered, and up to 50,000 cadre and supporters have reportedly been arrested.[7]

The negotiations that finally led to the PLO pull-out from Beirut in August 1982 gave traditional Muslim leaders international prominence. Saeb Salam (Lebanese ex-Prime Minister) and Chefic Wazzan, who later resigned as Prime Minister on 4 February 1984, acted as intermediaries between the PLO and US envoy, Philip Habib. These tactics helped legitimize confessional forces in the imperialist attempt to reconstruct the Lebanese polity.

When, in August 1982, Bashir Gemayel was 'elected' by the Lebanese parliament to succeed outgoing Lebanese President Elias Sarkis, all parties concerned (Saudi Arabia, the Lebanese traditional leaders as well as the US and Israel) were in agreement on the Phalangist Gemayel. This imperialist imposed president-elect and the PLO pull-out, left the LNM and the majority of the Lebanese to fend for themselves in the face of what seemed to be insurmountable odds. The task of defending the civilian Lebanese and Palestinian population was relegated to the multi-national force (MNF). Earlier the US had guaranteed that if the PLO would pull out from Beirut, no Israeli or Phalangist troops would be allowed into West Beirut. In an apparently orchestrated series of events, however, the MNF left Beirut after it had ended the supervision of the PLO pull-out. Soon after, on 14 September, when president-elect Bashir Gemayel (Amin's brother) refused to sign a peace treaty with Israel, he was assassinated in his 'impregnable' party headquarters. Israel was quick to blame the PLO. This was their opportunity to finish off the LNM forces who, with their PLO allies out of the picture, were easy prey. The following day Israeli troops rolled into West Beirut.

Israel's justification for this violation of their agreement not to invade West Beirut was their 'concern' to pre-empt right-wing reprisals against the population of West Beirut. Another deception provided was the compelling need 'to keep leftist militiamen from teaming up with Palestinians and launching a new wave of bloodshed'. When Israel moved in on West Beirut, they accomplished a strategic Israeli policy objective: the last hurdle to a right-wing Israeli-imposed Lebanese solution was wiped out. Israel's occupation of West Beirut set the stage for Phalangist troops (under Israeli guidance) to go into the Sabra and Chatila Palestinian camps and massacre about 1,000 human beings. A few days later, the MNF arrived in Beirut — once more to 'preserve the peace'.

As mentioned earlier, one of the negotiated conditions that allowed for the PLO evacuation from West Beirut, was the US government's and Israel's guarantee that Israel would not invade West Beirut. Further, both the PLO and LNM were guaranteed that there would be no reprisals against the civilian Lebanese and Palestinian population. In fact this US guarantee of the Lebanese and Palestinian population's safety and the promise that no Israeli or right-wing forces would enter West Beirut or attack the LNM, was the key factor that allowed the US to secure the PLO pull-out.

That none of these guarantees amounted to anything is quite clear. Israel proceeded with an invasion of West Beirut and soon after, hundreds of Palestinians and Lebanese civilians were massacred at the Sabra and Chatila camps.

The massacres at the Sabra And Chatila camps allows us to discern a pattern in which that particular fascist feast fits. During January 1976 LKP butchers also massacred over 1,000 people in the Karantina area, Tal al-Zatar and the Jisr-el-Basha Palestinian camp in an effort to depopulate the area of non-Christian Lebanese. They then proceeded to level the areas with bulldozers, displacing over 20,000 people. These same dispersal tactics upon concentrated areas of Palestinian population were also carried out by Israel in Southern Lebanon after the 6 June invasion, and is a continuation of a genocidal policy against the Palestinian people since the inception of the Zionist state. Ariel Sharon, then Israel's Defence Minister, was once quoted as saying, 'We will kill and arrest as many Palestinians as possible and leave the rest to the Arabs.' Israel and the Phalangists have historically been allies since, among other things, both share common exclusivist goals — 'Lebanon is for the Lebanese' (LKP slogan) and Israel for Jews.

The Israeli invasion of Lebanon and the events before and after present an opportunity for revolutionaries to evaluate their political positions, separate between fact and fiction and become better able to identify a wolf in sheep's clothing. Pertinent lessons can be drawn that may be helpful in a continuing struggle against imperialism. As the old adage goes, 'Actions speak louder than words.' It may be useful at this point to recapitulate and illustrate upon the pronounced justifications Israeli mouthpieces procured for the 6 June invasion of Lebanon and juxtapose them with the calculated policy objectives Israel hoped to achieve by this brash act of aggression.

The initial provocation Israel utilized for its incursion into Lebanon was to exact revenge for the attempted assassination of its Ambassador to the United Kingdom, Shlomo Argov, despite the fact that Scotland Yard found a hit list on the assassin's person containing the names of PLO officials as well as Argov's, and despite the fact that Israel had been amassing troops and equipment on the Lebanese border in preparation for a major military manoeuvre months prior to this assassination incident. When this excuse lost credibility, Israel claimed that the invasion was necessary to establish a 25 mile buffer zone on its northern border to protect its settlement from 'PLO attack'. Two weeks after the invasion Israel sent equipment into Lebanon to divert water from the Al-Awali river to their new settlements in the north of Israel. When the 25 mile buffer zone became discredited, Israel seized upon its 'rescue mission' alibi and declared that their objectives were to rid Lebanon of 'foreign troops'. Israel thus imposed its will, despite the Lebanese government protest and condemnation of the violation of their sovereignty, on several occasions at the United Nations during the Israeli invasion. The 'foreign troops' to which Israel referred was the Syrian army and the Palestinians. As mentioned in the previous chapter, the Lebanese government invited the Syrian army to crush the Resistance forces (LNM-PLO) during the Lebanese civil war in 1976. The Palestinians have been an integral part of Lebanon's history and economy since 1948 when the exclusivist state of Israel was created at the expense of the Palestinians there. Israel would not have to contend with the PLO or Palestinians in general if the creation of Israel had not been an unnatural aberration that disposed over a million of Palestinians in a country that was once called Palestine.

Israeli propaganda also provided another excuse: to rid the world of 'international terrorism' and the 'terrorist PLO'. This hypocritical rhetoric must also be seen in the light of the consistent and savage terrorism inflicted upon the Palestinians, not only in this recent invasion, in which over 17,000 people were killed, but also in light of the thousands of Palestinians who have been killed since the inception of the Zionist state. Let us also not forget that Begin, who so self-righteously denounced the 'terrorist' PLO was himself the leader of an underground organization, Irgun Zwai Leumi, that succeeded in terrorizing the Palestinian population into fleeing Palestine during the late 1940s.

Fighting the 'terrorist' PLO was a typical cover Israel frequently employed to manipulate public opinion and conceal their acts of aggression. All their 'defensive' rhetoric for their offensive acts were calculated propaganda ploys to mask deliberate plans for the expansionist Zionist state. Also, contrary to US media reports during the first few weeks of the invasion, Israel was not fighting the PLO but the Combined Forces of the LNM–PLO alliance.

Israel's objectives in Lebanon go beyond their claims to 'retaliation' or 'buffer zones'. Besides the contradictions that arose between the regional considerations mentioned earlier vis-à-vis the US and Israel, the other Israeli objectives in invading Lebanon were:

1. To break the back bone of the LNM–PLO alliance.
2. To strengthen the right-wing forces in Lebanon so that they could have the upper hand in the Lebanese Presidential election that year.
3. To defeat Syria militarily.
4. To crush the PLO and the LNM.

If fulfilled, Israel hoped these objectives would allow it to:

1. Sign a peace treaty with a Lebanese right-wing government.
2. Negotiate a phony autonomy with Israeli selected Palestinians who would be willing to sign away Palestinian national rights to Israel.
3. Annex the West Bank and the Gaza Strip.
4. Bridge the diplomatic gap and any secondary misunderstanding between Israel and the US that had arisen on the basis of the Camp David Accords.
5. Rest assured that it had quelled the revolutionary process in the area whose storm centre has been the LNM–PLO.

According to George Habash, General Secretary of the Popular Front of the Liberation of Palestine (PFLP), no Lebanese or Palestinian progressive organization, including the PFLP, had expected an Israeli strike of such an extent. Prevalent assumptions were that Israel would stop at Al-Awali river; the PRM/LNM alliance was ready to deal with the results of that. In addition, the military plan designed to counter these calculations rested on three stationary lines of defence that were supposed to inflict heavy losses upon enemy troops before they reached Al-Awali river.[8]

Israel's blitz, however, rendered the PRM/LNM strategy helpless. This faulty military analysis rested upon an erroneous political reading both of Israeli intentions and the tasks relegated to Israel, and the Lebanese fascists, by imperialism. PFLP's reading of the situation, for instance, assumed that the imperialist's main tool against the revolutionary movement in Lebanon would be the Lebanese state, especially its army institution. The building of this army, the PFLP had reasoned, would take several years. In that time the revolutionaries would be ready for the expected showdown. There was little reason to believe, however, that imperialism would wait for years before it attempted to deal a heavy blow to the revolutionaries in Lebanon. Imperialism has been facing a contracting capitalist market that is precipitating international instability unparalleled in the last 40 years. Imperialism would do its utmost to quickly stabilize a vital region such as the Arab market. These miscalculations were publicly and courageously criticized by the PFLP itself through its General Secretary and political report issued by the Fourth Session of its Central Committee (which met from 18 through 26 January 1983) dealing with the Lebanon invasion.

With the pull-out of the PLO from Beirut, that organization is now fragmented and geographically isolated; those PLO soldiers are now openly identified and marked.

## Rebellion Within Al-Fateh: 15 May 1983

It was these bungles that began to isolate Arafat from his mass base; he further discredited his legitimacy among the Palestinian masses when he entered into negotiations with King Hussein of Jordan during December 1982 for the purpose of delegating Hussein to negotiate on behalf of the Palestinians with Israel and the US. Hussein is anathema to most Palestinians since his massacre of over 20,000 Palestinians during 'Black September' in 1970. Clearly Arafat was moving in the direction of 'autonomy' and the Reagan initiative and thus abandoning the Palestinian Revolutionary Movement's major goal which calls for a democratic secular state in Palestine where Jews, Muslims and Christians can live in peace with full rights as citizens and equal protection under the law.

The Hussein–Arafat negotiations did not culminate in the signing of accords because the PLO forced Arafat to retreat from his position vis-à-vis Hussein. Arafat had misjudged Al-Fateh's and the PLO's opposition to these negotiations. His logical step then was to 'clean house' before proceeding any further with negotiations. In this endeavour, Arafat quickly replaced Abu Musa, hero in the fight against Israel and the fascist Phalangists, by Al Haj Ismael, who is known to have fled in the face of the Israeli enemy. Arafat also made a couple of other military appointments that Abu Musa rejected outright. Since 15 May 1983, when the rebellion within Fateh started, support for Abu Musa's action grew among Al-Fateh fighters. The demands of the rebellion were clear and simple:

1. Revoke the new appointments.
2. A complete and thorough appraisal of the 1982 war and the bringing to trial of those who may be responsible for botching things up in the fighting.
3. A stop to all negotiations and a declaration of rejection to all such negotiations on the basis of advancing imperialist plans which do not lead to total liberation of Palestine and the establishment of a democratic secular

state.
4. Insure that the Fateh leadership and the PLO leadership be collective and not individualistic as has been the case.
5. A call for an Al-Fateh congress to decide and resolve the problems within Al-Fateh democratically and legally.

The PLO's withdrawal from Lebanon spelled the end of a stage in the development of the revolutionary movement in the Arab East. The petty bourgeois radical leadership could, at one time, lead a guerrilla force and find a degree of tolerance or even patronage among the Arab regimes. This compromised and bankrupt leadership could even serve the interests of its 'enemy'. (It was revealed on US national TV in a June 1983 news report that on several occasions during the invasion of Lebanon, Israel had opportunities to assassinate Arafat but had given assurances to the US that this would not occur. This information had come from a confidential report from the US State Department.) Both Israel and the US recognized the role that PLO figureheads could play in realizing their objectives. When the PLO pulled out of Beirut they left their files and other important material in their headquarters for free perusal by Israeli intelligence; they also left tons of equipment, supplies and armaments. These oversights are incredible. The PLO has witnessed the decimation of its fighting capacity and the dispersal of its forces under this leadership while its Arab benefactors effectively washed their hands. It remains to be seen how long such leadership will be retained as its options become limited to those 'moderate solutions' permitted by such Arab reactionaries as Jordan's King Hussein, or by Ronald Reagan.

Despite these setbacks, the revolutionary movement in Lebanon forged ahead, broadening its support among the masses and improving its effectiveness in fighting the enemy. Military operations within Lebanon increased against Israel so much that Israel found itself fighting a war of attrition whose consequences Israeli society could not sustain for long. Military operations emanate not only from the Palestinian forces in the Bekaa, but also from the Lebanese Resistance Front (LRF). The LRF was formed in 1982 after the Israeli invasion and primarily consists of the Communist Party of Lebanon (CPL), the Organization of Communist Action (OCA), the Arab Socialist Action Party (ASAP) and the PFLP. Although the PFLP is a Palestinian organization, it is a member of the LRF due to the realization within the LRF that both the Lebanese and Palestinian peoples share common goals.

In view of the steadily increasing resistance, Israel was faced with several unpalatable options: 1) To continue with the occupation of Lebanon and suffer the consequences of a war of attrition. 2) To conduct a war against the Syrian and Palestinian forces in the Bekaa and the North of Lebanon. 3) Retrench further south to a more defensible position within Lebanon without losing the gains that resulted from the invasion (Israel becoming a regional power capable of influencing Lebanese policy, etc).

The first option was deemed 'unacceptable' by Israel. This pronouncement triggered speculation of an imminent Israeli strike in May 1983. The second

option would have exacerbated rather than solved Israel's problems in Lebanon. Israel would have had to pour in more troops and equipment in such an
eventuality and in all probability this still would not have saved her from a
war of attrition. Israel's third option allowed for the strengthening of the
LRF and the other LNM organizations. If Israel retrenched further south,
the PRM would also find it easier to reinforce the LNM against the right-
wing Lebanese army and the Phalangists. To aid the right-wing Lebanese
regime, Israel could conduct a strike against enemy forces in the Bekaa.
In all probability, however, such a strike would neither prevent nor seriously
delay the already growing resistance to the present Beirut regime. Cognizant
of this fact, Israel preferred to have the MNF assume Israel's role in those
areas that it pulled out from. This meant, however, that the MNF had to increase its forces to combat the LRF. Escalating the situation would also mean
more economic and social problems in those countries that have agreed to
participate in the MNF.

## The Israeli–Lebanese Agreement: 17 May 1983

In pursuit of the third option, Israel embarked upon negotiations which
eventually led to the signing of the Israeli–Lebanese agreement on 17 May
1983. In reaching this agreement, Israel was able to counter Arab diplomatic
efforts that were centring upon the Reagan Initiative and the Fez II Summit
plan of September 1982.

The Israeli–Lebanese agreement and the 15 May 1983 rebellion within
Al-Fateh, are perhaps the most important events that have occurred after
the 1982 PLO pull-out from Beirut. Consequently, any line of analysis that
seeks to unravel the post-Beirut political situation in the region must centre
around these two events.

The Israeli–Lebanese agreement was above all, an imposed one. Despite
what the parties to the agreement and the United States (who ostensibly
mediated the negotiations) claimed, Lebanon was forced to sign the agreement due to Israel's occupation of about half the country. The agreement was
also signed by an Israeli and US-propped-up government in Beirut which had
no control over most of Lebanon and only controls part of Beirut, and which
has the allegiance of less than 10% of the population. In short, it is a puppet
government of US imperialism.

The Israeli–Lebanese agreement also robs Lebanon of her sovereignty.
Israel and the US have decided what the Lebanese should and should not do
in their own territory. Only a puppet government could have signed such an
agreement. Some salient points of the agreement stipulated the following:
1. Joint Lebanese and Israeli army patrols of unspecified numbers of officers
to operate in the South of Lebanon. 2. An important role in the South for
Israel's puppet, renegade Lebanese army major, Saed Haddad (now dead).
3. Limitations on the number of weapons and the specifying of the kinds of
weapons that the Lebanese army may be equipped with in the South.

4. Lebanese army limitations to two divisions in the South with only one of these deployed on Lebanon's border with Israel. 5. A security area which would practically encompass the entire South of Lebanon from the Israeli border to the North of Sidon. This area would run inland along Al-Awali river. 6. Lebanon would not have the right to enter into treaties that may be interpreted to be hostile to Israel. 7. Lebanon would have to abrogate all agreements and treaties (with Arab countries) that might endanger Israel's security or Lebanon's rapprochement with Israel. 8. Lebanon must enter into trade negotiations in good faith with Israel.[9]

In exchange for all of this Israel would pull out her troops from Lebanon. Israel however, would still be in control of the South through her puppet, Saed Haddad and the joint patrols. Furthermore, Israel would secure her role as a regional power broker for minimum cost. In sum, the agreement, if implemented, would have severed Lebanon from the Arab countries and propelled her into Israel's lap. Lebanon would thus have become the first satellite of Israel.

Other interesting conditions were advanced by Israel for the implementation of that agreement. First, according to Lebanese Foreign Minister, Dr Elie Salem, Israel would not have begun her troop withdrawal unless the PLO returned the few Israeli prisoners it was holding.[10] (No mention was made of the 7,000 Palestinian and Lebanese prisoners Israel was holding in their makeshift concentration camp in Ansaar.) Second, Syrian and PLO troops would first have to withdraw from Lebanon before any Israeli troop withdrawal would begin.

The signing of the agreement was a triumph for both the United States and Israel. It was akin to the Kissingerian step-by-step diplomacy which in effect overcomes impediments to United States interests one-by-one. The Camp David Accords ensured Egypt's neutralization in Israel's fight against the PLO, Syria and Lebanon. And then came the Israeli–Lebanese agreement which is even more pernicious than the Camp David Accords. The conditions that Israel imposed before she would begin her troop withdrawal were unrealistic. As Israel well recognized, Syria would have to oppose the agreement outright because a Syrian withdrawal from the Bekaa would leave Damascus, Syria's capital, prone to attack and occupation. Furthermore, with Syria out of the picture, the LNM and the PLO would have been alone in countering a US trained fascist Lebanese army and possibly a beefed-up MNF.

This new agreement consecrated Israel's occupation of parts of Lebanon and baptized Israel as a regional power broker. Through the Israeli–Lebanese agreement Israel was able to circumvent the Camp David route to become a regional power broker via Lebanon. As an expansionist power, this regional power broker business is in fact, a matter of life and death to Israel. Israel has tried unsuccessfully for over thirty five years to achieve this status. The Camp David Accords were incapable of giving Israel that status since it was then dealing with Egypt, a regional power in its own right. Also the Accords were not able to pull Israel out of its isolation since Egypt itself was practically isolated from the Arab world once Sadat visited Jerusalem in 1977.

It is significant to point out that even without the implementation of the Israeli–Lebanese agreement, Israel has come a long way in becoming a controlling power in Lebanese and Arab politics. In fact, the third option that Israel was leaning toward needed a diplomatic cover before the international community. The agreement provided Israel with that cover: Israel was willing to withdraw from Lebanon 'completely' provided that all 'foreign' forces (except the MNF and the UN) withdrew first. Israel had itself covered from both angles: if these 'foreign' troops (Syrian and PLO) withdrew, the agreement would guarantee Israel's policy objectives. If, on the other hand, as was expected, Syria and the PLO did not withdraw, Israel would then effect its third option which could have included a 'surgical' strike against the 'foreign' troops in the Bekaa.

Ironically, the Israeli–Lebanese agreement that the United States was instrumental in bringing about was in contradiction to the much touted 1 September 1982 Reagan Initiative. Recognizing the need for increasing dependence upon the Arabs, the Reagan Initiative was introduced to serve as a basis for comprehensive negotiations. As it now stands, this initiative is dead. Some say that it was stillborn. Be that as it may, the fact of the matter is that the United States is not wedded to any particular plan when it comes to protecting its interests. The Arab reactionaries were able to see some 'positive' aspects in the Reagan Initiative. They also worked quickly in an attempt to pull the United States closer to their position regarding a comprehensive settlement. To this endeavour, they quickly assembled (right after the PLO Beirut pull-out) in Fez in September 1982 to adopt a sugar-coated version of the Fahd plan that failed to pass the Fez I Summit of November 1981.

The Unified Arab Peace Plan (the Fez II plan) allowed the reactionaries to proceed in their dealings with the United States and attempt to integrate Fez II and the Reagan Initiative. The Fez II plan (as opposed to the Fahd plan [Fez I]) recognized the PLO as the sole legitimate representative of the Palestinian people and specifically mentioned the Palestinian state (ministate) as one of the states in the region.[11] For these reasons, Arafat supported the Fez II plan which was later adopted in the Algiers meeting of the Palestine National Congress in February 1983 due to the hegemony of the Palestinian right wing at the Congress.[12]

Israel, for its part, had rejected the Reagan Initiative outright. Instead, Israel forced Lebanon into negotiations. Israel wanted an agreement that would allow it to successfully counter the Fez II plan as well as the Reagan Initiative.

One might wonder about the reasons that prompted the United States to 'mediate' the Israeli–Lebanese negotiations. Events have shown that all issues in the region are integrally connected. To separate the Lebanon issue from the regional one meant that the United States and Israel were not willing to conclude a comprehensive settlement. The United States, however, excused itself by saying that such an agreement would facilitate the withdrawal of all 'foreign' forces from Lebanon thereby creating a better climate for the Reagan Initiative. It is clear that this line of thinking was a distraction. The United States had other reasons for assisting Israel in reaching such an agreement.

There are indications that the United States had a change of heart about the Reagan Initiative. This had to do with an incorrect United States assessment of the Soviet position after the Beirut PLO pull-out. The Soviet position was in accord with the Fez II plan. Consequently, the United States was concerned that the Soviet Union might be able to establish a real role for itself in the comprehensive regional negotiations. The Israeli-Lebanese agreement was a hedge that the United States used in countering Soviet diplomacy in the area.

The other major event in the post-Beirut era was the rebellion of 15 May 1983 within Al-Fateh. It is significant to point out here that while Israel and the fascist Beirut regime were negotiating the agreement, Arafat and King Hussein of Jordan were also negotiating. The object of the Arafat-Hussein negotiations was to have Hussein represent the Palestinians in negotiations with the United States and Israel. This was a clear indication that the PLO and the Arab reactionaries were moving closer towards the Reagan Initiative (the Initiative did not recognize the PLO and dealt with a 'Palestinian' entity linked with Jordan). As mentioned earlier, the Arafat-Hussein negotiations did not culminate in the signing of an agreement due to the intense opposition within Al-Fateh and the PLO to these negotiations. Arafat's moves to put down the rebellion which opposed these negotiations and other moves on the part of Arafat, were backfiring. He found himself almost completely isolated from the Palestinian masses and troops especially after his ouster from Syria on 24 June 1983.

The opposition to Arafat and the right wing within the PRM was, in fact, a reassertion of the original strategic thrust of the PRM which is reflected in the slogan for a secular, democratic state in all of Palestine. Over the last 40 years events have consistently shown that the destiny of the Palestinians and their revolution is integrally tied with the destiny of the rest of the Arab masses and their revolutionary movement. This reassertion of the original strategic thrust of the PRM has derailed much of imperialism's and Arab reaction's plans.

The United States is now facing a dilemma in the area. The US would like the Arabs and Israel to reach an agreement yet it does not want to pressure Israel in conceding anything of significance from the Arab point of view. On the one hand, the US needs stability in the Arab East to protect its hegemony in the area. On the other hand the PRM and the LNM are still a viable force in countering imperialist designs. The US recognized that it is in the interest of its Arab allies to provide them with military bases, markets for their goods and aid for them in establishing US hegemony. These Arab capitalist states, however, also want the US to agree to a Palestinian 'ministate' which they feel would establish a material basis for a comprehensive regional settlement. But the growing 'rebel' faction within the PLO is against any type of co-optation, 'mini-state', 'autonomy', or whatever, that deviates from the original strategic goal of the PRM — a democratic secular state in all Palestine, where Jews, Muslims and Christians can live in peace with full rights as citizens and equal protection under the law. The US has been chasing a mirage. Although the US is a major actor and shaper of conditions in the region, it is incapable of fully controlling the situation. In its attempts to do so however, it finds itself wallowing deeper in the shifting sands of the Arab East.

# Notes

1. Hussein Abd El-Razaak, *Egypt on January 18 and 19* (Beirut, Dar-El Kalemah, 1979).
2. Jassem Al-Mutayer, *The Economic Opening* (Baghdad, 1976).
3. The Front was established at Tripoli, Libya after a conference between 2–5 December 1977.
4. The Iraqi plan appeared in the Baghdad *Ath-Thawra* daily newspaper on 3 February 1978.
5. Op. cit., 8 and 9 December issues 1977.
6. *Al-Watan*, newspaper, Kuwait, 10 September 1982.
7. 'Interview with CPI Secretary General', Aziz Mohammed, *Merip Reports*, No. 97, June 1981.
8. George Habash, *On Lebanon's War and its Results*, PFLP Central Information Department, March 1983.
9. The Arabic text of the agreement and discussion of the English text appeared in *Al-Watan* of 18 May 1983.
10. Ibid.
11. *Al-Watan*, 10 September 1982.
12. Text of the Sixteenth Session of the PNC appeared in *Al-Watan*, on 25 February 1983.

# Postscript

The day Israel withdrew from the central mountains to the south of Lebanon, 4 September 1983, was a watershed in the region's political development. To begin with, a three week battle ensued between fighters from the National Salvation Front (NSF) (SPP and Druze) and the Phalangist-led Beirut government. Israeli withdrawal also meant a more direct involvement of US (and other MNF) forces.

As has already been noted, a strategic Israeli goal since at least the 1982 invasion of Lebanon, has been to try involving the US more closely in the Middle East region militarily. The round of fighting of 4 September, for all practical purposes, accomplished that. In addition, the 1983 alliance between the US and Israel ensured that this increasing US involvement will not easily be reversed. Not, as has been suggested erroneously by some, that Israel has been using the US against the latter's international and Middle East interests. US foreign policy operates in fulfilment of strategic goals which serve those interests that have traditionally been represented by international corporations and financiers. Despite the US and Israeli commonality of interests that have arisen due to the 'dialysis effect' — the traditional support of Israel — tactical (and sometimes strategic) differences exist between the US and Israel concerning US hegemony and Israel's role in this kind of arrangement.

To interpret the meaning of what has taken place since 4 September 1983, including the crushing defeat and subsequent unceremonious withdrawal of Arafat from Tripoli (November 1983), it is necessary to present a picture of the events and the nature and relationship of the forces that have been fighting.

Israel's invasion made possible the seizure of government by the Phalangist party. The Beirut government had the support of the US (and the countries of the MNF) and most Arab countries (Saudi Arabia, Kuwait, etc.). From the outset, the sectarian Phalangists did not want to share power, even with other forces who wanted to change the National Pact (to reflect the new realities of Lebanon) but to stay within the confines of confessionalism. Clearly, anti-confessional forces were not to be considered (they were not represented in the November 1983 Geneva conference of warlords). By and large, anti-confessional forces were organized in the Lebanese Resistance Front (LRF) directly after the Israeli invasion of 1982. Initially, the LRF included the Communist Party of Lebanon (CPL), the Organization of Communist Action (OCA) and the Arab Socialist Action Party (ASAP). Other LNM organizations that stayed out of the LRF for political reasons, stayed on the fringes or entered into the Syrian backed NSF (Franjieh, Jumblatt and Karami).

The NSF brought together anti-Phalangist confessional leaders who wanted a better deal for themselves through reforming the Lebanese political process to reflect the new confessional realities in Lebanon. Realizing that such reform was impossible while Israel occupied Lebanon, these confessional leaders have come up against the Israeli–Lebanese agreement of 17 May 1983 and Israel's role in Lebanon.

The NSF interests were almost identical to those of Syria (17 May agreement, anti-MNF role which was perceived as aiding the Beirut government). By necessity, given the integral nature of the Middle East conflict, the NSF was in support of a comprehensive regional settlement along the lines of the Syrian version. Central to such a settlement is the creation of a Palestinian state through a Geneva type conference. This is different from Arafat's position that tended towards the Reagan Initiative and the so-called Jordanian Option.

Given that the main contradiction in Lebanon centred around the 17 May agreement, co-operation among Syria, the LRF and NSF was possible. It was also possible for Syria to isolate Arafat in Lebanon and support the rebellion against him in Al-Fateh. Arafat's only recourse in Tripoli was to rely on Muslim reactionaries whom he armed to massacre Tripoli Communists, in return for supporting him in his fight against the rebels and elements of the Palestinian movements that were supported by Syria and Libya.

Tripoli's war was central to Lebanese politics for a number of reasons: 1) To have undisputed control over Lebanese territory controlled by its forces, Syria had to oust Arafat from Tripoli. 2) Karami, the NSF leading figure of Tripoli, would then be in a better bargaining position vis-à-vis the Beirut government. 3) Control over territory would allow Syria to deal from a position of strength, with the US and the Arab countries in relation to a comprehensive settlement. 4) Israel would have liked Arafat to perish in Tripoli to further weaken her enemy forces and to prevent him from emerging as a viable force to negotiate along the lines of the Reagan Initiative or the so-called Jordanian Option.

Only pressure from the US and the European countries forced Israel to abandon its blockade of Tripoli, thus giving Arafat a safe passage out of Lebanon (November 1983). While the Palestinian rebellion was under way, LRF action, especially in the south of Lebanon, was a major factor that forced Israel to withdraw from the central mountains of Chouf. The withdrawal triggered a major war with the Beirut army and the Phalangists on one side and the NSF on the other. In this battle the US facade as a peacemaker fell. The battleship *New Jersey* began to pound 'Druze strongholds' in the Chouf mountains with huge guns. Direct intervention of this kind was a qualitative change in the US role (and the MNF) forces in the Middle East.

Not until 24 September did the major fighting stop to prepare for the November 1983 conference of warlords to try and buy time for the Beirut government. The major sponsor of such a conference was the US government. As expected, nothing came out of the conference for three main reasons: 1) The US government cannot hope to have hegemony except through the Beirut government. Other arrangements that include the NSF will, of necessity, have to bring in the USSR as an actor for a comprehensive peace settlement. And this would work against US hegemony. 2) As has been mentioned, this was a warlords conference, a section of the Lebanese represented by the LRF was not spoken for at the conference.

The warlords could only freeze the 17 May agreement, i.e. not deal with it; ostensibly, the agreement was the central point of debate. For Israel, such a freeze was favourable: it reinforced its rationale for staying in Lebanon and its desire for US and MNF troops to side with the Beirut government. The NSF tried to reach an agreement on expanding the Beirut government to include it, but to no avail. The role of the army, its structure and its positioning in the Chouf and other areas was central to the failure to agree. This showed that the Phalangists were in no mood to lose control of the army. What it also meant was that the Lebanese warlords would remain divided vis-à-vis Israel, despite the fact that the Beirut government was under pressure from many quarters, to at least amend the 17 May agreement.

The LRF was in a position to keep killing the Israeli enemy as its major response to the May agreement. The LRF position from the Beirut government emanated from the former's enemy status in relation to the MNF.

While secret contacts and negotiations have been under way for some time between the US and Syria to come to a compromise position on Lebanon and a comprehensive Middle East settlement, in the same breath the US was moving in a contradictory direction away from any plausible understanding with Syria. The recent US formal alliance with Israel, the increased and modified role of the US forces in the Middle East (since September 1983), the US tending towards Arafat after the latter had been ousted from Beirut were all indications that the US was moving towards directing a blow to Syria after isolating it almost completely from the 'moderate' Arab states.

The bombing of the US Marines and French compounds in Beirut on 23 October 1983 (and the earlier bombing of the US embassy in Beirut on 18 April 1983) did much to force the US to re-evaluate its position in Lebanon.

Events came to a head when Prime Minister Chafic Wazzan and his nine-member Cabinet resigned on 4 February 1984, in protest at President Gemayel's military actions against the opposition. On 7 February, the US announced its decision to withdraw its forces from Lebanon. Regardless of whether the decision was a withdrawal or a 'redeployment' of the Marines to the 20-ship flotilla off the shores of Lebanon, the Beirut government suffered heavily from that decision. A few days later, the NSF, Amal and other patriotic forces took over West Beirut in a matter of hours. The crushing defeat of the Beirut army left Amin Gemayel little hope of remaining President. Amidst calls for his resignation from Nabih Berri (leader of the Amal militia) and Walid Jumblatt (of the NSF), Amin Gemayel had to manoeuvre fast to protect his life and his position. To this end Amin Gemayel visited Damascus, Syria on 29 February 1984.

In Damascus, Gemayel accepted an eight-point Saudi plan which included the abrogation of the 17 May agreement. Syria rejected the Saudi plan, primarily because it called for negotiations to secure a simultaneous withdrawal of Israeli and Syrian forces from Lebanon and for giving Israel security guarantees.

Finally, due to pressure from Syria and the NSF, Gemayel had to agree to Syria's and the NSF's conditions. Basically, they called for the abrogation of the 17 May 1983 Israeli–Lebanese agreement, and political power sharing along the lines of a new confessional arrangement.

Having agreed to those conditions, Gemayel was able to work out with President Asad of Syria a Syrian-backed truce (2 March 1984) among the warring Lebanese factions. In addition, unity talks among the warlords were held in March in Lausanne, Switzerland. Several days after they began (21 March 1984), however, they collapsed.

Pressure intensified on Gemayel, from the Phalangists who did not want any capitulation to Syria, and from the NSF. With the US officially pulled out since 21 February 1984 and Israel's inability to counter Syria militarily at that stage, the Phalangists could not stop Syria's ascendancy. Amin Gemayel had to call upon Rashid Karami (of the NSF) to form a Cabinet on 25 April 1984.

At the time of writing (May 1984) after over ten years of war, Lebanon remains divided. Its political system remains confessional, and its fate remains tied to the rest of the region. Despite the US withdrawal from Beirut, its forces remain in Lebanon (Beirut, Beit Merry, Souk el Gharb, etc.). The US also remains with a military presence in other parts of the Arab world. Israel remains lodged in the south of Lebanon with no end in sight to its occupation.

Furthermore, the Iraq-Iran war and US and Israeli war-mongering threaten to encompass the entire region with more death and destruction.

## 1a The Lebanese National Movement, Military Arm – The Combined Forces (CF) (1975-76)

| Organisation | Founded | Main Leaders | Ideology | Political Presence | Fighters during the Battle | Fighters killed | Presence at war fronts | Main class composition |
|---|---|---|---|---|---|---|---|---|
| Socialist Progressive Party (SPP) | 1949 | Kamal Joumblatt *(Druze)* | Social Democrat Pan-Arab | All Lebanese districts | 2,500 professionals 15,000 militia | 300 | All main fronts: Mountain; Beirut; 250 men under CF | Rural and Urban petty bourgeoisie. Some workers. |
| Communist Party of Lebanon (CPL) or (LCP) | 1925 | George Hawi *(Christian)* | Marxist | All Lebanese districts | 1,000 professionals several thousand militia | 200 | All main fronts: Mountain; Beirut North | Rural and urban petty bourgeoisie. Workers. |
| Organization of Communist Action (OCA) | 1971 | Muhsin Ibrahim *(Muslim-Shiite)* Fawaz Tarabulsi *(Christian)* | Marxist | All Lebanese districts | Mostly militia volunteers (no numbers available) | 75 | All main fronts: South; Bekaa; Beirut | Rural and urban petty bourgeoisie. Some workers. |
| Arab Socialist Action Party (ASAP) | 1972 | George Habash *(of the PFLP)* *(Christian)* | Marxist | All Lebanese districts | Fighting is a condition of membership. No. of party members not available | 40 | All main fronts: Beirut; Bekaa | Rural and urban petty bourgeoisie. Some workers. |
| Independent Nasserist Movement (INM) | 1969 | Ibrahim Qulailat *(Muslim-Sunni)* | Arab Nationalist | Beirut | 1,000. With several thousand reserves | 200 | Beirut; Mountain | Urban petty bourgeoisie. Some workers |
| Arab Baath Socialist Party (ABSP) | 1947 | Abd al-Majid al-Rafii *(Muslim-Sunni)* Nicola Firizli *(Christian)* | Arab nationalist | All Lebanese nationalist | 2,000 | 100 | Main fronts: North; South; Bekaa; Beirut | Urban and rural petty bourgeoisie. Some workers |
| Syrian Nationalist Party (SNP) | 1932 | Inam Raad *(Christian)* | Syrian nationalist | All Lebanese districts | 2,000 | 200 | Main fronts: Beirut; Mountain; North | Urban and rural petty bourgeoisie |

## Ia

| | | | | | | | | |
|---|---|---|---|---|---|---|---|---|
| Arab Socialist Union (ASU) – Executive Committee | 1975 | Kamal Younis Mustapha Turk (*Both Muslim-Sunni*) | Arab nationalist | Beirut | No numbers available | 50 | Main fronts: Beirut; Mountain | Urban petty bourgeoisie |
| Arab Socialist Union (ASU) – General Secretariat | 1975 | Khalit Shihab (*Muslim-Sunni*) | Arab nationalist | Beirut; Mountain; North; South | No numbers available | 40 | Main fronts: Beirut; Mountain | Urban petty bourgeoisie. |
| Union of Working People People's Forces (UWPF) – Corrective Movement | 1974 | Issam Arab Fuad Itani (*Both Muslim-Sunni*) | Arab nationalist | Beirut | 250. Several hundred militia | 37 | Main fronts: Beirut; Mountain; South | Urban petty bourgeoisie. Some workers |
| Nasserist Popular Organization. Previously Popular Resistance of Maarouf Saad (1958) | 1975 | Mustapha Saad (*Muslim-Sunni*) | Arab nationalist | Sidon | 300 professional 1,000 militia | 50 | Main fronts: Sidon; Mountain | Urban petty bourgeoisie. Workers |
| Lebanese Movement in Support of Fateh | 1968 | Dr Usama Fakhoury (*Muslim-Sunni*) | Arab nationalist | Beirut; Tripoli, Sidon, Tyre | Not a fighting organization | | | Urban petty bourgeoisie |
| Kurdish Democratic Party (KDP) | 1960 | Jamil Muho (*Muslim-Sunni*) | Kurdish nationalist | Beirut | Not a fighting organization | | | Petty bourgeoisie. Workers |

## 1b The Front of Patriotic and National Parties (pro-Syrian)

| Organization | Founded | Main leaders | Ideology | Political presence | Fighters during the Battle | Fighters killed | Presence at war fronts | Main class composition |
|---|---|---|---|---|---|---|---|---|
| Baath Party Organization (BPO) | 1947 | Issam Qansy *(Muslim)* | Arab nationalist | All Lebanese districts | 2,000 | 200 | All | Urban petty bourgeoisie |
| Union of Working People's Forces (UWPF) – Nasserist Organization | 1970 1970 | Kamal Chatilla *(Muslim-Sunni)* | Arab nationalist | Beirut | 300 | 15 | Beirut | Urban petty bourgeoisie |
| Movement of the Deprived – Lebanese Resistance Legions (AMAL) | 1975 | Imam Musa al-Sadr *(Shiite religious leader)* | Shiite sectarian | Beirut; South; Bekaa | 800 | n/a | Beirut; South; Bekaa | Rural and urban petty bourgeoisie. Workers |
| Lebanese Progressive Vanguards | 1973 | Muhammad Z. Itani *(Muslim-Sunni)* | Arab nationalist | Beirut | 200 | n/a | Beirut | Urban petty bourgeoisie |
| Syrian Nationalist Party (SNP) | 1932 | Elias Kunaizeh *(Christian)* | Syrian nationalist | All Lebanese districts | n/a | n/a | Beirut; Mountain | Rural and urban petty bourgeoisie. |
| Kurdish 'Razkari' Party | 1975 | Faisal Fakhro *(Muslim-Sunni)* | Kurdish nationalist | Beirut | Not a fighting organization | | | Petty bourgeoisie. Workers. |

## 1c Organisations Outside But Fighting Alongside the LNM (1975-76)

| Organization | Founded | Main Leaders | Ideology | Political presence | Fighters during the Battle | Fighters killed | Presence at war fronts | Main class composition |
|---|---|---|---|---|---|---|---|---|
| October 24th Movement | 1969 | Farouk Al-Muqqadam *(Muslim-Sunni)* | Arab nationalist | Tripoli | 200 | 50 | Tripoli; North | Small peasants; workers; students |
| The Muslim Group | 1964 | Muhammad Danawi *(Muslim-Sunni)* | Sectarian Muslim | Tripoli; Beirut; Sidon | 200 | n/a | North; Beirut | Urban petty bourgeoisie |
| Reform Pioneer Movement | 1973 | Saeb Salam *(Muslim-Sunni)* | Bourgeois | Beirut | 250 | n/a | No military role | Urban petty bourgeoisie and lumpen elements |
| Najjadah Party | 1936 | Adnan A Al-Hakim *(Muslim-Sunni)* | Sectarian Muslim/ Pan-Arab | Beirut | 300 | n/a | No military role | Urban petty bourgeoisie. Some workers |
| God's Soldiers | 1975 | | Sectarian Muslim | Tripoli *(Abu Samra neighbourhood)* | 100 | 20 | Tripoli *(Abu Samra neighbourhood)* | Urban petty bourgeoisie |

## 2 The Maronite Right Wing* – Military Arm – The Lebanese Forces (1975-76)

| Organization | Main leaders | Ideology | Political presence | Fighters during the Battle | Presence at war fronts | Main class composition |
|---|---|---|---|---|---|---|
| Lebanese Kataeb Party (LKP). Also known as Phalangists | Pierre Gemayel | Fascist capitalist | All Lebanese districts | 7000 | All | Urban and rural petty bourgeoisie. Bourgeoisie. Some workers. Lumpen elements |
| Party of Free Nationalists (PFN) | Camille Chamoun | Fascist capitalist | Beirut; Mountain; South | 2000 | All | Urban and rural petty bourgeoisie. Bourgeoisie. Lumpen elements |
| Cedar Guards | Said Akl | Fascist capitalist | Beirut; Mountain | 250 | Beirut; Mountain | Urban and rural petty bourgeoisie. Lumpen elements |
| The Maronite Order of Monks | Charbel Kassiss | Fascist capitalist | Mountain | 300 | Mountain | Urban and rural petty bourgeoisie. Lumpen elements |

*The Maronite right wing was originally organized under the name of 'Front of Freedom and Man' and later under 'The Lebanese Front'. There is also an entity called 'the Maronite League' headed by the fascist Chakar Abu Suleiman. This League brings together the Maronite establishment. Edde, for instance, belonged to the League, but he was the only opposition to the fascists who dominated it.

Note – Franjieh, the President of Lebanon during the Battle, was in conformity with the organizations listed above. He also had his private militia in the northern town of Zgharta. He also had a section of the Lebanese Army aid the 'Front of Freedom and Man' in its battles with the LNM. Since the Battle, Franjieh has been co-operating with the Syrians against the 'Lebanese Front'.

## 3 The Palestinian Resistance (Revolutionary) Movement (PRM) in Lebanon Under the Palestine Liberation Organization (PLO) (1975-76)

| Organization | Main leaders | Ideology | Political presence | Presence at war fronts | Main class composition |
|---|---|---|---|---|---|
| Fateh | Yasser Arafat | Nationalist | All Palestinian camps | All | Petty bourgeoisie. Workers |
| Popular Front for the Liberation of Palestine (PFLP) | George Habash | Marxist | All Palestinian camps | All | Petty bourgeoisie. Workers |
| Democratic Front for the Liberation of Palestine (DFLP) | Nayef Hawatmeh | Marxist | All Palestinian camps | All | Petty bourgeoisie. Workers |
| Arab Liberation Front | Abd Al-Rahim Ahmad | Nationalist | All Palestinian camps | All | Petty bourgeoisie. Workers |
| Saiqa | Zuhair Muhsin | Nationalist | All Palestinian camps | All | Petty bourgeoisie. Workers |
| PFLP – General Command | Ahmad Jibril | Nationalist | All Palestinian camps | All | Petty bourgeoisie. Workers |
| Popular Struggle Front | Bahjat Abu Garbiyeh. Samir Ghoshe | Nationalist | Most Palestinian camps | No significant military role | Petty bourgeoisie. |

The above are the main guerrilla organizations. The Palestine Liberation Army (PLA) is a separate entity and is the official military arm of the PLO. Fateh dominates the PLO and is the largest guerrilla grouping. The PRM has fielded close to 25,000 professional fighters and militia during the Battle of Lebanon.

# Bibliography

Agwani, M.S., *The Lebanese Crisis, 1958* (New York, Asia Publishing House) 1965.

Almond, Gabriel and James Coleman (eds.), *The Politics of the Developing Areas* (Princeton, Princeton University Press) 1960.

────── and Bingham G. Powell Jr., *Comparative Politics: A Developmental Approach* (Boston, Little, Brown and Company) 1966.

────── and Sidney Verba, *The Civic Culture* (Boston, Little, Brown and Company) 1965.

Aly, H. and N. Abdun-nur, 'Appraisal of the Six Year Plan of Lebanon (1972–1977)', *Middle East Journal* XXIX (Spring 1975).

Apter, David, *The Politics of Modernization* (Chicago, University of Chicago Press) 1965.

Appelbaum, R., 'Born-Again Functionalism? A Reconsideration of Althusser's Structuralism', *Insurgent Sociologist* IX (Summer 1979).

Attalah, A. and S. Khalat, *The Lebanese Industrial Sector: Its Growth and Development,* A Study for the Ministry of National Economy (Beirut, Bureau of Industrial Development) 1969.

*At-Tariq* XXXV (January–August 1976).

Aziz, A., *On the Settlement, Change and the Kata'eb's War* (Baghdad, Ath-thaer Al-Arabi) 1977.

Baaklini, Abdo, *Legislative and Political Development: Lebanon 1842–1972* (Durham, Duke University Press) 1976.

Badre, A. and A. Altounian, 'National Income of Lebanon' Monograph 2, 'Income Arising in the Construction Sector' (Beirut) November 1951.

────── and Asad Y. Nasr, 'National Income of Lebanon' Monograph 3, 'Income Arising in the Industrial Sector' (Beirut) May 1953.

Baker, Robert, *Egypt's Uncertain Revolution under Nasser and Sadat* (Cambridge, Harvard University Press) 1978.

Bannerman, M., 'Saudi Arabia', in P. Haley and L. Snider (eds.), *Lebanon in Crisis* (New York, Syracuse University Press) 1979.

Barakat, Halim, 'Social and Political Integration in Lebanon: A Case of Social Mosaic', *Middle East Journal* XXVII (Summer 1973).

────── *Lebanon in Strife: Students Prelude to the Civil War* (Austin, University of Texas Press) 1977.

Bassat, Hisham, 'The Lebanese Economy — Problems and Solutions), *Arab Studies* VIII (March 1972).

Best, Michael and William Connolly, 'Politics and Subjects: The Limits of

Structural Marxism', *Socialist Revolution* IX (November–December 1979).

Binder, Leonard, *Politics in Lebanon* (New York, John Wiley and Sons) 1966.

Bodenheimer, Susanne, 'The Ideology of Developmentalism: American Political Science's Paradigm – Surrogate for Latin American Studies', *Berkeley Journal of Sociology* XV (1970).

Bridges, Amy, 'Nicos Poulantzas and the Marxist Theory of the State', *Politics and Society* IV (Winter 1974).

Cooley, J., 'The Palestinians' in P. Haley and L. Snider (eds.), *Lebanon in Crisis* (New York, Syracuse University Press) 1979.

Cooper, C. and Sidney Alexander, *Economic Development and Popular Growth in the Middle East* (New York, American Elsevier Publishing Company) 1971.

Crow, Ralph, 'Religious Sectarianism in the Lebanese Political System', *Journal of Politics* XXIV (August 1962).

Deeb, Marius, *The Lebanese Civil War* (New York, Praeger) 1980.

Dekmajian, Richard H., 'Consociational Democracy in Crisis', *Comparative Politics* (January 1978).

Dib, George, 'Selections from Riad Solh's Speech in the Lebanese Assembly, October, 1943', *Middle East Forum* XXXIV (January 1959).

Dos Santos, T., 'The Structure of Dependence', *American Economic Review* II (May 1970).

Easton, David, 'Introduction: The Current Meaning of Behavioralism in Political Science', *The Limits of Behavioralism in Political Science*. American Academy of Political and Social Sciences. October 1962.

Emerit, M., 'The Syrian Crisis and French Economic Expansion of 1860', Arab Studies VIII (March 1972).

Enloe, Cynthia, *Ethnic Conflict and Political Development* (Boston, Little, Brown and Company) 1973.

Entelis, John P., 'Structural Change and Organizational Development in the Lebanese Kata'ib Party', *Middle East Journal* XXVII (Winter 1973).

———— *Pluralism and Party Transformation in Lebanon: Al-Kata'ib, 1936–1970* (Leiden, Netherlands, E.J. Brill) 1974.

———— 'Reformist Ideology in the Arab World: The Case of Tunisia and Lebanon', *Review of Politics* XXXVII (October 1975).

Farah, Tawfic, *Aspects of Consociationalism and Modernization: Lebanon as an Exploratory Test Case* (Lincoln, Middle East Research Group Inc.) 1975.

Faris, Fuad, 'The Civil War in Lebanon', *Race and Class* XVIII (Autumn 1976).

Farsoun, Samih and Walter Carroll, 'The Civil War in Lebanon: Sect, Class and Imperialism', *Monthly Review* XXVIII (June 1976).

Fei, Edward and Paul Klat, *The Balance of Payments in Lebanon: 1951 and 1952* (Beirut) 1954.

Fisher, Sydney, *The Middle East* (New York, Alfred A. Knopf) 1960.

Frank, Andre G., *Capitalism and Underdevelopment in Latin America* (New York, Monthly Review Press) 1967.

Gold, David A., Clarence Lo, and Erik Olin Wright, 'Recent Developments in Marxist Theories of the Capitalist State', *Monthly Review* XXVIII (November 1975).

Gramsci, Antonio, *Prison Notebooks* (New York, International Publishers) 1971.

Hall, S. and A. Hunt, 'Toward Further Modernization of the Study of the New Nation', *World Politics* XVII (October 1964).

———— 'Political Parties and the Crisis of Marxism' Interview with Nicos Poulantzas in *Socialist Review* IX (November–December 1979).

Harfouche, Jamal, *Social Structure of Low-Income Families in Lebanon* (Beirut, Khayat's) 1965.

Harik, Iliya, 'The Iqta' System in Lebanon: A Comparative View', *Middle East Journal* XIX (Autumn 1965).

———— *Politics and Change in Traditional Society: Lebanon, 1711–1845* (Princeton, Princeton University Press) 1968.

———— 'The Ethnic Revolution and Political Integration in the Middle East', *International Journal of Middle East Studies* III (July 1972).

Hassan, H., *Lebanon from Ayn-El-Rummaneh till Riadh* (Baghdad, Thawra Publications) 1977.

Hess, Clyde J.G. and Herbert L. Bodman, Jr., 'Confessionalism and Feudality in Lebanese Politics', *Middle East Journal* VIII (Winter 1954).

Hitti, Philip, *Lebanon in History* (New York, Macmillan) 1957.

Hourani, Albert, *Syria and Lebanon: A Political Essay* (London, Oxford University Press) 1946.

———— *Minorities in the Arab World* (London, Oxford University Press) 1947.

———— *A Vision of History: Near Eastern and Other Essays* (Beirut, Khayat's) 1961.

———— 'Lebanon from Feudalism to Modern State', *Middle East Studies* II (April 1966).

Hudson, Michael C., *The Precarious Republic: Political Modernization in Lebanon* (New York, Random House) 1968.

———— 'Democracy and Social Mobilization in Lebanese Politics', *Comparative Politics* I (January 1969).

———— 'The Lebanese Crisis: The Limits of Consociational Democracy', *Journal of Palestine Studies* V (Spring/Summer 1976).

———— 'The Precarious Republic Revisited: Reflections on the Collapse of Pluralist Politics in Lebanon'. Presented at the Annual Meeting of the Association of Arab–American University Graduates. New York, 2 October 1976.

———— *Arab Politics* (New Haven, Yale University Press) 1977.

International Monetary Fund, *Lebanon — Recent Economic Development SM/75/18.* 21 January 1975.

Institut International de Recherche et de Formation en vue du Developpement Integral et Harmonise. *Besoin et Possibilite de Developppment*, Vol. I. (Beirut, Ministere de Plan) 1961.

Johnson, Dale, 'Strategic Implications of Recent Social Class Theory', *Insurgent Sociologist* VIII (Winter 1978).

Jumblatt, K., *This is My Will* (Al-Watan Al-Arabi) 1978.

Kazziha, Walid, *Revolutionary Transformation in the Arab World* (London, Charles Knight and Company Ltd.) 1975.

Khalaf, Samir, 'Primordial Ties and Politics in Lebanon', *Middle East Studies* IV (April 1968).

Khalil, K., 'South Lebanon Between the State and Revolution', *Arab Studies* XI (February 1975).

Khuri, Fuad, 'Changing Class Structures in Lebanon', *Middle East Journal* XXIII (Winter 1969).

Koury, Enver, *The Crisis in the Lebanese System: Confessionalism and Chaos.* American Enterprise Institute. *Foreign Affairs Study 38*, July 1976.

Kuwait Fund for Arab Economic Development, *Report on the Lebanese Economy and its Developmental Projects*, 1976.

*Lebanon's War* (Beirut, Dar-Al-Masseerah) 1977.

Lenin, V.I., *Selected Works* (New York, International Publishers) 1971.

———— *On Organization* (San Francisco, Proletarian Publishers) 1971.

———— *What is to be Done?* (Peking, Foreign Language Press) 1973.

Lerner, Daniel, *The Passing of Traditional Society: Modernizing the Middle East* (New York, The Free Press) 1958.

Lijphart, Arend, 'Typologies of Democratic Systems', *Comparative Political Studies* I (April 1968).

———— 'Consociational Democracy', *World Politics* XXI (January 1969).

Longrigg, Stephen H., *Syria and Lebanon under French Mandate* (London, Oxford University Press) 1958.

Mahmoud, Hussein, 'Reflections on the Lebanese Impasse', *Monthly Review* XXVIII (November 1976).

Marx, Karl and Frederick Engels, *Selected Works* (New York, International Publishers) 1970.

Marx, Karl, 'The German Ideology'. In Lloyd Easton and Kurt Guddat (eds.), *Writings of the Young Marx on Philosophy and Society* (New York, Doubleday) 1967.

Meo, Leila, *Lebanon, Improbable Nation: A Study in Political Development* (Bloomington, Indiana University Press) 1965.

*Message from Fateh to the Lebanese People* (Beirut, Fateh) 1969.

Middle East Research and Information Project, *Lebanon Explodes* XLIV (February 1976).

Miliband, Ralph, *The State in Capitalist Society* (New York, Basic Books) 1969.

Nordlinger, Eric, *Conflict Regulation in Divided Societies.* Harvard Center for International Affairs. Occasional Papers, No. 29, January 1972.

O'Brien, Donald, 'Modernization, Order and the Erosion of a Democratic Ideal: American Political Science 1960–1970', *Journal of Developmental Studies* VIII (July 1972).

Polk, William, *The Opening of South Lebanon, 1788–1840* (Cambridge, Harvard University Press) 1963.

———— *The United States and the Arab World* (Cambridge, Harvard University Press) 1975.

Packenham, Robert, *The New Utopianism: Political Development Ideas in the Dependency Literature* (Stanford University Press) 1978.

Poulantzas, Nicos, 'On Social Classes', *New Left Review* LXXVIII (March –April 1973).

———— *Political Power and Social Classes* (Thetford, Norfolk, Lowe and Brydone) 1975.

———— *Classes in Contemporary Capitalism* (London, NLB) 1975.

———— *The Crisis of the Dictatorships* (London, NLB) 1976.

—————— 'The New Petty Bourgeoisie', *Insurgent Sociologist* IX (Summer 1979).

Qubain, Fahim I., *Crisis in Lebanon* (Washington DC, Middle East Institute) 1961.

Salem, Elie A., *Modernization Without Revolution: Lebanon's Experience*. Indiana University International Development Research Cener; Studies in Development, No. 6. Indiana University Press, February 1973.

Salibi, Kamal S., *The Modern History of Lebanon* (London, Weidenfeld and Nicolson) 1965.

—————— *Cross Roads to Civil War: Lebanon 1958-1976* (New York, Caravan Books) 1976.

Sayigh, Yusif A., *Entrepreneurs of Lebanon* (Cambridge, Mass., Harvard University Press) 1967.

—————— *The Economics of the Arab World: Development Since 1945* (New York, St. Martin's Press) 1978.

Sharabi, Hisham, *Nationalism and Revolution in the Arab World* (Princeton, New Jersey) 1966.

Shukri, G., *Urs Ed-Dam Fi Lubnan* (Beirut, Dar-Et-Taliya) 1976.

Smock, David and Audry Smock, *The Politics of Pluralism: A Comparative Study of Lebanon and Ghana* (New York, Elsevier) 1975.

Stauffer, Robert, *Western Values and the Case for Third World Cultural Disengagement*. Paper presented to a Conference on 'Intercultural Transactions for the Future', held at the East–West Cultural Learning Institute, Honolulu, Hawaii, 22–26 June 1975.

Stoakes, Frank, 'The Supervigilantes: The Lebanese Kata'eb Party as a Builder, Surrogate and Defender of the State', *Middle Eastern Studies* XI (October 1975).

—————— 'The Civil War in Lebanon', *World Today* XXXII (January 1976).

Suleiman, Michael, *Political Parties in Lebanon: The Challenge of a Fragmented Political Culture* (Ithaca, New York, Cornell University Press) 1967.

Sweet, Louise (ed.), *Peoples and Cultures of the Middle East* II (New York, The Natural History Press) 1970.

*The Two Year War* (Beirut, Dar-An-Nahar) 1976.

Wallerstein, Immanuel, *The Capitalist World Economy* (Cambridge, Cambridge University Press) 1979.

Zartman, William, *Political Modernization in the Middle East and North Africa* (Princeton, New Jersey, Princeton University Press) 1966.

Zubian, Sami, *The Lebanese National Movement* (Beirut, Dar-Al-Masseerah) 1977.

Zuwiyya, Jalal, *The Parliamentary Elections of Lebanon, 1968* (Leiden, E.J. Brill) 1972.

# Index

# MIDDLE EAST TITLES FROM ZED

## POLITICAL ECONOMY

Samir Amin
**THE ARAB ECONOMY TODAY**
(with a comprehensive bibliography
of Amin's works)
Hb and Pb

B. Berberoglu
**TURKEY IN CRISIS**
**From State Capitalism to Neo-**
**Colonialism**
Hb and Pb

Samir Amin
**THE ARAB NATION**
**Nationalism and Class Struggles**
Hb and Pb

Maxime Rodinson
**MARXISM AND THE MUSLIM**
**WORLD**
Pb

Ghali Shoukri
**EGYPT:**
**Portrait of a President**
**Sadat's Road to Jerusalem**
Hb and Pb

Fatima Babiker Mahmoud
**THE SUDANESE BOURGEOISIE**
**Vanguard of Development?**
Hb and Pb

## CONTEMPORARY
## HISTORY/REVOLUTIONARY
## STRUGGLES

Kamal Joumblatt
**I SPEAK FOR LEBANON**
Hb and Pb

Gerard Chaliand (Editor), A.R.
Ghassemlou, Kendal, M Nazdar,
A. Roosevelt and I.S. Vanly
**PEOPLE WITHOUT A**
**COUNTRY:**
**The Kurds and Kurdistan**
Hb and Pb

Rosemary Sayigh
**PALESTINIANS:**
**From Peasants to Revolutionaries**
Hb and Pb

Bizhan Jazani
**CAPITALISM AND**
**REVOLUTION IN IRAN**
Hb and Pb

Abdallah Franji
**THE PLO AND PALESTINE**
Hb and Pb

Suroosh Irfani
**REVOLUTIONARY ISLAM IN**
**IRAN:**
**Popular Liberation or Religious**
**Dictatorship?**
Hb and Pb

People's Press
**OUR ROOTS ARE STILL ALIVE**
Pb

Anouar Abdel-Malek (Editor)
**CONTEMPORARY ARAB**
**POLITICAL THOUGHT**
Hb

Michael Jansen
**THE BATTLE OF BEIRUT:**
**Why Israel Invaded Lebanon**
Hb and Pb

Regina Sharif
**NON-JEWISH ZIONISM:**
**Its Roots in Western History**
Hb and Pb

Alain Gresh
**THE PLO: THE STRUGGLE**
**WITHIN**
**Towards an Independent Palestinian**
**State**
Hb and Pb